American Ambassadors
in a
Troubled World

Recent Titles in
Contributions in Political Science

American Ambassadors
in a
Troubled World

Interviews with Senior Diplomats

Dayton Mak
and
Charles Stuart Kennedy

Contributions in Political Science, Number 303

GREENWOOD PRESS
Westport, Connecticut • London

Library of Congress Cataloging-in-Publication Data

Mak, Dayton.
   American ambassadors in a troubled world : interviews with senior
diplomats / Dayton Mak and Charles Stuart Kennedy.
      p.   cm.—(Contributions in political science, ISSN 0147-1066
; no. 303)
   Includes index.
   ISBN 0-313-28558-6 (alk. paper)
   1. United States—Foreign relations—1945-1989. 2. Ambassadors—
United States—Interviews. 3. United States—Foreign relations
administration. I. Kennedy, Charles Stuart. II. Title.
III. Series.
E840.M335   1992
327.73—dc20   92-7398

British Library Cataloguing in Publication Data is available.

Library of Congress Catalog Card Number: 92-7398
ISBN: 0-313-28558-6
ISSN: 0147-1066

First published in 1992

Greenwood Press, 88 Post Road West, Westport, CT 06881
An imprint of Greenwood Publishing Group, Inc.

Printed in the United States of America

The paper used in this book complies with the
Permanent Paper Standard issued by the National
Information Standards Organization (Z39.48-1984).

10 9 8 7 6 5 4 3 2 1

Contents

Preface

The material for this book has been taken from transcripts of taped interviews of over seventy U.S. ambassadors and other senior diplomatic officers who served in embassies abroad and whose experiences were recorded under the Association for Diplomatic Studies' Foreign Affairs Oral History Program. The texts are verbatim with minor editing in the interests of brevity and clarity. The transcripts in their entirety may be read at the Lauinger Library of Georgetown University or at the Department of State's Foreign Service Institute.

The authors, retired Foreign Service officers, wish to thank all of the persons whose experiences are recorded here as well as those who volunteered their time to conduct the interviews. Our particular thanks go to William Morgan and Norman Pratt, retired Foreign Service officers, and Ambassador Andrew Steigman of Georgetown University for their most helpful advice and assistance throughout the project. We also want to thank our transcribers, Marion Henderson, Thomas Stern, Debbie Read, and Elizabeth Beuter.

Special thanks are due to the librarian of the Lauinger Library, Dr. Susan Martin, and her assistant, Karen Laufman, and the Special Collections Division's George M. Barringer and Jon Reynolds, all of Georgetown University.

1

The American Ambassador:
A Historical Perspective

Representing the president and the American people abroad as ambassador of the United States of America to another nation is a singular honor. Men and women, successful in their various careers, have been proud to serve their country as ambassador. To a Foreign Service officer, it is the acme of a career.

There have been times when the life of the ambassador abroad was a comfortable one; a handsome place to live, a fine office in which to work, domestic and office help to assist and a place of honor and privilege in the foreign community. In those times the persons of the ambassador and his family as well as the staffs of the chancery and residence were protected as a matter of accepted diplomatic courtesy.

The world has changed. The virtual end of colonialism and great power domination has let loose a host of ideas, interests and goals sometimes considered inimical to American interests. Some elements, viewing the United States an obstacle to their goals have turned to street violence and terrorism against American commercial establishments and U.S. embassies. Ambassadors themselves have become favored targets. The once quiet embassies and comfortable residences of ambassadors have been turned into armed fortresses, heavily guarded with access carefully restricted. In some capitals ambassadors, their families and their staffs have become virtual prisoners in their own embassies. Transportation for the ambassador is often now an armored sedan surrounded fore and aft by a convoy of armed guards.

The traditional view of the American ambassador has been replaced by a more vivid one. Television cameras catch American envoys climbing into helicopters, surrounded by U.S. Marines in combat gear as they are whisked off the embassy compound just ahead of enemy forces or mobs, or perhaps inspecting their just blown-up embassy. The list of embassies bombed, sacked, attacked, or threatened by angry mobs is long, as the accounts in this book attest.

One has only to recall the American ambassadors who have been kidnapped, taken hostage, or murdered at their posts since World War II to appreciate the risks involved in representing the U.S. Government abroad. Burke Elbrick was kidnapped in Brazil in 1970. Gordon Mein was assassinated in Guatemala in 1968, Cleo Noel in Sudan in 1973, Rodger Davies in Cyprus in 1974, Francis Meloy in Lebanon in 1976, and Adolph Dubs in Afghanistan in 1979.

In view of these risks, why would one want to become an ambassador? Why, for that matter, should we send ambassadors to such dangerous places? Why not, in this day of instant communications, rely on the telephone, telegraph or fax to conduct our relations in such capitals? The answer is that it simply does not work. A major country such as the United States needs an official on the spot to represent its interests.

United States ambassadors are relatively new arrivals on the international scene, appearing in 1776 on the birth of the nation. Ambassadors of some sort, however, have always been around; somebody was needed to resolve disputes between tribes and nations, and from this imperative developed the profession of diplomacy and the role of ambassadors.

As the American colonies struggled to free themselves from the British during the Revolution and in the early years of independence when foreign support and recognition were vital to the preservation of the new country, America sent its best as representatives to Europe. The major figures were Benjamin Franklin, Thomas Jefferson, John Adams, and John Jay who served in Europe during the Revolution and Confederation periods. Under the new constitution of 1787, George Washington chose as envoys to represent the newly-minted United States men whom he knew well, whose judgment he could rely on, and whose integrity was unquestioned. They were cultured, educated gentlemen who could hold their own in the highest political circles abroad and who had strong political ties to the small ruling elite that was forging the new nation.

As the nation became stronger and its interests more far-flung, it became increasingly necessary to establish ties, diplomatic and consular, for representing American commercial interests around the globe. This required an increasing number of people, and soon the responsibility for selecting persons for these roles shifted from the president and his immediate entourage to others in his government. Increasingly the ranks were filled by those fortunate enough to have political influence and support in their states, who had the desire to live abroad and the financial resources to supplement the meager compensation offered by the U.S. government. From about the presidency of Andrew Jackson on, the guiding principle to the selection of American chiefs of diplomatic missions was, "To the victors belong the ambassadorial or ministerial appointments." Both U.S. embassies and consulates were staffed by politically appointed Americans until the turn of the twentieth century.

The United States had no actual ambassadors abroad until 1893. Prior to that, American chief representatives were ministers, or to give them their full diplomatic title, envoys extraordinary and ministers plenipotentiary, a rank below ambassador. While the major European countries exchanged ambassadors among themselves, the United States was considered to be a second-class power and rated only ministers. By 1893, however, the United States had become an industrial giant, and the ranks of its envoys were accordingly raised from minister to that of ambassador, or ambassador extraordinary and minister plenipotentiary, in Great Britain, France, Italy, and Germany. The system of "first- and second-class powers" with regard to the ranking of diplomats broke down completely in the post-World War II era of rapid decolonialization. Today most countries, no matter how small, are represented in Washington by ambassadors. In turn, American chiefs of mission abroad have the title of ambassador.

The ranks of those who have been ambassadors or ministers represents an unusual cross section of American meritocracy and plutocracy. Seven presidents have been diplomats abroad; John Adams, Thomas Jefferson, James Monroe, John Quincy Adams, Martin Van Buren, James Buchanan and, after a more than a century's hiatus, George Bush. Several American writers were appointed as ministers as rewards for their literary accomplishments; James Russell Lowell, Washington Irving and Richard Henry Dana, Jr. being prime examples. Historians such as George Bancroft, John Motley, and John Hay headed missions abroad. [Hay was also a secretary of state]. Many Civil War officers were given posts abroad after the conflict. Two generals, James Longstreet (Confederate) and Daniel Sickels (Union), who fought each other at Gettysburg, served as ministers to Turkey and Spain, respectively.

African-Americans were not represented during the pre-Civil War period by appointment to diplomatic positions. However, Frederick Douglass, a leading figure in the abolition movement and a former slave, did serve as minister to Haiti in the 1890s. Women did not break into the minister/ambassador club until 1933 when Ruth Bryan Owen, daughter of former Secretary of State William Jennings Bryan, was appointed as minister to Denmark. Gradually, especially since the 1960s, both African-

Americans and women were increasingly included in ambassadorial appointments, albeit slowly.

In 1906, the Consular Service, mainly concerned with United States shipping and commercial interests was reformed, and made more professional, with entry examinations required for aspiring consuls. The Diplomatic Service followed suit shortly thereafter, with the major exception of appointments to ambassadorial positions; these remained mainly in the hands of the politicians. Politically appointed ambassadors (or ministers), however, could now be supported by professional staffs.

By 1924 both the Diplomatic and Consular Services, which until then had been separate, were combined into the single Foreign Service. More ambassadors or ministers were appointed from its ranks, mainly to non-European countries. The United States, except in Latin America, was still not a major player in the diplomatic world between the two world wars.

The end of World War II in 1945, however, found the United States a superpower with vastly increased international interests and responsibilities. There was a dramatic growth in diplomatic representation throughout the world. From the 1950s on there was the rapid decolonization of Asia and Africa. As each of the newly independent countries from these continents entered on the world scene, the United States established diplomatic relations with them, broadening thereby the opportunities for ambassadorial appointments.

Today, as has been the rule since the first days of the Republic, appointments of nonprofessionals to ambassadorial positions have largely been awarded for success in other fields. The preponderance of those going to the major capitals of Europe have been drawn from the wealthy. Traditionally American ambassadors to such posts as London and Paris found it necessary to dig deeply into their own pockets to compete on the diplomatic circuit with their colleagues representing other countries. Not until 1991 was a career Foreign Service officer appointed ambassador to the Court of St. James in London. Those nonprofessionals sent to posts where representation responsibilities do not require such personal wealth are drawn from a broad cross section of American society. But in general they have done well in business, politics, the academic world, or the arts. The Foreign Service still supplies the preponderance of ambassadors to the more volatile areas of the world. Despite their diverse professional backgrounds, however, no distinctions are made in the tasks that await the ambassador at an embassy.

It is true that instant communications and peripatetic Washington-based envoys have changed the nature of diplomacy. Nevertheless, they cannot substitute for the person on the spot whose duty it is to convey to foreign leaders and discuss with them U.S. policies; to listen, observe, and report the views of such leaders; and to analyze and report on all aspects of the local environment--in effect, to serve as the eyes, ears, and voice of the United States of America abroad.

The general public has little information about these men and women, who they are, where they come from, or how they became ambassadors. Except for a few of the famous or near-famous, the American ambassador remains an unknown quantity. The next three chapters of this book are designed to give the reader, in the words of the ambassadors themselves, a sense of their background, how they became ambassadors, and how they prepared themselves for their missions. Three chapters, 5,6 and 7 describe how a number of ambassadors organized and conducted the day-to-day operations of their embassies and how they dealt with the host governments and the U.S. bureaucracy.   The remaining chapters are accounts of ambassadors recalling their experiences in carrying out their missions, often in difficult or unusual circumstances.

While these accounts by no means cover all aspects of an ambassador's activities nor provide instruction in the art of diplomacy, they may give the reader a view of ambassadors at work.   They are all, of course, accounts of events as seen from one point of view, that of the ambassador or deputy.   Others sitting in Washington or elsewhere might see and recollect the same events in a different light.

2

Ambassadorial Backgrounds: Who Are They?

To have a better understanding of who our ambassadors are, it is useful to know where they came from and how they happened to become interested in a career in the diplomatic service. In this chapter twenty U.S. ambassadors, career and non-career, tell of their family backgrounds, education and the origins of their interest in foreign affairs.
Together these comments convey a sense of the variety of backgrounds--family, geographic, educational and financial, of U.S. ambassadors.

CECIL BURTON LYON was born in New York in 1903. Educated at Harvard, he entered the Foreign Service in 1930. He served in the Far East, Latin America, and Europe and was ambassador to Chile, 1956 to 1958; and Ceylon, 1965 to 1967. He retired in 1968.

Lyon: People often ask me about why I went in the Foreign Service. I think it was a mixed bag. I think in the first place when I should have been reading *The Rover Boys*, I was reading E. Phillips Oppenheim, where the young junior secretary would always be lunching with the glamorous spy in the Ritz bar somewhere. I think also--it may sound corny today, but I had a desire to serve my country. And finally, I think it was a yearning to travel, to see the world, to go to far places, to have some experience and a life which would broaden one with some adventure in it. I must say I was looking for that. I had an English father and he did everything he could to dissuade me from going into the Foreign Service. We didn't have much money and he said in the British Foreign Service you had to have a private income--"which you won't have,"--he told me. So I took the course of least resistance. I roomed with a fellow called Cassat in college whose father had a brokerage firm. I went into that and spent three miserable years in Wall Street. The day of the big crash in 1929 I went into the toilet at that office, and the senior New York partner came in and he said, "Cecil, this is a hell of a business. I've been in it 20 years and I've just lost everything I have." So that made me decide that I was going to go into the Foreign Service.

Born in Oklahoma in 1906 and graduating from the University of Oklahoma 1929, EVERETT FRANCIS DRUMRIGHT entered the Foreign Service in 1930. Drumright was a China Hand, having served in a variety of posts in China from 1931 until 1944 and was ambassador to the Republic of China on Taiwan from 1958 to 1962.

Drumright: I was graduated from the University of Oklahoma with a degree in business administration in 1929. After graduation I returned to my home where, for a few months, I did some work for my father, who was in business. Then, you may recall, that the Great Depression came upon us and the chances of getting a job were greatly diminished.

I considered going to Stanford University for further study in business administration and, in fact, in February of 1930 I even went out there to look into it. But I decided that I didn't want to pursue that, so I came back to my home. And one day, by chance, I happened upon a friend, a young lawyer, in my town. The town is Drumright, Oklahoma, by the way. And this friend told me that he was preparing to take the examination for the Foreign Service. I said, "What is that all about?" So he proceeded to tell me what he knew about the Foreign Service and gave me the booklet he had received from the State Department, which I read with considerable interest. After giving the matter some thought, I decided that I would take a fling at it.

I think about June, this friend and I decided to take the examination in Denver, where the climate was good, rather than in St. Louis, where we knew it would be hot. So we decided to go in advance to the University of Colorado and study for the exam in the University of Colorado Library. We accordingly did so, spending about six weeks, every day, in the library going over the examination questions   from previous examinations.   I believe in early September, we proceeded to Denver where we had two days of written examinations. After that we returned home and, in due course, I received word that I had a passing grade of 80. Whereupon, I applied for the oral exam, which was given in November. I duly went to Washington and took the oral exam before Wilbur Carr and several others who were prominent in the Foreign Service.

A midwesterner, JOHN WESLEY JONES was born in 1907 and raised in Sioux City, Iowa. Joining the Foreign Service in 1930 he served mainly in Europe, with an assignment to China during the Communist takeover. He served as ambassador to Libya and Peru.

Jones: When I was a junior, I think, in Sioux City Central High School, the registrar of the high school had been a clerk in the American embassy in Paris during the First World War. She took a fancy to me and talked to me about the Foreign Service and suggested that I might think about it as a career. Then also a maiden aunt, a sister of my father, thought this would be a great career so she encouraged me in it, too. So for the last two years of high school and my four years in college, I determined that that's the career I wanted to follow.

For my last two years in college, I persuaded my father to send me to Washington, D.C. since in Sioux City, Iowa, not many people knew much about the Foreign Service and I thought that perhaps in Washington I would learn more about it. Because of my father's religious prejudices, I knew that it was useless to ask him to send me to the Foreign Service school at Georgetown run by Jesuits, but I learned that George Washington University had received that year a grant of a million dollars to establish a foreign service school. The Masonic Lodge was apparently worried about the influence of the Jesuits on the future of Foreign Service officers and decided they would like to have a foreign affairs school in a non-religious university.

So I enrolled at G.W. [George Washington University] as a junior in 1928 and graduated in 1930 in liberal arts, took the Foreign Service examinations the summer of 1930 here in Washington. On the 31st of December I received a letter in Sioux City, Iowa, telling me that I had not only passed the Foreign Service exams but that also my appointment as a career Foreign Service officer had been approved by the Senate.

RALPH ELIHU BECKER was raised in New York State. A lawyer by profession, he was active in cultural and civic affairs as well as in the Republican Party. He was a founding trustee of the John F. Kennedy Center for the Performing Arts in Washington, D.C. and served under several presidents in national and international affairs. In 1976 he was appointed ambassador to Honduras by President Ford.

Becker: I have had a long career, first as a lawyer in Westchester County in New York State, and then in Washington. I came to Washington in the '46 campaign (the 80th Congress) as the national chairman of the Young Republicans. I was involved in the Eisenhower campaign. As national chairman of the Young Republicans I travelled the country (150,000 miles and organized every state) and became very much involved in national and international affairs. In addition to practicing law, I have been a civic and cultural leader as well as being a decorated World War II veteran. Also I was a Presidential appointee for 20 years as well as serving as minority counsel to the U.S. Senate Committee on Election and Privileges 1951.

ROBERT FORBES WOODWARD, a midwesterner, after an unpromising academic career, entered the Foreign Service in 1931 and eventually rose to be ambassador to Costa Rica, Uruguay, Chile, and Spain, as well as assistant secretary for Latin American Affairs.

Woodward: I came from a family of very modest circumstances in Minneapolis. I had a public school education. I went to the University of Minnesota, because every person who graduated from high school in Minnesota was eligible for education in the university. I was working after school and was much more interested in my work than I was in the university courses. I finished the university with very mediocre grades. I elected, for my last year in the university, a course in preparation for the diplomatic and consular service which was offered in the university catalog. Toward the end of that year, when a written examination for the Foreign Service was offered at the St. Paul Post Office, my advisor said that he didn't think I should take the examination because I wasn't a good enough student. I, nevertheless, did take it, and qualified, at least, to take the oral, which I failed. I took the written examination right over again, in July 1931. Living in Minneapolis, I was close to one Foreign Service post, and they were saving money on transportation [during the Depression]. They assigned me to Winnipeg as my first post.

DOUGLAS MACARTHUR II was born in Pennslyvania in 1909. His father was a naval officer, his uncle a distinguished army officer. He joined the Foreign Service in 1935. Interned for some time during World War II by the Germans, he became a political advisor to General Eisenhower during the period before and after the invasion of France and later was Eisenhower's political advisor when NATO was formed. When Ike became President, MacArthur was made counselor of the Department of State, the number three position. He was later ambassador to Japan, Belgium, Austria, and Iran.

MacArthur: I think navy families are a little bit like those ladies of easy virtue; they follow the ships or fleet around, wherever it happens to be--East Coast, West Coast. So at a very young age, we got used to different environments, totally different, East Coast, West Coast, New England, Virginia, Washington. I wouldn't say that one develops a wanderlust, but one develops a curiosity after a while about what's happening in the outside world.

In my case, when I was about 12 or 13 years old, my father was asked to command a ship that took the secretary of the navy on a good-will tour to Japan and China. Because the secretary had a boy my age, he wanted to take the boy along. So my father was invited to take myself and my brother. When we came to countries like Japan and China, where there were all sorts of ceremonial events and important people, we were often left in the charge of a vice consul. This made a very deep and lasting impression on me at that age. Because they spoke the language of the country, they seemed to know a lot, and showed us and explained to us all sorts of things about the country that otherwise we never would have understood. That was when I decided that I would probably like to be a member of the Foreign Service.

ANGIER BIDDLE DUKE, a New Yorker, was educated at St. Paul's School and Yale University. Although not a "career" Foreign Service officer, Ambassador Duke has had more experience over a longer period of time at the ambassadorial level than all but a handfull of senior career officers, having served as ambassador to El Salvador, Spain, Denmark, and Morocco, as well as Chief of Protocol in the Department of State.

Duke: I was born in 1915 in New York City. My father died when I was seven years old; my mother remarried and we moved to Long Island where I went to school and grew up. And at the age of twelve or on my 13th birthday I went off to St. Paul's School in Concord, New Hampshire where I stayed for six years. I then went to Yale University. During the summers we would visit my mother's brother, Anthony J. Drexel Biddle, who was minister to Norway and subsequently ambassador to Poland.

I regret to say I left Yale in my junior year, always intending to come back, but the war intervened and one thing led to another, and I never did graduate. I did go to service schools and graduated from Officer Candidate School at Ft. Meade, Maryland, and I feel that life has given me a pretty good education. Although I regret not getting my degree, I take inordinate pride in the honorary degrees that have been given me.

Yes, it was my uncle who was serving in the embassy in Europe and of course my own experience during the war in North Africa, England and France and to some extent, Germany which gave me a great feeling for service abroad.

CAROLINE CLENDENING LAISE [CAROL LAISE BUNKER] was born in Virginia in 1917. She was ambassador to Nepal and Director General of the Foreign Service. Laise was married to the late Ellsworth Bunker, also an ambassador.

Laise: I graduated from American University on the eve of war. I studied at their School of Public Affairs and became deeply interested, because of the creative and pioneering work which that school was doing, in government, and public administration primarily. When I came out of school, I took the junior professional examination, one of the earliest ones that had been devised in an effort to upgrade government. I managed to pass it. I entered government basically as a result of the defense buildup as a junior professional officer working in the Civil Service Commission. That meant I worked primarily in personnel work, both setting up a placement system as well as working on personnel utilization with defense industries in order to reduce staff turnover. After the war was over, this led me to be posted to UNRRA [United Nations Relief and Rehabilitation Administration] in London.

I came back to Washington as a result of the experience I was having and the cooperation I had developed with people in the State Department in turning the activities over to the successor organization. It just followed naturally that I came back and joined the Bureau of the United Nations Affairs (in the State Department) and helped to look after U.S. interests in the U.N.

CLAUDE GEORGE A. [TONY] ROSS , a native of Illinois, entered the Foreign Service in 1940 and served at a variety of posts ranging from Quito in Ecuador to Noumea in the South Pacific. He was ambassador to the Central African Republic, Haiti, and Tanzania.

Ross: I became aware of the Foreign Service at the age of 15, and from that point on, I never really seriously considered any other career. To explain, I should say that there were probably three factors that attracted me to the Foreign Service and then sustained me in preparing myself for the examinations. From earliest childhood, I had been fascinated by pictures of foreign lands and exotic peoples. I remember that geography was my favorite subject in grammar school. As a seven-year-old, and eight-year-old, I was fond of drawing maps. For some reason, Iceland and Greenland fascinated me, and I don't know how many reproductions of those places I made. Another bit of memory was my fascination with the Tigris and Euphrates Rivers and their confluence, and the delta going into the Persian Gulf. Also at an early age, I became interested in stamp collecting. I remember that the stamps of the British and French colonies were my favorites, probably because they had very colorful representations of those areas. One I remember in particular was from French Equatorial Africa, which showed a crouching leopard, and the stamp was surcharged Ubangi-Shari. I didn't know at that point that some years later I was going to be in the Central African Republic, which had earlier been known as Ubangi-Shari.

My grandmother taught me some German. So all of these factors worked when in my last semester of my high school, I took a class in international relations. That's where I heard about the Foreign Service. From that point on, my attention was focused.

WILLIAM TAPLEY BENNETT, Jr., was raised on a plantation in Georgia, graduated from the University of Georgia in 1937 and entered the Foreign Service in 1946. He later served as ambassador to the Dominican Republic, Portugal, and NATO. He was also assistant secretary for Legislative and Intergovernmental Affairs.

Bennett: I did not dream of the Foreign Service from birth onward as some have claimed. In fact, I remember the precise moment when it hit me. I grew up in the rural South on what you might call a cotton plantation although we also had cattle and wheat and other grains. But it was a simple childhood by today's standards. And I'm grateful for that. We lived five miles in the country from Griffin, Georgia, a town of about 10,000 people. And my first year at school I was taken to town each day in a horse and buggy, which shows how things have changed in my lifetime.

Then I went on to the University of Georgia. I was rather ticketed for a family law firm. Then, after graduation, the following year I had started law school and was suddenly picked up and given an exchange fellowship to Germany just because there was a vacancy.

Well, I went to Germany and that, obviously, was an exciting year, 1937-38, just before the war broke out in Europe when Nazism was rising to its infamous heights. It was an interesting year with travel as far east as Vienna and down the Danube to the Balkans into Turkey and back through western Europe. So I came home thoroughly embued with an interest in foreign places. And that obviously had changed my life.

I did go back to law school at Georgia, but I found law school rather dull after this adventuresome year of wandering around Europe. I remember going to the college library one day and looking into some of the shelves. And there was a pamphlet about the Foreign Service. And that's the precise moment when it struck me that this is what I would like to do.

It was his expertise in management and international finance that prompted President Kennedy to ask WILLIAM TRUE DAVIS, Jr. to become his ambassador to Switzerland. A midwesterner from Missouri, Mr. Davis was a U.S. Navy test pilot during World War II and has been the chairman of the board, president, or director of twenty-eight corporations. He served in Switzerland from 1963 to 1965 and then became assistant secretary of the Treasury from 1965 to 1968.

Davis: In adult life, I was in the Navy, and coming out, formed a small pharmaceutical company. It grew very well, and I eventually realized I couldn't finance it by myself. I had either to go public or merge it with a larger company. At that point I merged it with the Dutch Philips Lamps of Holland. Then I became eventually their president here in the United States. Our better-known products are Norelco and Philips. At that time, they had a chemical pharmaceutical division.

More than that, I became their merger specialist for the free world, and thereby developed a self-educated form of expertise in international finance. Then eventually, I was asked by President Kennedy to be ambassador to Switzerland.

JEAN MARY WILKOWSKI was born in Wisconsin in 1919, graduated from St. Mary-of-the-Woods College in 1941 and received a master's degree from the University of Wisconsin. Toward the end of World War II she planned to become a foreign correspondent for United Press and had no thought of entering the Foreign Service. But somehow she got side-tracked and ended up as a vice consul in Trinidad in 1944. Thus began her Foreign Service career. She became ambassador to Zambia in 1972.

Wilkowski: When I was in college, I certainly had no idea of going into the Foreign Service. But my first job was down in Miami, Florida. I was doing publicity for a college, and I had to cover a very interesting meeting of the American historians who were down there and who had just come back from Lima, Peru. I thought their experiences were fascinating, and I was on my way up to Chicago to take a job with the United Press, because journalism and political science had been my field. I really wanted to get into work as a foreign correspondent.

So this sociologist who was at the conference said, "I'll tell you what. Why don't you take this letter to the Foreign Service at the State Department in Washington on your way to Chicago?" And I said, "It's a little bit out of the way." But I did.

I went to an assistant secretary of state, who suggested I go to "employment", which, of course, is where you do go if you're looking for a job. But I wasn't terribly serious about it since I was interested in the United Press job in Chicago.

But I did apply, and I never will forget what the man said, "You don't know how lucky you are."

I said, "Why is that?" This is October 1944. He said, "we've lost a lot of men and we're really scraping the bottom of the barrel. We're looking for 4.Fs [males physically ineligible for the military services] and women, in that order"--4.Fs came first. I said, "Oh, that's interesting."

And he said, "I'll tell you what. They're taking in vice consuls."

I said, "What's a vice consul?" So he sent me over to [Personnel in] the old Walker Johnson Building, and then from then on, it became history.

I came in as Foreign Service auxiliary, went to Trinidad, and then later took the examination and came in. So that's how I got started.

ARTHUR WILLIAM HUMMEL, Jr. was born in China to missionary parents in 1920 and spent his early years there. He was interned by the Japanese in World War II, eventually escaping with a British friend and spent the rest of the war years with Chinese guerrillas. After his wartime adventures he joined the Foreign Service in 1950, initially specializing in public affairs and serving mainly in the Far East. He eventually returned to China as ambassador from 1981 to 1985. He was also ambassador to Burma, Ethiopia, and Pakistan as well as assistant secretary for East Asian and Pacific Affairs.

Hummel: My parents were missionaries and I was born in China, and spent my early years mostly in Peking. I left when I was eight years old.

My father moved to Washington where, being more of a scholar than a missionary, he was asked to be the head of the Library of Congress Oriental Division. He stayed there from 1928 or late '27, I forget which, to 1954. I more or less grew up here in Chevy Chase. However, like a number of missionary kids, I think, coming back to the States was traumatic and I sort of put all that away and didn't even want to speak Chinese anymore. As a matter of fact, because of the Chinese servants and the fact that my parents were practicing their own Chinese, I spoke Chinese before I spoke English but that withered away considerably.

My father became a Quaker and I went to a Quaker prep school. I was one of the rebellious young people, like a preacher's son very often will be. As a matter of fact, I got kicked out of prep school, but then returned. I went to Antioch but dropped out for lack of interest, and spent a couple of years roaming around, mostly in the Midwest, doing odd jobs and floating from town to town. I had a great time.

Then my father was invited to go back to Peking for a book buying and research stint of several months; so my parents decided to take me with them and sent me ahead. I arrived in September 1940. Then, their trip was cancelled because of tension in the Far East, but I was too dumb to leave.

When I arrived there, I immediately went to a Chinese language school, the same school where my father had been part of the faculty and where I used to live as a child, the Peking Language School. My language came back in a rush but, of course, I had to study the written language for the first time.

I was studying Chinese with a tutor and teaching English to support myself. I was too dumb to leave before Pearl Harbor. I got interned by the Japanese, first, one year in Peking, a very loose kind of internment.

Then they shipped all of us enemy aliens--British, Canadians, French and so on--down to a camp in Weihsien in Shantung Province. I was there for a year and then eventually escaped with a British friend and joined Chinese guerrillas nearby and stayed with them until the war was over.

After the war was over, I spent a year working for UNRRA in North China doing survey trips into Communist areas; that was my first contact with the Chinese Communists. Then I went back to the States and worked for a while for the United China Relief Organization.

HERMANN FREDERICK EILTS was born in Germany in 1922, came to the United States as a child and graduated from Ursinus College in Pennsylvania. He joined the Foreign Service in 1947 and became a specialist in Arab affairs. He was ambassador to Saudi Arabia and Egypt.

Eilts: I had long had an interest in diplomacy. My father had been in the German Diplomatic Service and, although he had been in the United States for many years and out of diplomacy, it was something that was very much talked about in the family. So when I went to college it was always my intention to try to get into the Foreign Service. When the appropriate time came at the end of World War II and examinations were again given, I took the examination and was fortunate enough to pass.

The son of Professor Carleton Coon, Sr., a well-known anthropologist, CARLETON S. COON Jr., was born in France in 1927. After military service, he joined the Foreign Service in 1949. His wife, Jane Abell Coon, also a Foreign Service officer, was ambassador to Bangladesh. He was ambassador to Nepal.

Coon: My mother and father were on an expedition in the Riff mountains of Northern Morocco when I was carried there and dropped in Paris on the way home, so to speak, in 1927. My parents were always interested in overseas and expeditions. My father was an anthropologist at Harvard until about '48 or thereabouts when he moved down to Penn. There were always foreigners around when I was growing up. Just at the end of the Second World War I was drafted. V-J Day came just in time, during my basic training. I spent the year 1946 in Germany, first as a private and then as a reward for excellent behavior--a private first class. I was offered chances at OCS [Officer Candidate School], Japanese language training, but my feeling at the time was that the war was over and I just wanted to do my time and get out. So I did. I was out by the end of the year.

But I had a year in Germany during which I became fairly fluent in German. So naturally by 1948 when I was looking around in college for something to do the idea of the diplomatic service appealed to me.

WILLIAM REX CRAWFORD, Jr. was born in Pennsylvania in 1928 and graduated from Harvard. After military service he entered the Foreign Service in 1951 and served in the Middle East. He was ambassador to Yemen and Cyprus.

Crawford: I had a somewhat unusual childhood. Both parents were teachers. My father was a professor at the University of Pennsylvania, my mother a teacher of French in the public high school system in Philadelphia. When I was five years old, we spent a year in Europe, when my father had a Guggenheim Fellowship, primarily in France. Then later in 1940-41, he was an exchange professor at the University of Chile, and my brother and I went along on both of those trips. From 1943 to 1945, he was drafted into government service during the war as our first ever cultural attaché. He was stationed at the American embassy in Rio, and I went along for two years of that, from 1943 to '45.

By the time I got out of secondary school, I had lived quite a lot in Europe and in Latin America and had a pretty good background in French, Spanish, and Portuguese. I went to Harvard as an undergraduate. More and more, international relations was the thing that naturally came most easily and that I became most interested in. By my junior year in college, that was what I wanted to do.

WILLIAM BOWDOIN JONES, a native Californian, was active in international affairs before his appointment as ambassador to Haiti from 1977 to 1980.

Jones: I graduated from UCLA in 1949. I majored in political science, and I applied for a fellowship to study at the University of Southampton in England for a semester; fortunately, I was granted it. It was an IIE fellowship.

I was born and raised in Los Angeles, and other than going to Mexico, I had not been out of the state of California. I had a cousin who was then studying in Paris; he had been in the war and had gone back to Paris. He was at the Sorbonne. I went to Paris and stayed with him for a while and traveled. It gave me an entirely different view on life. I then became very much interested in international affairs, particularly in travel and seeing people in different cultures. I came back and entered the University of Southern California Law School, graduating in 1952. I was Law Review and had done very well in school, and I was vice president of my class. I was the only black student in the entire law school at that time. But I received no opportunities to practice law the way that I wanted to, which would have been with one of the larger firms. So I went into law practice on my own and eventually joined up with two other classmates of mine from USC and practiced law for ten years.

All during that time, I was interested in international affairs. I became the attorney for the African Students of Southern California, and I was a founding member of the World Affairs Council. I began to entertain leader grantees that came through California for the State Department. I became known to the State Department and in 1962 they mounted a recruiting drive, and they sent someone out to interview me. As a matter of fact, it was Richard Fox who subsequently also became an ambassador. He persuaded me to give up my law practice and to join the Foreign Service.

HERMAN W. NICKEL, born in 1928, was a news correspondent by profession and had served as a correspondent for Time magazine in South Africa, where he was expelled by the South African Government after one year. In 1982 he returned there as United States ambassador.

Nickel: I've spent most of my professional life as a journalist; as a foreign correspondent. I started as a foreign correspondent for *Time* magazine in 1958 and in the course of my career, had all kinds of foreign assignments, including one in South Africa. The irony of my appointment was that my tenure as *Time* correspondent in Africa, based in Johannesburg from 1960 to 1961, ended with my expulsion by the South African Government after exactly one year.

It was amusing that when I arrived in South Africa [as ambassador] in April of 1982, that very same afternoon the foreign minister, Pik Botha, asked me to come by and because I was going to present my credentials the following day, they were in a great hurry to get me properly installed. And at the end of our discussion, he said with a rather thin smile, of course the South African Government remembered the circumstances of my departure from South Africa some years ago, and he added, with this touch of Boer-humor, that they hoped they wouldn't have to do this again.

JAY P. MOFFAT was born in New York in 1932 and joined the Foreign Service, after military duty, in 1956. He served in the Far East, Europe, the Caribbean, and North Africa before becoming ambassador to Chad in 1983.

Moffat: I'm a third generation Foreign Service officer, so in a sense it was somewhat predestined. I went to Harvard College and like many of my era I went into the the military, spending three years in the Army, which taught me Russian.

My grandfather, Joseph Clark Grew, was an ambassador in a number of posts, ending up in Japan. He was also the under secretary of state in the days when they only had one. And then my father, who was already in the Foreign Service married Mr. Grew's daughter, and I'm the next generation down.

DAVID B. FUNDERBURK, from North Carolina, was a staff officer in the U.S. Information Service in Romania in 1975, an exchange fellow to that country 1971-72, an exchange professor, 1976-77, and finally U.S. ambassador to Romania, 1981-85.   He is the director of the Jesse Helms Institute for American Studies & Foreign Policy and a professor at Campbell University.

Funderburk: To go back to childhood, I grew up with my mother in a small town in North Carolina.   She was the school teacher and a *World Book Encyclopedia* salesperson.   She worked in two or three jobs, but we had *World Book Encyclopedias* in the house, and I used to read through these, country after country.   I lived in a room by myself and had three sisters.   In my room, on the wall, as wall paper, a map of the world.   And I just remember a very intense interest and fascination with geography and history and the study of the people of the world.   So I looked through the countries of the world in this *World Book Encyclopedia* and on the map and so forth, and studied this through the years.   In college, I developed an interest in history and international affairs.   And what really led me to Eastern Europe, which is my area of expertise and special interest at Wake Forest University, was study under a professor whose field was the Austro-Hungarian Empire and Romania, in particular.   And though it really didn't hit me at the moment, I certainly started to develop an interest in Romania; I saw it as an exotic area, an area that had a history of tragedy--the Romanians as an island of Latins in a sea of Slavs, and so forth.

And so some years later, I decided to pursue it and got grants for the study of Romanian.   My wife and I went from North Carolina to California one summer and studied Romanian. The next summer we drove to Seattle, Washington, and studied it again.   And then after that I received a Fulbright grant for study in Romania for a year.   And the ball kept rolling after that in terms of research grants and study grants in that part of the world.   We also took advantage of being in that part of Europe to see other countries, to visit other ones there.   In fact, my doctoral dissertation was on relations between England and Romania, so we spent some time in the archives in Great Britain, as well.   So that's pretty much how the interest developed in that part of the world.

3

Appointments:
How to Become an Ambassador

An ambassador is the personal representative of the president of the United States. He or she is the embodiment of the term "embassy" and is customarily resident abroad in the country of accreditation. While the proliferation of international organizations requires the appointment of special representatives with the rank of ambassador, it is the appointment of those accredited to a specific country that is discussed here.

The selection and appointment of American ambassadors is a unique process involving presidential preferences, domestic politics, professional abilities from within the Foreign Service, and special qualifications from without. There is no sure route to an ambassadorship. Perhaps the simplest is the selection by the president, personally, of a specific individual in whom he has confidence and whom he wishes to represent him abroad. Another is the recommendation of a candidate by a political party chief, member of Congress, or close associate of the president as being someone particularly worthy. The largest group, about 70 per cent, is that comprised of officers chosen from the ranks of the Foreign Service and proposed by the secretary of state. While climbing the ladder in the career Foreign Service is one route to an ambassadorship, it is an uncertain one. Only a small percentage of all officers entering the service can expect to become ambassadors.

Although the selection process can vary, the final appointment system is fairly standard. Except for those chosen personally by the president, the names of nominees are sent to the White House by the proposing organizations (State Department, political party, congressional leaders, etc.), where they are reviewed by members of the president's staff. The list is culled and a "short list" of candidates is sent to the president, who then makes his decision and submits the candidate's name to the Senate for examination by the Senate Foreign Relations Committee and confirmation by the whole Senate. If the Senate does not approve, the appointment is withdrawn.

Rather than the process itself, the circumstances surrounding a number of ambassadorial appointments are described here by the ambassadors themselves. Their comments illustrate the variety of factors that can play a part in the final selection of an ambassador by the president.

LANGHORNE A. MOTLEY was born in Brazil of American parents and eventually became a career U.S. Air Force officer. He left the service and moved to Alaska where he became involved in state politics and supported the Reagan election bid in 1980. In 1981 President Reagan named him ambassador to Brazil. He later served as assistant secretary of state for Inter-American Affairs.

Motley: Sometime after the election and the elation had died down, I decided that I would like to go to Brazil as ambassador. It was a dream I had had from high school and college days. There were two jobs I wanted in my youth. They were assistant secretary of state for Latin American affairs and U.S. ambassador to Brazil.

My interest in the job of assistant secretary came from my studies at the Citadel. I was the president of the International Affairs Club there. I had studied the hierarchy of the State Department and had learned that the assistant secretary ran U.S. foreign policy in Latin America. So these were the two goals I had set out for myself in my youth. I hadn't spent my life plotting to get them, but all of a sudden the opportunity for one of them looked viable. Unlike many of my colleagues, who say that they were perfectly happy with what they were doing in private life, but agreed to accept when the president got down on bended knees and begged them to take this job or that, I make no such claims. I set out to get that job and I worked full time at it. I lobbied hard for it for six months.

You do it in a manner quite similar to any process to achieve any goals. First of all, you have to draw a roadmap. You've got to figure out who makes the decisions on ambassadorships. Each White House is different, but I sat down with the guys I knew who knew the White House and the State Department and found out who made the decisions regarding ambassadorships. I found out that the decision makers were an informal group consisting of Jim Baker, Mike Deaver, Bill Clark--then deputy secretary of state--and Wendy Borchert, deputy director of White House personnel. Those were the four decision makers.

Wendy collected the information and was very influential. Clark would look to her because she brought the political dimension to bear. The process then and now, which I believe to be wrong, was for the

Department to put up a candidate; then the political system, through the Office of Presidential Personnel, would put up a candidate for every job. This committee would then decide between the two. That is generally the way it worked, although obviously there were exceptions. It is not a very formalized process, but it was used in the Reagan years and now in the Bush Administration. I think it was also used by President Carter.

These ambassadorial appointments were all Presidential appointments. So there is a lot of push and pull. First I found out how the system worked. That told me that I had to get my name favorably supported before this committee. It had to be supported by people for whom they had respect. That is where the road map comes in. Al Haig was then the secretary of state. Frank Murkowski, although just a freshman Senator for Alaska, was willing to help. He wanted to see Haig, but was being put off. One day he went to the Department, to the secretary's office and introduced himself. He said he knew that the secretary was very busy, but he was prepared to wait. That threw the seventh floor [the location of the secretary's office] in a tizzy; they didn't know how to handle that. What were they going to do with a United States Senator? I was amused by Murkowski's action. The secretary's office is not geared up to handle surprises, and the appearance of a senator who was willing to wait for the secretary was that. I am sure they didn't know how to handle the situation. Haig was bemused. He asked Murkowski why he came to see him; it should have been the other way around. Murkowski told him that it was very simple. He had a candidate for the Brazil job who was very qualified and he wanted Haig to give me serious consideration. The fact that I spoke Portuguese was certainly in my favor since we don't have a surplus of Portuguese language experts, unlike Spanish.

The same type of approach was made to other members of that small group, Baker, Deaver and Bill Clark. I went to see the latter myself. I also saw Baker and Deaver, but I had friends who interceded with them on my behalf.   Let's face it, the president is going to appoint a number of political people. Hopefully, they are all qualified. That is not always the case, just as some foreign service officers are also not qualified. For every vacancy there may be four or five candidates. The issue is how you come out on top. So you have to find out when the Brazil assignment is coming up. You have to make sure you have your forces arrayed. I went to see Clark, who in turn sent me to see McFarlane, who was the counselor of the Department at the time. He in turn sent me to Tom Enders, then the assistant secretary for Inter-American Affairs. I felt pretty good about the process to that point and I wanted to see Enders to get off on a good foot with him. I was not under any illusion that Tom had any part to play in the selection process. He himself had not yet been confirmed, but had considerable sway in determining which Foreign Service officer would be nominated for Brazil by the Department. In fact, he had not focused on

Brazil when I saw him. I also had some friends in the system and knew what officers were vying for the job. They were formidable. I kept persisting and people would say to me: "Motley, if you can't have Brazil, what about Uruguay?" And I kept saying that I wanted to be U.S. ambassador to Brazil and if I couldn't have that, I was not interested in being an ambassador. I had made that fundamental decision earlier; I was not going to fall in the trap of just wanting to be an ambassador; there are a lot of people who do that--who are interested in the title. My stand surprised a lot of people; they found it hard to believe that I would return to Alaska if I couldn't get the Brazil job.

Then I had waited long enough and had done all the things I thought needed to be done. Finally, the decision was made. I was the recommendation that went to the president, who accepted it. Anyone who tells you appointments just fall out of the sky doesn't know whereof he speaks; it is a full-time job for a political appointee to get what he wants. For a Foreign Service officer to be the Department's nominee is a job for which he also has to work. If he is not willing to do that, then he doesn't understand how the system works

SHELBY CULLOM DAVIS, an investment banker, had long been active in Republican political circles. He served from 1969 to 1975 as ambassador to Switzerland.

Davis: I was named ambassador for a very simple reason, really, but the fact is, I had known Bill Rogers, who was secretary of state, since he had been a young Dewey man. I had had the title of Economic Advisor to Thomas E. Dewey in the 1940 campaign for the Republican nomination for the presidency, and in 1944. He knew about my interest in Switzerland and that I had been there. They needed someone who had some connections in Switzerland, which I, of course, had, having gone to the university there. I knew a lot of people, and I had skied there also, really every year since 1959. It had been discovered, actually through Bob Morgenthau, who was then the district attorney for the southern district of New York, that the Mafia and other criminal elements were taking satchels of money over to Switzerland on the new fast planes (the planes had become much faster in the sixties) and were depositing them in a bank which was kind of laundering the money. Then the funds would be brought back, and the Mafia could buy into legitimate enterprises. Morganthau had known that, but no one else had realized that this was happening. He had taken it up with the State Department and, in particular, Bill Rogers. Bill had known that I had lived in Switzerland and knew a lot of people there. I think that's the reason I was selected for, I might say, six happy years there. But it was really to look into the banking secrecy; that's why I was chosen. That was my mission, actually, to get a treaty with the Swiss.

OLCOTT HAWTHORNE DEMING entered the Department of State in 1943 and joined the Foreign Service in 1947. He was assigned to various posts in the Far East and Africa before being recommended by the secretary of state to become ambassador to Uganda, where he served from 1963 to 1966.

Deming: One morning Henry Tasca, assistant secretary and subsequently our ambassador to Greece, called me in and said, "We're going to make an ambassador out of you!" I expressed my appreciation, and Tasca added that he didn't know where or when this would take place but suggested Mauritania. I noted that it didn't have a capital yet. Tasca said the Department was going to put the embassy in a trailer. I said I wasn't terribly attracted by that. I didn't want to be an ambassador so badly that I'd live in a trailer in a country with no capital. He laughed.

Shortly after that Tasca told me that Assistant Secretary [Mennen] Williams wanted me to go to Uganda three months before independence and take over there from the present consul. He did not want any present representatives of the United States who had served under the British in Africa to stay on after the date of independence. It would look as though there had been no change in our point of view between colonial status and independence.

So in August 1962 I was sent out to take over as consul general in Uganda until independence came in October, when I would become chargé d'affaires. This left the Department free to appoint somebody else as ambassador or to later confirm me as ambassador.

MAXWELL M. RABB, a staunch supporter of the Republican party, had a long career in Wall Street and public service before being offered the ambassadorship to Italy by President Reagan in 1981. He served in Rome until 1989.

Rabb: I think people would say I was a moderate Republican, but I think I was the first of the establishment figures (I then was in New York) to come out for Reagan. We had been friends for a long time, even though I was a delegate to the Republican Convention of 1976 and had voted against him. I was for Ford in New York, but we were good friends. He finally talked to me and asked me to come out to see him in California. He didn't tell me what it was, but it wasn't difficult for me to guess. And so I went there and, sure enough, they wined and dined me. I was prepared for it.

Then he called me on the telephone and offered me a very important post. I said no to him. It was a big one, yes, but even a foreign one--I think I was then the senior partner in a very large Wall Street law firm with close to 350 lawyers, and I had my problems. I just thought, "Look, I'm going to be a good citizen and not take it."

That ended it. Very shortly thereafter, he came back. He said, "Max,"-- this is verbatim--"Max, I am going to make you an offer that you can't turn me down on. I want you to be my ambassador to Italy."

And I, who had always thought there might be moments that would be of consequence to me in my life; those would be moments that I would react to with pear-shaped words, words that would ring down through the ages for my children, and my children's children.

And, when he said this, I blurted out, "Wow, wow!"

He laughed on the other side of the telephone and said, "I take that as an assent."

I said, "Yes."

ROBINSON McILVAINE, a career Foreign Service officer, had his problems getting past the eagle eye of President Johnson when his first appointment as ambassador came to the White House. He later served as ambassador to Dahomey (now Benin), Guinea, and Kenya.

McIlvaine: I was working for Averell Harriman. He was ambassador-at-large, so he was not very busy; he wasn't doing anything. I wasn't terribly busy except when he was busy. What had happened was that my name, I discovered later, had been sent over to the White House to be ambassador to Senegal. LBJ, who was noted for his testiness, looked at it and said, "I won't have another goddamned Harvard guy in this thing," and threw my name out. So I didn't get that job. So that's when Averell Harriman took me on. I had gotten to know him pretty well while running the Congolese Task Group. So I was just lodged there until we could try another ploy. So six or eight months later, a vacancy came up in Guinea, and my name was sent over, and sure as hell, nobody wanted to go there, so I didn't have any competition. I got through. I guess the President wasn't looking at what he was signing.

Career Foreign Service officer EILEEN ROBERTA DONOVAN had served previously in Barbados as consul general. Her familiarity with the country and its leaders led to her appointment to return there as ambassador, where she served from 1969 to 1974.

Donovan: Barbados' independence was coming to fruition. I went down with Chief Justice Warren to the ceremony in November, 1966.

Early in 1969 I was one of six women in Washington who won the Federal Women's Award. Under Secretary of State U. Alexis Johnson stopped me in the corridor one day and said, "Eileen, don't get excited about the Barbados possibility because no one is going to appoint anybody that the Department of State recommends. It'll be a political appointment made by the White House." I said, "I'm not excited about it. I'm just grateful that the Department would include me among the others." So, one day they announced that it was I. I would go back again. Sayre and others said, well we thought it was about time we sent somebody there who knew something about it, and you seem to be the only one. So, off I went again.

MALCOLM TOON's Foreign Service postings had been primarily in Eastern Europe and the Soviet Union. However, he had a special quality that caused the secretary of state to send him to Israel. Toon also served as ambassador to Czechoslovakia, Yugoslavia, and the Soviet Union.

Toon: Henry Kissinger had become very upset with the Israelis, because he claimed that they had sabotaged and ruined his diplomatic shuttle exercise. So he wanted to send, as he put it, I think, rather crudely, "a tough-minded S.O.B." to Israel as ambassador in order to put the Israelis in their place.

I had gained a reputation, whether justified or not--it depends on your own point of view--of being rather blunt, outspoken, tough, in dealing, primarily, with eastern Europeans and the Soviets. So Henry decided it would be a good idea to send me there.

JAMES WILMER WINE was a Kentucky lawyer, whose interest in religious freedom prompted him to become involved in the campaign of John F. Kennedy in 1959-1960. This early tie to Kennedy eventually sparked Wine's appointment to the Ivory Coast as ambassador from 1962 to 1965.

Wine: The president of the Ivory Coast, Houphouet-Boigny, was the first African chief of state to come here on a state visit during the Kennedy Administration. Houphouet-Boigny and John Kennedy got on personally very well. At this point I'm reciting what I've been told from the White House. On his departure he asked Mr. Kennedy, "When you send your ambassador down there, would you send somebody whom you know personally, because then I'll feel as if this linkage of friendship is being maintained."

I was called on the phone from the White House and asked about it. I said, "I'm going to have to think about this a little bit. I don't even know where the place is."

They said, "Well, send us a cable tomorrow."

That day I did learn that Abidjan was probably a most modern city. I talked with a friend on the phone in Paris who knew the Ivory Coast quite well. He told me about it. I was also interested in education. I understood that   President Kennedy and Houphouet-Boigny had talked about the establishment of the university in Abidjan and that they were very much interested in having people in key places in Africa. This was a presidential policy decision. Then there was a pause and he said, "Hell, you're an adventurer. You certainly shouldn't have any objection to going down there."

I sent a cable the next day accepting.

JEAN MARY WILKOWSKI, a career foreign service officer and a specialist in economic policy, recalls her reaction to the offer of an ambassadorship to Zambia.

Wilkowski: Graham Martin [then ambassador in Rome] had called me down and said, "I want to know how you feel. Do you want to be an ambassador?" I just kind of gulped, and he said, "Well, what's your answer?" Instead of saying, "I have to go home and ask my mother," which was about what I would have done about ten years ago, I simply said, "Well, what do you think, Graham, Mr. Ambassador?"   He just leaned back in his chair and shook his head, you know. "How could this woman be so dumb? " was written all over his face. He leaned forward in the chair. He just eyed me very keenly and intensely, and he said, "I think you can do anything you set your mind to."

I said, "Well, thank you, Mr. Ambassador. I would welcome your recommendation when you go back to Washington." So the next thing I knew, dear Cleo Noel [later ambassador to the Sudan where he was assassinated] was on the telephone, calling me from Washington. He was in Personnel then, and he said, "Well, Jean, how would you like to go to Zambia?"

And I said, "What as?"

And he said, "Oh, knock it off. Chief of mission?"

So I was pretty excited, of course. Some people say, "Endsville, Africa. Why do they send all the career people and the women to Africa." But I thought, "Gee, you know, it's fine. I'll go." And so then back to Washington for the usual swearing in and briefings and consultations with the academics and all of that jazz, and then I went back to Rome to buy a lot of clothes which were totally inappropriate for Zambia.

President Lyndon Johnson was not the easiest man to please, and he had little affection for professional diplomats. Yet the president was personally responsible for LEWIS DEAN BROWN's being named ambassador to Senegal and The Gambia in 1967. He was later ambassador to Jordan.

Brown: There were many ways to communicate with the president of the United States, and Lyndon Johnson was president. If you understand

Lyndon Johnson, you understand how to communicate. That is, at 3:00 in the morning, he's got nothing to do and he wants something to read. So there was a piece of paper produced by the secretariat in the State Department called "The President's Evening Reading." It was done about 9:00 or 10:00 at night, and if you were around, you could get something in it. And there wasn't anybody to check with; you just put it in. Because no one was going to see that except the president. The secretary of state wasn't going to see it or anybody else.

So I produced a lot of stuff for that thing on various matters, and Lyndon Johnson liked it. He called in his chief of staff and said, "How long has he been in Washington?" They said, "A while." He said, "Get him an embassy." So they called me to the White House. A guy says, "What do you want?" I was smart enough not to say, "What's vacant?" I knew what was vacant. So I said, "I'll take Senegal." He said, "Good. I thought you were going to ask for one of the impossible ones."   You had to make sure that Lyndon Johnson understood that you worked your way through college. If you told him that, you were okay. But if he thought that your father had paid for you to go to Harvard, you were dead with him.

So then I went to Senegal.

JACK BLOOM KUBISCH joined the Foreign Service in 1947 and served in a variety of posts in Latin America, South Asia, and Europe, mainly with AID missions. In 1974, upon the recommendation of Secretary of State Henry Kissinger, President Ford appointed Kubisch ambassador to Greece.

Kubisch: It turned out that in July of 1974, while I was assistant secretary, the then Greek military government endeavored to cooperate with Greek Cypriots on the island of Cyprus to overthrow the government of President Archbishop Makarios on Cyprus, to assassinate him, and for a group of Greek Cypriots to take control of Cyprus and unite Cyprus with Greece. This led to a crisis and a near war between Greece and Turkey. It led to the fall of the military regime in Greece that had been in power for seven years and the reassignment of the American ambassador in Greece, Ambassador Tasca, who had been closely associated with the regime of the Greek colonels.

Kissinger asked me if I had any interest in going to Greece as ambassador, and I said, "Yes, I would" in line with earlier conversations that we had had. I said, "I would welcome such an assignment." And he said that he would talk to the president about it. The matter dragged on for a couple of weeks because these were the final days and weeks of the Nixon administration leading to President Nixon's resignation on Friday, August 9, 1974, almost at the height of the crisis between Greece and Turkey. Kissinger called me that day and said he had spoken to President

Ford, and President Ford was prepared to name me as ambassador to Greece and would I come to the White House. Nixon resigned at noon on Friday, August 9 and about 5:00 P.M. that afternoon I was at the White House privately with our new President Ford and Secretary Kissinger talking about the Greek-Turkish problem.

President Ford, whom I had known fairly well as a congressman and as vice president, called me by my first name; "Jack, Henry tells me that you're willing to go to Athens as our ambassador. Is that right?" And I said, "Yes, I would welcome the assignment." He said, "All right, that settles it. You can go."

HARRISON MATTHEWS SYMMES entered the Foreign Service in 1947 and spent most of his career in the Arabic-speaking world. Despite his own doubts about the wisdom of his going to Jordan as ambassador (1967-1970), he was appointed primarily because of his reputation for toughness, a quality which Deputy Secretary Katzenbach thought was needed.

Symmes: When the idea of going to Jordan as ambassador was put forward, at least one of my dear friends who was in a position to make his views known, made his views known to higher authority. "You shouldn't send Harry there. It's not right for Harry and it's not right for Jordan." He was mainly concerned about its not being right for me because of my reputation for being "Mr. No" that had been developed and because he thought the agency (CIA) was suspicious of me. I recall that when I was first told by Rodger Davies about this, I told him, "Rodger, I don't know. I think Jordan is a lovely place to be and I would like being in the country with all the archeological advantages, and that kind of thing. Nevertheless, I don't think the Jordanians are going to like it. And you know my reputation."

And he said, "Nick Katzenbach," Katzenbach then being the deputy secretary, "and I have discussed this and we want you to go because of your reputation. In other words, we want you to go because you have stood up against the Jordanians in the past. In our view you have a balanced view toward Jordanian relations with the United States and you have the kind of integrity we want. We want somebody who isn't just going to lie down and let the Jordanians walk over us."

It was a combination of expertise in the Arab world, felicitous personnel shifts, and recommendations of George Ball, David Bruce, and the Near East Bureau of the Department of State that led to HERMANN FREDERICK EILTS' appointment by President Johnson as ambassador to Saudi Arabia in 1966.

Eilts: Just before I was to leave London, the man who was to go as DCM to Tel Aviv was given an embassy in Africa and the Tel Aviv post was vacated, and I was named to it. I was delighted. It was Governor Harriman, however, who was undersecretary at the time, who broke my Tel Aviv assignment and insisted that I go to Tripoli, Libya. He did so because we were having problems with the Wheelus Air Force Base negotiations, and he wanted me to get involved.

I was very unhappy when I left London in order to go to Tripoli, very unhappy. And I remember expressing to David Bruce [U.S. ambassador to London] my unhappiness. He said, "Don't worry about it, you won't be there more than a year." About a year after I had arrived in Tripoli, David Newsom was named ambassador to Libya, and there was clearly no longer any need for me to be there. At that particular time I received a message from the State Department, from the Director General, saying that President Johnson wanted me to go as ambassador to Saudi Arabia. I was asked, if offered the job, would I accept it. I subsequently discovered that there were three elements in the Department that had pushed this assignment. One was the NEA Bureau, which wanted me to go there. Another was George Ball with whom I had worked on the Cyprus thing; and the third was David Bruce. They had all, apparently around the time that I left London to go to Tripoli, proposed to the White House that I be named ambassador to Saudi Arabia. However, when the post became vacant, William Porter was named. Porter was very quickly moved--he never went to Saudi Arabia--he became deputy ambassador to Vietnam, where Henry Cabot Lodge wanted him. The position therefore again became vacant and all of these three recommendations then came together. As a result, I was named ambassador to Saudi Arabia.

THEODORE ROOSEVELT BRITTON, Jr.'s successful career in public and private life had caught the attention of Senator Strom Thurmond and others in the Republican Party. This led to his appointment as ambassador to Barbados and Grenada by President Nixon in 1974.

Britton: Having met so many people at embassies and having had to work closely with State Department, again, whetted my interest in international matters. I was getting some publicity from my travels from organizations such as *Jet* magazine, and so on. I always have to thank Simeon Booker who did kind of publicize my travels. He's the Washington editor. So out of it, eventually, the White House [I had good friends over at the White House] became interested in what I was doing, and about 1973 I was asked if I might be interested in an embassy, and I said, "Oh boy! Yes, of course." But it was a long time between the summer of 1973 and the fall of 1974.

Nixon was still president. Yes. It was interesting, from my early days in New York I began to feel more comfortable with the Republican party.

We had in Harlem at that time what was called the United Young Republicans. I wasn't living in Harlem, but I worked over there at the Carver Federal Savings and Loan Association, which is located right in the center of Harlem--and I met people, for example, Sam Pierce and others. And, of course, Nelson Rockefeller had just become governor and he was very active. His son was a member of the group--Rodman, that is. Steven, the other son, was teaching Sunday school at my church, the Riverside Church. Stan Scott, who was then a special assistant to President Nixon, called me one day and asked if I would be interested in an ambassadorship. I think the same thing had been asked in one of Simeon Booker's columns in *Jet*. He said that I would be interested in an ambassadorship if offered. Stan Scott called me and said, "Are you really interested?"

I said, "Yes."

"Well, we're going to have a number of them coming open, including Upper Volta. If you're interested, I'll certainly start pushing your name."

Eventually, Ouagadougou was filled by a career Foreign Service officer. But we continued to talk, and I continued to put material forward whenever I was asked for something.

Things were drifting along and I chose at that point to go back to call on the friendship of a person whom I had met earlier, Senator Strom Thurmond. I was born in South Carolina and still have a big interest in South Carolina. Senator Thurmond and I had met during the time I was working on what was called an "add-on bathroom" for South Carolina houses. It was going a long way to help out in South Carolina. He was very grateful, and we struck up a good friendship. I pointed out some of the terrible things that happened in South Carolina and things that had not been done even though he and others had held the highest positions--there was so much to be done. As I say, he accepted this in good spirit and we began to be in regular touch. He had sent me a note and said that any time he could be of help to me, let him know--"to use him," to quote his words. So I sent a note to him telling him of my interest and the fact that I could use his help at that time, and he sent a long personal letter to the new secretary of state, Henry Kissinger. Apparently, when that letter arrived, it triggered an immediate response and my telephone really began to ring. It was almost as if everybody was told to get on it right away. I was invited to come over to see Deputy Secretary Kenneth Rush, plus other people. I have to interject the name of Gregory Lebede who was in charge of my interest in the position over there at the White House. He was in the personnel office and stuck with me throughout. He called to say, "They're going to offer you Barbados, and I hope you're interested." He added, "You'd better be interested."

While serving as ambassador to the Yemen Arab Republic, WILLIAM REX CRAWFORD, Jr. was urgently transferred to Cyprus in 1974 by President Ford at the urging of Secretary Kissinger following the assassination of Ambassador Rodger Davies at Nicosia.

Crawford: I was summoned back to Washington to be interviewed by Secretary of State Kissinger, to go to Syria as ambassador. Three of us were interviewed separately by Dr. Kissinger. But in my file that went up to him, the assistant secretary of NEA, then Roy Atherton, put in a note which he was kind enough to inform me of. Apparently it was along the lines of: "You asked to see him, but we'd really rather not pull Crawford out of Yemen because we've just got things going there." So that was the way it would have worked, except for the events in Cyprus. I went off on summer vacation hiking in Norway. In the end it was only for a few days. When Ambassador Rodger Davies was killed in Nicosia, Kissinger summoned me back urgently, and within what was then a record time in U.S. history confirmed by the Senate, briefed by President Ford and Secretary Kissinger, and on my way back, not to Yemen but Cyprus.

DAVID B. FUNDERBURK had considerable knowledge of Romania, having been a staff officer in the U.S.Information Service in Romania in 1975, an exchange fellow in 1971-72 and an exchange professor in 1976-77. His impressive knowledge of Romania and the support of such influential figures as Senator Jesse Helms and Senator Strom Thurmond assured his appointment by President Reagan as ambassador to Romania in 1981.

Funderburk: I was being sponsored, primarily, by Senator Jesse Helms, and some other southern conservatives. The fact that Senator Helms had held up the nominations of some of the favorite golden boys of the Foreign Service certainly meant that in order to try to get retribution from Senator Helms, they were going to do tit for tat. So, in other words, when Senator Helms held up the nomination of Lawrence Eagleburger for various positions, many people in the Foreign Service took it upon themselves to say, "Well, we should inform some Senators to do the same to Senator Helms' nominees." So it was simply the fact that I was a favorite of Senator Helms and Strom Thurmond and a few other southern conservatives. I don't think it had that much to do with me personally. Nobody knew about me personally. And when I got into the Senate Foreign Relations hearings, people from Chuck Percy to Howard Baker to others were very friendly and said, "We're amazed that here is a political appointee who's been to the country and knows the language of the country." So they thought this was an asset and that this would be a good thing. But it was a political thing.

This [my comparative youth] was basically dismissed as not being a paramount factor in view of the fact that I had lived in that country four years and knew something of the language, had written a dissertation about it, many articles, and so forth. So the familiarity with the country itself, and the people seemed to outweigh this concern about youth. There were some others who were appointed during that same year who were about the same age.

My initial request, or preference, was to be head of the Office of Eastern Europe inside the State Department, or the Bureau of East European Affairs. And, in fact, after the election of Ronald Reagan, Senator Helms' office said, "Would you list some positions that you might be interested in?" And I listed about six places, and I think fourth on the list was ambassador to Romania. I hadn't really given it that much thought. And so my name was thrown in the hopper by seven senators who endorsed my nomination, and the Heritage Foundation, and some other groups, some generals and other friends of mine. My name was thrown in initially to be in the East European area of the State Department. And, eventually, some many months later, I got a telephone call from White House personnel saying that the position that I was opting for was really a career position.

Well, I wouldn't say it was distasteful--the period of waiting to be approved for an ambassadorship, but it certainly was a period of some trauma and uncertainty in our family. There was some concern and anxiety, being unsure of whether the nomination was going to be held up indefinitely or going to be shot down. There was worry over being treated unfairly by the media just looking for sensationalism, and maybe from leaks of people in the Foreign Service who resented a political appointee in such a position. There are many right now whose only qualification is that they gave $150,000 to the Bush campaign.

WALTER C. CARRINGTON's path to an ambassadorship was through his experience as a Peace Corps director, which brought him to the attention of the Carter White House. He held various positions in the Peace Corps and was the executive vice president of the African-American Institute until his appointment in 1980 by President Carter as ambassador to Senegal.

Carrington: I had been involved in African affairs almost since I graduated from college. In fact, I remember two weeks after graduating going off to Senegal as part of an American youth delegation to the Conference of the World Assembly of Youth which was held in Dakar, Senegal, in 1952, marking I think the first international conference ever held in Africa. When I came back, I went on to law school but kept an interest in international affairs, and then a few years later took a group over to Nigeria for the Experiment in International Living. Then in 1961 when the Peace Corps began, I got involved with the Peace Corps very early and was part of the original group of seven overseas directors that Sargent Shriver appointed. My assignment was to go out and negotiate with the government of Sierra Leone to have the Peace Corps come there. After the successful negotiations, I became the first Peace Corps director in Sierra Leone and served there from 1961 to 1963.

I left the Peace Corps and went to New York to become executive vice president of the African American Institute and served there until 1980, when I was appointed by President Carter to be ambassador to Senegal. I was getting ready to leave the Institute. I wasn't sure what I was going to do, and I had been down in Washington in January of 1980. President Carter had a meeting to reassess foreign policy and to bring in a lot of support because there were many things happening. I remember going into this meeting at the White House, and there were all of the famous names of American foreign policy. You had Schlesinger, you had everybody who had served in either a Republican or Democratic administration. They were all there. And then there were some others of us who were sort of representing organizations involved in international matters.

I remember we left that meeting, and as I was coming from the White House with a couple of friends, limousines were waiting and all these big names got in the limousines and zipped off. Some of us who had to grab taxis walked down to the entrance and all the reporters were there. Well, they weren't able to get any interviews from anybody else, so they grabbed us. I remember a reporter asking me a question about what had gone on and so forth and asked me a question about this very issue that I had raised serious questions about. I gave a little thing about extending the cold war in Africa and how I thought that was unwise.

I got on the shuttle back to New York. I walked into my apartment and my son, who was then 5 years old, came running up and say, "Daddy, Daddy, I just saw you on TV." Then my wife came in and said, "You've just had a call from the White House." And I said, "What in the hell is going on?" So I called back and it was Louis Martin, who was one of the advisers to the president. Louis was a person I had known for a long time. In fact, I first met Louis in Nigeria back in 1958. Louis called me and said that the president wanted to put my name forward for an ambassadorship. I said, "Well, what country are they talking about?" He said, "I don't know." He said, "It's Cameroon, or Senegal. I don't know." And so he said, "Can I tell him yes?" And I said, "Well, you know, Louis, I'd like to know exactly what country plus I've got to talk to my wife and so forth. I'll have to get back to you.".

So I remember the next morning I got a call from a friend of mine who said, "What the hell is going on? Louis Martin thinks you're crazy. Here the president has offered you this ambassadorship and you're waffling and so forth." I told him I was waiting to find out what country it was. My friend said, "Well, Louis tells me it's Senegal." And so as soon as I heard it was Senegal, I called back and said yes I'd be happy to take it. Senegal is a country that I had very special kind of relationship with. And so this was in January of 1980.

4

Ambassadorial Seminar:
Preparation for the Post

When the ambassadorial appointment appears to be certain, and confirmation by the Senate and agrément [acceptance] by the host government assured, briefings at the Department of State and other appropriate organizations are set up. In 1973 the Department of State established at its Foreign Service Institute an Ambassadorial Seminar to acquaint newly appointed ambassadors with the various embassy functions and, through discussions with experienced ambassadors and specialists, with some of the problems they are likely to encounter.

This seminar has been a prime tool in preparing new chiefs of mission for their assignments. Both career and non-career ambassadors-to-be are invited to attend, along with their spouses. BRANDON HAMBRIGHT GROVE, Jr. former U.S. ambassador to Zaire, a career Foreign Service officer and currently director of the Foreign Service Institute, conducts the seminar along with LANGHORNE A. MOTLEY, a former non-career ambassador. The two ambassadors describe some of the matters discussed in the seminar, emphasizing the nature and extent of the responsibilities and authority placed in the hands of the ambassador by the president of the United States. They also give their views as to the relative strengths and weaknesses of career and non-career ambassadors. Ambassador Grove concludes by stressing the duty of all ambassadors, as personal representatives of the president, to reflect the philosophy and goals of that president and his administration.

Motley: In the State Department, there is a process by which every new ambassador, career and non-career, before going to his new post attends an ambassadorial seminar. It used to be one day, then it became three days. When I went through it, it was a five-day session; now it lasts almost two weeks. In July 1985, when I left the Department, George Shultz asked me to get involved in the seminar. So Shirley Temple Black [ambassador to Ghana and Czechoslovakia], the Director of FSI Charles Bray, and I became co-chairpersons of the seminar. I have conducted every seminar since July 1985. I have lost count of the number of seminars I have participated in, but it is well over twenty. There are twelve in a seminar, which would make more than 240 ambassadors. I have some repeats when after their first ambassadorial stint, they were assigned to another, and decided to take a refresher course.

BRANDON GROVE emphasizes that the source of an ambassador's authority is the president of the United States.

Grove: The heart of the seminar is the matter of ambassadorial authorities--where does an ambassador get authority to act?   Then we discuss how that authority can be used, and how it can be the basis for uniting people from various agencies in the country team within the embassy.

After the introductory portion of the seminar on the first day, which is always a Monday, we make that the first item of business and discuss Section 207 of the Foreign Service Act of 1980, which contains the definition of ambassadorial authority, as well as the president's letter to each ambassador. [Each administration issues such a letter spelling out the responsibilities and authority of ambassadors. The text of President Bush's letter to ambassadors is included as Appendix A to this book.]

These two documents, in particular, form the basis of specific authority, rooted in the law itself, for anyone who becomes an ambassador. Whether you're at a very big post or a very small one, the authorities are exactly the same. The president's letter is circulated by the president to the head of every department and agency in Washington, so employees of all agencies know exactly what the ambassador has been told and is empowered to do.

In discussing the president's letter I actually go through it phrase-by-phrase to discuss not only what it says and what it means, but how it came to read that way. We make comparisons with earlier versions of the letter. We walk people through every word and phrase, and open up discussion as to what they mean throughout that letter. There isn't anybody who leaves the ambassadorial seminar who hasn't given serious thought to every word in that letter.

Motley: I make the point that they [the ambassadors] have an extraordinary set of authorizations, more powerful than any others in the

U.S. government with the exception of the president. Their authorizations are more powerful--in the sense of clear and defined--and succinct than those of cabinet officers. The authorizations stem from a series of sources, one of which is the Foreign Service Act and the other is the presidential letter which each ambassador receives. These authorizations, in essence, have the president saying that the ambassador has responsibility for the activities of all United States Government operations and for the conduct of all employees of the executive branch, with the exception of a couple of specifically stated entities, such as certain military commanders. But all the other military staff are included.

I tell them that an ambassador sends signals. They have a problem which I call the "pedestal" problem. Historically, the embassy staff will want to put you on a pedestal. That is what embassies like to do for their ambassadors. It is a wonderful thing. It is part of the lore and tradition-- "Yes, Mr. Ambassador" or "No, Mr. Ambassador" or "Right away, Mr. Ambassador." You drive up in your car, flags flying, and somebody rushes up to open your door. You speak and people write down your every word. The down-side is that you begin to believe your own press notices. You have to be careful. The embassy will try to put the ambassador on a pedestal. We try to keep them human.

An ambassador sends signals from that pedestal. One of my predecessors was shy, and he tended to walk around with his head down. The embassy staff thought he was mad at them because he wouldn't say "hello." It was nothing of the kind. He just behaved that way and was not expressing any feelings, one way or the other. So an ambassador can send signals without even knowing it. Ambassadors have to remember that if they smile or frown or say "hello" or don't say "hello," their demeanor will be interpreted, rightly or wrongly. They are the unelected mayors of the community and are always on display. They should never forget that. Ambassadors send signals and that is the way they exercise their authority.

The ambassador must be scrupulous in conduct and ethical in all dealings and not only avoid wrongdoing but avoid all appearance of wrongdoing.

Grove: One of our biggest growth areas, in terms of time we spend in this seminar, is the area of ethics. We now spend two hours with a legal advisor at the State Department, who deals with ethical matters and explains in detail what ambassadors and their families can do, should not do, should not even appear to be doing.

The whole question of monies and how they can be spent is discussed. Expenses for the residence, expenses for entertaining, whom can you entertain at the taxpayers' cost, whose entertainment you must yourself pick up. For instance, if you have an American business group visiting a post and you give a luncheon for them, that is a legitimate expense under reimbursement. If you want to give a Christmas party for your own staff, even though all of them work directly for the United States government, that's entirely out of your own pocket.   We speak of business people. There are many things you can and should do to help them. There are also a few things that you cannot do, in terms of giving preferential treatment to a particular company when there are other American companies who are interested in the same kind of market. We discuss that.

You can talk about some seemingly small things, like who gets to use official cars. To what extent should a spouse (let's assume it's a woman in this case) use a car? Is it legitimate, for instance, to go down to the beauty parlor and get your hair done and tie up a driver for two hours or so, even if the visit is for some official entertaining that the spouse will be going to? There are many specific questions that need to be talked about. Can you pay for Christmas cards by charging the cost of those cards, for example, or of any holiday greeting cards, to the United States government?

The list is long. The issues are serious. I just picked some of the more colorful ones. But the seminar portion with the legal advisor is one that has grown considerably and focuses, as the Bush administration has itself focused, on appearance as well as wrong-doing itself.

We have a yardstick we apply, which is not a bad one to think about. If you, as an ambassador, are in a quandary about what you ought to do, and you're wondering a little bit whether it is all right or maybe has some question attached to it in terms of its propriety or its wisdom, our solution for that is: In your own head, make up a brief account of what you are planning to do as if you had actually done it. Write it up, in your mind, as a news story. And then ask yourself how you would like to read that account in, say, *The Washington Post*. If you feel comfortable with that, well, that's fine, you're probably on the right track. If you have a queasy reaction, you'd better take a second look. And that has to do with the matter of appearances.

A portion of the seminar is devoted to discussions on security, terrorism, and counterterrorism.

Grove: We spend considerable time on the matters of security and counterterrorism. These are difficult times. The security briefings cover the kinds of information an ambassador and the immediate family need to know about the residence and the chancery. We talk at some length about the Marine guards we now have at virtually every overseas post. We also talk about counterterrorism and how you handle threats from the outside that are specifically directed against an embassy or a person.

Included are such matters as protocol, medical problems, and relations with the press.

Grove: We have a session on protocol. What are state visits. What are the different kinds of visits by foreign dignitaries; when is an ambassador likely to come home if the chief of state of his country visits the United States; or when that is not likely to occur; the occasions, for instance, on which a spouse will be brought back at government expense. There are a number of questions in the medical area that a State Department doctor discusses. Acquired Immunity Deficiency Syndrome [AIDS] has become a global problem and is frightening. There are problems of AIDS at a number of posts. There are certainly many countries, and not just in Africa or Haiti, in which the AIDS rate is very high. What are the threats, really? How do you handle that at a post? What do you do, for instance, about the residence staff who are people from the country itself to which you are accredited? If the cook is fixing the salad and slices his finger, and a drop of blood falls in the salad, are you endangered? (The answer is no.) But we talk about these questions. Do flies, or mosquitoes more specifically, carry AIDS if they've bitten a person who has AIDS and have drawn blood from that person? These are real life questions.

We discuss alcoholism. What is to be done if a person in a family or a member of the embassy staff is an alcoholic. What procedures should the chief of mission follow in dealing with that person? What authority does the ambassador have if the problem is as serious as that?

We talk about medical evacuations. More often than we like, people become ill or are involved in an accident at a post and need to be taken out of a country . How do you handle it? Who pays for it? What kind of help can you get in transportation? These are examples of some of the subjects that come up.

We try to talk about what one might call a media policy for the ambassador. What kinds of relations with the press should there be? Should there be regular briefings? Should there ever be a press conference? How do you want to handle that? Are you going to have backgrounders for maybe just the American correspondents? There are a great many questions that a press officer helps an ambassador with. That's another aspect of public diplomacy we now address.

The ambassador is often required to deal with all sorts of crises, those resulting from riots and violence, natural and economic disaster, and so forth. A discussion of some such situations in the past and their relevance to the human equation is included in the seminar.

Grove: A third new area for us is what we call the human side of crisis management. Things go wrong abroad. Sometimes they're natural disasters. You will remember the earthquake in Mexico. Sometimes it's a plane crash. For example, we talked about Pan Am 103, which crashed at Lockerbie. Sometimes there are riots and violence caused by political instability or economic chaos in a particular country. There have been many examples of that.

What are the responsibilities of an ambassador in dealing with that sort of crisis? At what point do you evacuate Americans from your post? What are the authorities for sending Americans home? We've had many evacuations throughout the world in the last two and a half years. How do you handle the American community, including those that are not government people, as you see a crisis building up? How do you deal with grief? How do you handle people when your consular section and others must convey the bad news that someone has lost their life? Very often it's the embassy that first has this news.

We now have special films FSI [Foreign Service Institute] has developed in bereavement counseling. We have developed training in stress management under crisis. If there is one of these disasters, a small number of people at a post or in a consular section can get overworked very quickly. What do you do about that? How can you mobilize the whole mission to work as a team and spell each other when the going gets tough and will be prolonged because of the nature of the problem? What are your responsibilities to the American community? We have business people, missionaries, private citizens, students, and of course the Peace Corps, who can be far-flung throughout the country. How do you get in touch with them? What do you tell them if you think a crisis is brewing? How do you help get them out?

The two ambassadors discuss the matter of when to and when not to carry out instructions from Washington.

Grove: When an ambassador gets an instruction that he or she doesn't like, it's a difficult problem. If it's a bolt from the blue, it suggests that the ambassador may be more out of touch with what's going on in the department than he should be. If it is within the context of a known issue but off the mark, we suggest that there is nothing wrong in going back and either questioning it or pointing out your assessment of what the consequences would be, the adverse consequences, if indeed you were to carry out these steps the way you've been asked to. Not only is there nothing wrong in that, it's the responsibility of a chief of mission to raise such questions.

There are some instructions that you must not carry out. The subject of ambassadorial authorities has drawn a lot more interest after the Iran-Contra Affair, Tony Motley tells me, than it had before. This was simply because there was an ambassador who had taken an instruction from a member of the staff of the National Security Council who had no business instructing an ambassador.   This became a cause célèbre, and the ambassador was reprimanded by the secretary of state.

Motley: If an ambassador receives an instruction that he or she doesn't like, negotiate right then and there. Tell Washington that you would be happy to do whatever was requested, but that it should be reconsidered one more time. Ask whether Washington really wants the ambassador to charge up that hill and then fall on his sword? Is that really what we want? The multi-lateral instructions--that is, when all posts are instructed to do the same thing within a similar time frame--you can't really do anything about them. Depending on what country you are assigned to, the ambassador may have the freedom to decide whom he should see and when. Washington understands that. However, that situation is different from a bilateral one; yet a good ambassador will find an informal way to get the instructions changed. The Foreign Service "Bible" says you write your own instructions, and that is correct. If an ambassador is aggressive, he or she will be way ahead of the curve and in effect will have written his or her own instructions. That ambassador is not sitting back waiting for someone in Washington to tell him or her what to do. That ambassador has already prepped that Washington official and primed him; he or she may have even sent a draft of the instructions to Washington. I firmly believe that this is the right course. Washington is usually in gridlock with sixteen different agencies wondering what is going on, and the Department is concerned about how it will look in public. No one worries more about bilateral relations than the ambassador; no one spends as much time on the issue as she or he does, except maybe the desk officer. So the ambassador is really in the driver's seat as far as the policy is concerned. You can write a message that starts with: "Unless I am otherwise directed, I am going to do the following." That is one of the things I tell the seminar people. You have to be intellectually honest about it. You can't write on a Friday afternoon that you will tear down the embassy walls on Monday morning. You have to give Washington a reasonable period of time for reaction. Nine times out of ten, Washington will be glad that something is being done. If they want to say "No" someone has to feel very strongly about it. The reverse of that coin is to ask for guidance, which is a favorite technique in the Foreign Service.

I had a rule in my embassy that no one was allowed to ask for guidance unless I authorized it. I didn't care whether it was guidance for lost household effects or anything else. We didn't ask for it because [a] nine times out of ten nothing happened, and that puts you in a dilemma and [b] nine of ten times the embassy could resolve the problem and come up with the best solution. If Washington didn't like it, it would let you know. And thirdly, sometimes the guidance is not what you wanted, and then you have a problem on your hands.

Ambassadors GROVE and MOTLEY discuss some of the differences in style and approach between career and non-ambassadors as they have observed them.

Motley: If we have a seminar with both kinds in it, I get into that right away. I'll speak to the non-career officers and tell them not to listen to the "freaks downtown" who warn you about the Foreign Service. It is in the best interest of the career service that they succeed. They should believe that. They look at a non-career ambassador somewhat differently, because they are a different breed. But they will be loyal, supportive. They want to be led. Foreign Service officers want and are happy to be led. They will question an ambassador because they are taught to question. They are not questioning an ambassador's authority, but they do want to probe ideas.

I tell both career and non-career ambassadors that if they fail as ambassadors they will fail for different reasons. A Foreign Service officer who fails, or runs into trouble, will most likely do so because he or she has said to themselves that, after twenty-two years, or whatever, they have arrived and that the assignment was owed to them. Or worse, your spouse thinks that. If you are a non-career and you run into trouble, it will be more than likely because he or she believes that the president has given them a fiefdom and they can do whatever pleases them. They will feel that they have only one master and that is the president. If ambassadors have that view, they will get into trouble. That is a major difference between the two.

Grove: Let me talk first about non-career people who come to us and become ambassadors, and in the sense of pluses and minuses, or strengths and weaknesses. Very often these people are successes in what they did before, and they're accustomed to success. They have come to public prominence and to a candidate's knowledge because they have been in politics or headed corporations or have done one thing or another that permitted them, for example, to make large contributions to a campaign. The point is that they are used to success.

This can be a minus and a handicap once they are ambassadors if they go to difficult countries. I think one of the toughest things for non-career people to understand is that holding the line, in terms of an American/foreign country relationship, can itself be a good outcome, that surviving real stresses and strains can be a reflection of success in a relationship. People who don't know this by having been in our profession are often shocked that they can't get more done more quickly and achieve the public recognition they are used to having, for their work as ambassador. Accolades don't come the same way they have been coming, for a great many of them, up to that point in their lives.

Non-career people are often good with other people. They've got a good sense of public relations. Many of them are extroverted in a positive sense. They have a keen nose for public diplomacy, for dealing with the media. Many of them are smart negotiators, particularly those who have come from the business world. A good sense of how to cut a deal. Many of them are gifted leaders in terms of organization, sophisticated in the kinds of training that they have had and experience they have had in running things--not immediately translatable in every way to running an embassy. But there is a lot there of managerial experience and sophistication that can be very impressive. They tend also to be problem solvers. Their instinct is to get things resolved and to move on from there, something, as I suggested earlier, that doesn't happen that readily in foreign policy, where monstrosities like the Berlin Wall go on for decades, and you learn to live with them. At the same time, such people can lack depth in understanding the foreign policy issues themselves, and are often inexperienced in how the bureaucracy works. I think one of the most notable differences between even the very best non-career and Foreign Service ambassadorial appointees is that the Foreign Service side of the house knows the bureaucratic map, and the political people tend to be increasingly horrified as they understand how our bureaucratic system either does or does not work.

People who come from outside the Foreign Service, on the other hand, often have a very sophisticated understanding of our political system and how it works. This is true of somebody like Mike Mansfield or John Sherman Cooper, both senators, people who have been very much involved in elections, who understand the way other politicians think. To a remarkable extent, such people can quickly empathize with leaders of other countries. They feel that they've shared the same dilemmas, that they have a unique understanding of what political heat is really all about.

On the debit side of the ledger, again, political appointees sometimes come to their jobs with too much enthusiasm about what they can get done, an unrealistic view of the prospects in the relationship, and an insecurity which can be quite translatable to an embassy staff, about their role, about their authority, and about what they should do when they get out of bed in the morning and go to the chancery.

I happen to have served under more political ambassadors than career ambassadors. They need careful handling (and this is where the DCM [deputy chief of mission] comes in), careful understanding in terms of what their sense of goals and objectives is, and an understanding, on the part of the DCM and the embassy staff, of the inevitable adjustment that a non-career person goes through in arriving at an embassy if they haven't had a lot to do with embassies before. That said, non-career people can be a lot of fun at a post, for many of the reasons I mentioned before.

At FSI, we emphasize the DCM function strongly. I alluded to it earlier because the most intimate relationship at an embassy is between the ambassador and the DCM. It becomes very complicated, potentially at least, if the ambassador is non-career and inexperienced in foreign affairs. FSI has a two-week, mandatory DCM seminar, in which we talk about many things, but none more strongly than the need for a "psychological contract" between the ambassador and the DCM. It's critical, in the relationship, to the prospects for success of an inexperienced political ambassador or of a veteran Foreign Service officer.

Foreign Service people, and I would include in that people who have had extensive experience in foreign affairs in other agencies--USIA, AID, occasionally the military, occasionally CIA, very often have great depth in languages, areas, and issues in specific context, when it comes to individual countries or regions, and even globally. They have a sense of U.S. purpose worldwide which they have acquired over many years of experience. They are the experts in a very real way more often than not. They are, if they're any good at all, very savvy about bureaucratic politics. They know how the sixth and seventh floors in the State Department work. [The Secretary of State's office is on the seventh floor and the assistant secretaries on the sixth floor.]

Just as important, they understand the interagency process, the legitimate roles of other departments, sometimes the preponderant role in specific issues of departments such as the military, Treasury, Agriculture, for example, but not to the exclusion of the primacy of the Secretary of State in foreign affairs. On occasion foreign affairs issues are the legitimate, preponderant interests of other departments and agencies, something which is clearly understood by good people on the Foreign Service side.

They are experienced in the conduct of diplomacy because, from vice consul on, they have had a number of assignments, probably in different parts of the world. And by the conduct of diplomacy, I mean their being at home within the foreign culture itself. Not just among other diplomats at a post, and not just with the government, but in that culture. They are, in fact, recognized by everyone in the host country concerned with foreigners as being professional outsiders from the United States. There are subtleties. I think style is important. And there are certain rules that govern this. We all know people who have this quality of being experienced and at home in the conduct of diplomacy in its largest measure. Those within the Foreign Service, I think, have a concept of service itself, of service to country, which is very strong. It transcends the partisan feelings that each one of us has, is more extended and expansive than the immediate allegiances of political appointees to any given administration, but does not in any sense mean that the Foreign Service person would be less loyal or less dedicated or less supportive.

It's just qualitatively different, this concept of service, because you've lived it all your life. You've lived it through hardships. You've lived it in the sense of developing a long view of the U.S. purpose and of the nature of U.S. representation, the financing of programs, the structure of embassies, the staffing of embassies, the communications between embassies and the department, and the whole world of what that relationship means. All of these things are matters on which we've worked one way or other in our careers.

To refer to a point I made earlier about non-career people, those in the Foreign Service often recognize that strained relations with the host country can be the best you can hope for under the circumstances, and are not so "success driven" as some of their political colleagues can be.

Now there are also, of course, weaknesses that Foreign Service people have and display, and they're not necessarily generic any more than the strengths or weaknesses of political people. But they are, to some extent at least, recognizable in people who have, particularly for the first time, become ambassadors from among our own ranks. These weaknesses can include micro-managing--the ambassador who just can't let go of the details of the operation of an embassy, or the economic section if that person primarily had economic experience, or of the political section if that person is primarily someone who has been a political officer--can't release to the DCM what the DCM needs to have to be the manager of an embassy under the direction of the ambassador. That's a big problem for many of our colleagues

Sometimes I think Foreign Service people tend to take a smaller view of their responsibilities than they should. By that, for example, I mean that the outreach to the American business community is sometimes astonishingly poor. It is hard for some of us to realize that dealing with American business representatives, actively promoting American trade and exports, is a central responsibility of an ambassador. It's a new function for some people; they're not as good at it sometimes as they should be.

I also think Foreign Service officers occasionally are media-shy and public relations-shy, too timid in public diplomacy. I don't mean any heavy-handed propagandistic efforts. I do mean utilizing those tools that USIA provides, speaking engagements, a press policy, for maximum effect toward accomplishing U.S. purposes. Sometimes maximum effect means lying low and doing practically nothing. But, on other occasions, we could do better in seizing the possibilities, in a media age, for very broad communication with the people of a country about ourselves as people, that modern-day media techniques provide.

Sometimes Foreign Service officers are too much focused not just on Washington but on the Department of State. This is not to denigrate the primacy of the Secretary of State, the responsibility of assistant secretaries for conduct of our foreign policy, or their origins within the State Department themselves. It is to say that there are other legitimate players, and that you are the president's ambassador and not the State Department's ambassador.

This may shock some people, but Tony Motley and I stress that throughout the ambassadorial seminar.   You are the president's ambassador.   And there are times when you will disagree with the State Department, when you will, from your vantage point, believe that another agency is closer to the mark in what it is advocating than are the views of the Department of State.   This is a tough dilemma.   Handling that, arguing it, is very delicate.   It takes a certain amount of courage, but it's essential to do it.   When I say that some of us have too much of a fixation on Washington, what I mean is that we sometimes don't do that enough. When we fail to provide a broader view about the interagency aspects that you deal with in an embassy, I think we're letting the team in the State Department down.

Finally, it's also true that how you fare as an ambassador, if you're a Foreign Service officer or from other agencies in the government, is likely to affect your future.   You are within a personnel system as such.   It is very hard not to remember that.   It is hard not to think of perhaps another chief of mission post if you do well in this job.   You want to do it right.   You want to please your superiors in Washington.   You don't have a president to go to who is backing you, the way many political people do in relations that are genuinely personal ones with the president. Your home and the place to which you will return after three years in your assignment is the Department of State.   And that can be inhibiting.

Motley: [Giving his impression of the ambassadors that he has observed.] It is a mixed bag. It is up and down. Over a period of time I have found that the early Bush appointees were not up to the standards that I expected. I found that the second round of Foreign Service appointees was also not up to the standards I expected. They were adequate but perhaps not the best. I guess part of the problem was that I knew some that didn't get appointed, and I knew them well enough to know that they were better qualified than those who got appointed. The Department has gone overboard on Equal Employment Opportunity. If you are a woman of sufficient high rank, you will be appointed as ambassador. That may sound chauvinistic, but it is that simple. It is a fact. One of the senior female members of the Foreign Service, for whom I have a lot of respect, told me after her tour as an ambassador, that some of the jobs being offered to her were only because she was a woman. They were jobs to which she would normally not aspire. But it is not only women; it is minorities in general.

The Department is on a "quota" system. If anybody thinks differently, they don't know whereof they speak.

GROVE reminds us that an ambassador is the president's personal representative abroad and, as such, is expected to reflect the views and political viewpoint of the president and his administration.

Grove: On the question of policy, an ambassador is, after all, supposed to reflect the president personally. You are the personal representative of the president of the United States and therefore of the policy views of the president and of the administration. This is as true of Foreign Service ambassadors as it is of political appointees. You serve a president personally, and you take on the character of the administration as you represent our country abroad, at any given moment and under any given president. This can sometimes be difficult for Foreign Service people who, after all, have their own sets of values and political beliefs. It can cause non-career people to be excessive in their zeal, in an ideological way, in representing the United States abroad, and often insensitively in this event. But at the heart of the matter is that any ambassador is not the Department of State's ambassador but the president's ambassador.

5

Managing an Embassy

Embassies come in all sizes. Those in such capitals as Tokyo, London, or Cairo have hundreds on their staffs with dozens of departments or agencies represented. Others, in capitals such as Doha, Bujumbura, or Bandar Seri Begawan function with only a handful of employees. Whatever the size, the ambassador is charged with insuring that all elements of the embassy are functioning efficiently and accomplishing their common mission.

Large embassies customarily are a conglomerate of representatives from a number of U.S. government departments and agencies, each with its own agenda but with a common goal. These are in addition to the specialists from the State Department's Foreign Service in economic, political, and consular matters. It is the duty of the ambassador to supervise and coordinate these various functions, and it is his right to be informed of all aspects of embassy operations. While the styles and methods of operation vary among ambassadors, their overall duties and responsibilities are constant.

In this chapter a number of ambassadors explain how they organized the work of their embassies to make use of the expertise of their staffs and achieve the best results. Several give their views as to the optimum size of an embassy under both normal and unusual circumstances and comment on their attempts to overcome the perennial problem of overstaffing.

GREECE (1974-1977)

Following is Ambassador JACK KUBISCH's suggested daily routine at a large embassy such as Athens.

Kubisch: The first thing one needs to realize is that an ambassador abroad, an American ambassador, is really on duty 24 hours a day, 7 days a week.   There are no holidays.   He is on call all the time, and he has to be well informed all the time.

In my own case, I would go into my office in the morning, and during the period from about 8 A.M. to 9 A.M. every morning, either at my residence, where someone would bring me overnight telegraphic traffic and messages, or at my office, I would go through the traffic.   I would also meet with my personal secretary and assistant and discuss my schedule and appointments for the day.

Then at 9:00 every morning, I met with the DCM [deputy chief of mission].   We had a fifteen minute discussion every morning.   By that time, he also was well informed of what had happened since we parted company the evening before, in terms of overnight developments.   We would meet and discuss these things and who in the embassy was going to do what, when.

Then, from 9:15 to 10:00 every morning there are usually two briefings for the ambassador, the DCM, and a few others.   One is the CIA briefing, and the other is a press briefing.   In Paris, for example, the ambassador and I, and usually three or four other key members of the country team, would meet in his office every morning.   We would have a French speaking person from the press office come, who had been up, maybe, since 4 or 4:30 in the morning going through all the newspapers, listening to all the radio and news programs, seeing the morning television shows, looking at new magazines that had just come out, clipping and choosing and picking.   Then he would do about a 10-or 15-minute summary in French of important press developments, a kind of press briefing for us early in the morning.

We'd then go into the "Tank," as it is called, the secret, enclosed room, which is not penetrable by foreign intelligence agencies, and have a CIA briefing.   At about 10 in the morning, three days a week, I would have meetings with the country team.   There are really two elements of the country team.   There is the immediate country team consisting of the DCM, the counselors of the embassy, the defense attaché, and the CIA station chief, about 6 or 7 people, and I used to meet with them twice a week, usually Monday and Wednesday.

Once a week, usually on a Thursday or a Friday morning at 10:00, we'd have about an hour meeting with an enlarged country team, which would include all the attachés.   That sometimes went to 20 or 25 people.   I felt those meetings should be rather longish meetings.   I wasn't one for conducting, and don't favor having quick, sharp country team meetings, but rather fairly full exchanges of views.   This is an opportunity for officers to present the biggest issues and have an exchange with the ambassador and other key members of the country team about them.   And if any subject required more intensive discussion then we could set up a separate meeting and get a group together for that discussion.

When I had meetings in my office, the meetings were always scheduled for 15 minutes, 30 minutes, or 60 minutes, depending on the number of people to be present, and the complexity or detail that I felt we should go into. I think when people know, in advance, how long the meeting's going to be, they tend to control their presentations, with that in mind. If not, the person presiding or chairing the meeting has to keep it moving along. I felt those meetings were a very important instrument for me in directing such a large and disparate organization.

After these meetings, I would spend the rest of the day, when I was in town and in the office, with appointments, with dictation, with writing, with thinking, just quiet spells, and maybe some meetings or visits outside the embassy. Then at the end of the day, about 6:00, a second meeting with the DCM to go over events of the day, and to be available to him to review, consider, and approve outgoing messages from the embassy in the name of the ambassador that I personally needed to review. Usually, there were two, three, or four of those everyday, out of many dozens.

FRANCE (1974-1977)

SAMUEL RHEA GAMMON III served as the deputy chief of mission to Ambassador Kenneth Rush in France [1974-1977] and to Ambassador Arthur Hartman (1977-1981). He shows how the two ambassadors differed in their methods and describes how he performed his duties as deputy under each at this large embassy. He later was ambassador to Mauritius.

Gammon: Ken Rush who was a previous Deputy Secretary of State and who had dealt with me in S/S [Staff Secretariat of the State Department] picked me for the job. I like Ken. He knows the great game, knows it very well, but he was not hyperactive. He was in a sense "energy efficient," shall we say. He would say basically, "I will deal with the prime minister and the president of the Republic."

Giscard d'Estaing was president in those days, the Prime Minister Jacques Chirac, the mayor of Paris, a fascinating man. And usually Ken would see the foreign minister, and say to me, "You do everything else." This meant all the rest of the cabinet with their business to be done, and the director general of the Quai d'Orsay, the whole schmeer. Then, of course, he would be gone at least four months out of the year, out of the country, so I did an awful lot of chargé time. Whenever anything went wrong or something hit the fan, I was chargé [chargé d'affaires], that's a paranoid's rule of thumb. It became very different under his successor [Ambassador Arthur Hartman] for my last year.

I switched to being the floor manager and particularly looking after the huge mission. We had something like thirty agencies in Paris, including the Veterans Administration and Social Security!

Interestingly enough when Kingman Brewster came in as ambassador to London in the early Carter period and fairly late in the day for me in Paris, I had this funny message from London shortly after he arrived, that he was going to be in Paris and needed an hour's time with me. I said, "What was all this?"

When he duly came he said in effect that he was thinking about how he should organize his embassy in London and somebody in Washington said come and talk to Sam Gammon across the channel. So I told him in effect it's like, where does the 800 pound gorilla sleep? You organize the embassy in the way which will be most effective for your operation. Then I talked a little bit about Rush's role and how the embassy functioned. And about Hartman's role, he had been there three or four months and how obviously he was starting to function. In fact I think he experimented, somebody told me, with merging the political and economic sections or some adventurous innovation of that sort. I said, "Whatever works for you is fine. There ain't no you got to do it this way or you got to do it that way."

To a very considerable extent the section heads managed the store. I tried to get to all of the constituent posts and I think I got to all of them at least twice during my three and a quarter years in Paris. For some reason I seemed to have made it to Nice more often than to Lyon, I can't think why! And similarly I stayed in touch with the other agency operations, the Secret Service, the Treasury, the Social Security and the Battle Monuments Commission, and all of the rest of them. But I relied very heavily on the counselors. In fact, when I visited Moscow a couple of years after I left the service, Warren Zimmerman, who came to Paris with Hartman as political counselor, said to me--I was ravished with pleasure, very decent of Warren because he was then DCM Moscow,--"I'm trying to operate this job the way you did in Paris. I was very impressed that you never peered over my shoulder or joggled my elbow as political counselor and I'm trying to do the same here."

FRANCE (1977-1981)

CHRISTIAN ADDISON CHAPMAN was deputy chief of mission to Ambassador Hartman, France 1977-1981. He comments on Hartman's method of operation and describes how the ambassador used him in running one of our largest embassies, Paris.

Chapman: It was a totally pleasant three years with an ambassador who was thoroughly professional and very highly regarded. Arthur Hartman is one of the most politically sensitive persons I have ever known. He has antennas, that pick the essence of situations out of the air, with very good judgment and with very broad views. He was a strategic thinker and highly respected in Paris and Washington.

He and Donna are very culturally inclined. They genuinely love the arts, particularly music. They put a lot of effort into it and received a lot of American artists and went out virtually every night to concerts or something. So they established a climate around the embassy of being receptive to the arts and to the world of the artists. This in France plays big. As far as running the embassy, he left it largely to me. I ran the embassy, but Arthur always kept an eye on what he considered problems that had to be dealt with. He was also very sensitive on personnel matters. Professionally as a Foreign Service officer it was a fascinating job. On one side you run the embassy and at the same time, you have to maintain a presence in town so that when the ambassador leaves, the embassy doesn't become faceless. In effect, you are doing two jobs. It means thirteen to fourteen hour days every day, but it was professionally very satisfying.

We had 27 different agencies represented in the embassy. One great advantage of being the Paris embassy was that the agencies sent, by and large, very good people. There was never a dearth of volunteers. As a result, we dealt with first class professionals in all agencies, which makes all the difference in the world, as you know.

I let my colleagues deal primarily with the bureaucracy. I tried to have as few operational questions to deal with as possible. Otherwise operations and contacts become layered and confused. If I were to deal with the foreign office exclusively, that would mean the political counselor would be squeezed out. It was much better to give him full rein. I had a State Department house with four servants, and I tried to provide support for my colleagues in every field, as they considered it useful and necessary. For instance, I had luncheons for senior people at the foreign office to let the more junior political officers get to know them. When American businessmen came through, the economic and commercial officers would organize an event for their counterparts in the French government. I found this kind of support for our colleagues a very good use of our rather elegant appointments.

As regards our consular posts, it was a real problem because we were under pressure to reduce the number of consulates. The case had to be made that they served an important purpose. It is a very good thing to have consulates, to have an American presence around a country like France which keeps tabs on what is going on around the countryside. Though the reality is that French political power remains very largely centered in Paris, the power of politicians remains anchored in local communities in the provinces. Typically, a French deputy spends each weekend in his department nurturing his constituents.

It is also good to have consular affairs officers and commercial officers closer to people throughout the country. But consular posts cannot be a top priority; yet powers that be in Washington remain very attached to some of these posts, all for different reasons. The most amusing was the case of Nice. We went through a painful exercise of justifying this post, pointing out among other things that closing it would save really very little. Nevertheless, the decision was made to close it. Then, Grace Kelly wrote a "Dear Ron" note to President Reagan, and presto it was reopened--on a more modest scale. We lost a magnificent property in the heart of the city, and the consulate general was reopened in a more modest setting.

HAITI (1977-1980)

WILLIAM BOWDOIN JONES was ambassador to Haiti from 1977 to 1980. Jones explains how he allocated the work of his staff at his small embassy in Port-au-Prince.

Jones: I divided my embassy in this way. I was the main liaison with the senior levels of the Haitian Government, which meant the Duvalier régime. Only the ambassador can do that. You cannot have relations with a country, whether you agree with what they are doing or not, and ignore them or insult them. Then you are simply freezing yourself out of decision making and freezing yourself out of information which is vital. So I was the major contact with the high-level political controllers of the country, Duvalier and his ministers and the head of the army.

I was also designated as the main contact with the elite group in Haiti, the business elite, the people who control the economy. These were fair-skinned mulattos who were frozen out of government entirely. They were very well educated, very sophisticated. They were not land owners. (There were no big land owners in Haiti. The peasants owned the land in Haiti.) But they owned the industry. They owned the computer chip factories, the baseball factories, the textile mills, the light industry sector that was developing in Haiti, patterned on Taiwan and Hong Kong.

So I developed close relations with the Mevs family--Pritz Mevs, whose grandfather had come to Haiti from Germany to avoid service in the Kaiser's army and had married an African woman. The Mevs family controlled the sugar mill and shoe factory in Haiti. They controlled the soap making and toothpaste manufacture. The Brandt family, Clifford Brandt, who was a Jamaican, was also of German-African origin. The Brandts owned all kinds of different factories. Brandt was the wealthiest Haitian with a reported worth of $150 million. Mevs was probably worth $70 million.

George Leger, who later became ambassador from Haiti to the United States--his grandfather had been president of Haiti--was the leading lawyer in Port-au-Prince. He was a great fisherman, as I am, and we would go deep sea fishing together frequently. When we would get out on the boat, of course, we could talk freely with no one listening.

With other members of that group, no one else in the embassy could have access to because they wouldn't be bothered with anyone else in the embassy below the level of ambassador. They simply wouldn't.

My DCM, of course, was the manager of the embassy, and he had contacts. But my political officers were instructed to develop contacts with potential opposition groups. We had direct liaison with Gerard Bourge, who founded the Haitian Civil Rights League, and Jean Dominique who was the young broadcaster who was openly anti-Duvalier.

The political section was tasked to develop contacts with potential opposition groups in the country and so on down the line in the embassy, with the military attaché dealing with the military, and the information people with the press, and the AID people out in the country, out in the field in the rural areas.

So I thought we had the country pretty well covered. I think we knew what was going on in Haiti, in those days, very well. I had a good staff there.

JORDAN (1966-1967)

FINDLEY BURNS, Jr. was ambassador to Jordan from 1966 to 1967, during the Six-Day War between Jordan, Syria, and Egypt on one hand and Israel on the other. In such times of stress the ambassador must have a clear idea of how best to use the staff. Burns describes how he conducted his embassy during the war after dependents and some staff had been evacuated.

Burns: There are two things an ambassador would think about in a situation like that. The first is you want the people there whose functions most directly relate to the crisis that will confront you. For example, you want the chief of the political section, the station chief of CIA, and the administrative officer (because you've got the problem of keeping the embassy--the guards, the security, the communications--all running). You also want competent people. In Jordan, I went so far in one case as, to select a deputy, but not the top man, to remain in the embassy to work with us through the crisis. Of course, this was not appreciated by the top man, but the matter was too important to follow protocol. His deputy, in my opinion, was infinitely more capable.

In a situation like that, in your immediate circle of advisors, you don't want many more than about six working together. That does not count necessary security and administrative personnel who have to be there, like Marine guards or the cryptographic personnel and stenographers, personnel of that sort. I'm talking about the immediate circle of officer personnel that you're going to work with. I've seen country teams with up to 25 people. That's fine for peacetime, because those meetings are more for improving inter-agency relations than they are for working purposes. But when the chips are down and you've got a serious crisis on your hands, you just don't have time to play games. It would be irresponsible of you if you did.

I had a large staff meeting once a week, and smaller staff meetings two or three times a week. The smaller group were the officers whom I have described as having stayed at the embassy during the Six-Day War. We could usually get the smaller group meetings done in 20 to 30 minutes, because I was dealing with each bilaterally continuously. I dealt with each one of the six probably several times a day on a one-on-one basis. The conclusion you might draw is that six people is enough to run an embassy, and you don't really need 70. Two comments on that. First, you are working under intense pressure, and you're working not eight hours a day; you're working 24 hours a day. You can't keep that up for a long period of time, obviously.

Secondly, there are a great many functions which are most desirable to perform. However, normal economic reporting or agricultural research are not relevant to getting through a war that is going to last less than a week. You need the economists back right afterwards to ascertain what the economic effects will be, but during the actual hostilities, it isn't necessary. One of the officers I had there, one of the six, was an economic officer (the AID Mission Director), but basically he was there because he was a very able officer and he could do all sorts of things that were necessary to do, other than economics.

BRAZIL (1961-1966)

ABRAHAM LINCOLN GORDON was ambassador to Brazil, 1961-1966. He discusses the reporting requirements of a large post such as Brazilia, emphasizing that the ambassador must exercise his right to see all official communications emanating from his embassy regardless of source or classification. He discusses the difficulties in doing this in view of the volume of reporting.

Gordon: It couldn't all be absorbed by any one person. The question is was all of it being read by anybody or was it just dropped in people's wastebaskets or left totally unread. I didn't read all of it myself. I could have spent the whole day doing nothing but reading our outgoing material. After Niles Bond left, my deputy was Gordon Mein [later ambassador to Guatemala, where he was assassinated in 1968], an extremely diligent officer. He read a great deal that he screened for me. We had rules about who could authorize outgoing telegrams. He and I could do so, and on certain subjects we delegated authority down to the counselor level, but within limits. If it were really important or controversial either Gordon

Mein or I was to see it before it went out. And with the CIA there was a complete understanding: I didn't try to clear all their communications in advance, but I saw them all afterwards, and if there was some line of reporting on which I had a difference of opinion the station chief and I would talk about it and, if necessary, he would send a correction.

People have asked me whether by any chance there might have been a so-called "Track Two" as in Chile under Nixon with poor Ambassador Korry. He was almost driven mad by what he later learned about what was happening around him in Chile without his knowledge. By definition, one can't be a hundred percent sure that things done without one's knowledge didn't happen, but I am morally certain there was no such action in Brazil. The instructions from Kennedy were absolutely clear-cut. Under Eisenhower, ambassadors did not have to be told about everything the CIA was doing in their country, but Kennedy had changed that rule. My personal relations with each of my CIA station chiefs were good. The last one who was there at the time of the military take-over seemed to me exceptionally good. He was a very cautious fellow and worked very hard on improving intelligence collection in the literal sense.

ECUADOR (1947-1949, 1960-1965)
MAURICE MARSHALL BERNBAUM discusses embassy staffing in Ecuador.

Bernbaum: When I was in Ecuador as DCM [1947-1949], we had a small, lean staff. I thought we functioned very well. I was DCM, executive officer; occasionally I'd write political reports, economic reports, always working with the people in charge. When I returned to Quito as ambassador in 1960 I found a great many more people there. I didn't have the feeling that we were much more efficient.

Bureaucracy, the demands of Congress for information, the progressively greater curiosity of the State Department, the interest of the other government departments to have representation all contributed. We would find commercial attachés there. Of course, we always had military attachés, but one good example of this; when I arrived in Quito as ambassador, we had one armed services attaché, who covered the three services. I think after the Bay of Pigs problem, President Kennedy was supposed to have made some comment about our ability to have good relations with the military, to know what they were up to. So I had a request to appoint an air attaché. I checked around with our armed services attaché, who in effect said we didn't need one. And after exchanging about two or three telegrams each way, I found myself forced to accept one. Well, the man had nothing to do. He was just a pest, he was always on the back of the MAG [Military Assistance Group] to fly their plane and to do things. Eventually I had a request to appoint a naval attaché. Here we were, two miles above sea level, and they wanted a naval attaché. Well, I was able to ward that one off.

I learned later that after I left Ecuador we had a reduction in force, and there was an effort to eliminate the air attaché. However, our ambassador had become accustomed to having an air attaché and fought tooth and nail to keep the guy, which was an indication of how things worked.

GUATEMALA (1965-1968)

JOHN OSCAR BELL, ambassador to Guatemala, 1965-1968, tells of problems caused by rivalry within his embassy between the different American intelligence gatherers as well as frictions between the economic section and the AID office.

Bell: There was an ongoing competition for intelligence reporting which was sometimes irritating and sometimes amusing. The military had originally the army attaché, the navy attaché and the air attaché and then later they had the defense attaché which was supposed to foster integrating the military components, but actually simply added one more customer in Washington. And then they had the Military Assistance Advisory Group which reported to the commanding general of southern command in Panama. The commanding general in Panama was no more interested in being scooped by G2 in Washington or the air or navy or CIA than they were interested in being scooped by each other. Of course you had the CIA to report intelligence and you had the State Department reporting various degrees of intelligence. It took a lot of effort to try to force them into what I would call "all addressees" forms of communication. So that they would all receive this material simultaneously and, hopefully, with some degree of coherence and some similarity of emphasis. Yet it was never entirely successful. What the CIA people reported of course you never really knew for sure.

Before I went to Guatemala there had been some discussion of this because Mr. Muccio, who was my predecessor in Guatemala, had been the lucky ambassador who discovered through the *New York Times* that we were training in Guatemala, through the CIA, people to invade Cuba and the operation was being run by his supposed subordinate on the floor above him in the Embassy building, a CIA man. He got a call from Mr. Herter wanting to know what was happening. That's how he found out about it. Well they had a hoo-hah in Washington. I was told, before I left that that had all been straightened out and the CIA had promised to be good and not do that anymore without the ambassador's knowing. Actually, the CIA had been blamed improperly in my opinion. The person who should have been blamed was the assistant secretary of state, who was on a committee that decided whether or not you would conduct these kinds of operations. He had participated in the decision to conduct such an operation in Guatemala and had participated in the decision that the ambassador did not need to know. This I think was unforgivable.

We had the normal problems of some friction between the economic section and the AID mission but we were able to get that hauled away pretty well because I'd had enough experience with that on both sides to be able to instinctively know what was what. [Ambassador Bell had been AID director in Pakistan.] I had more trouble, I guess, with the AID regional office in Guatemala than any other government agency. The so-called ROCAP, Regional Office Central America Panama, was an office which in many ways I thought I had suggested in earlier conversations with Ted Moscoso, who was then running the Latin American part of AID. But the fellow who was in charge of it, a man named Henry Duflon had been assistant secretary of defense for manpower or something, a political appointee. Duflon was very aggressive and he was determined to spend as much money as he could in Central America, theoretically promoting Central American economic integration, but in my opinion frequently just wasting money. So we had some friction. They were headquartered in Guatemala and it wasn't too easy.

KENYA (1969-1973)

ROBINSON McILVAINE was ambassador to Kenya, 1969-1973, one of the most comfortable posts in Africa. There is an understandable tendency for U.S. departments and agencies to set up branch offices in these spots, rather than the less comfortable capitals. As a result he got a Federal Aviation Agency attaché, a Library of Congress attaché, Peace Corps, and AID missions--and others.

McIlvaine: I recall one time a gentleman arrived, and he turned out to be a representative of the federal aviation agency. He wanted to talk to me about having a federal aviation attaché. I absolutely horrified him. I said, "What for?" "Oh, oh, oh." Nobody had ever asked him that before.

He said, "We have a requirement." I hate that word. A lot of people use that for self-serving purposes. I said, "Who requires you?" "Well, the president and Congress." And I said, "Well, tell me about this requirement." He said, "That is, we're responsible for U.S. airlines and how they operate, and we have to have a guy out here to check on Pan Am and TWA."

I said, "Well, you know, I date way back to when Pan Am was the first airline we had, and its slogan is "The World's Most Experienced Airline." My guess would be that if Pan Am can't get from New York to Nairobi without your help it ought to be abolished. In any case, if it does require your help, why can't you put your guy in New York and he can do a round-trip and see how they fly both ways?"

Well, he was furious about that.

And we had a Library of Congress attaché, and what did he do? He went around and bought books everywhere, and magazines. We had a huge Peace Corps, a huge AID mission, and I guess there must have been 500 or 600 Americans getting a government check one way or another.

CHAD (1961)

As a young officer FREDERIC LINCOLN CHAPIN opened our first embassy in Chad in 1961 as chargé. At that time we had one ambassador who represented the United States in four of the newly independent African countries, including Chad. The Embassy office and living quarters at Fort Lamy were all in one house, from which the staff managed to carry on as a functioning embassy.

Chapin: I volunteered to go to Chad. Although I had never been to Africa before, I did speak French, and that was asset. So I did volunteer. I actually arrived in Brazzaville in the French Congo at the end of January 1961. The three other members of my staff had already arrived at Fort Lamy and had taken up residence in the house which had been rented for me, or for us. It became the office and mess for the entire staff and was a rotating residence for all of us at one time or another.

There wasn't an office. When I arrived in early February I had brought along a portable typewriter and a French keyboard typewriter which I had borrowed from the AID agency in Leopoldville in the Belgian Congo. We set up office on the dining room table. The way it worked was that I would come over from the hotel around seven o'clock and all four of us would have breakfast; namely, the Administrative Officer, Walt Silva, the Administrative Assistant, Tom James, and his wife, who was the secretary.

We had problems in locating properties. There was only one property which had been rented by the advance team and that was the small house that we were occupying. It had no airconditioning, and it had two bedrooms which were separated from the dining room-living room area, so that you had to go outside. It was not secure by any stretch of the imagination, but that was the office that we had to work from. We subsequently hired a French-English lady who was the wife of a local French school teacher to come on board and use our French keyboard typewriter, and we persuaded the Embassy in Brazzaville to ship us a filing cabinet/safe so that we could begin to receive one time pads. Those are the old style code pads so that we could transmit confidential messages through the Chadian telegraph system. That meant also that we could receive classified pouches and that a courier could come in.

The first courier to arrive was somewhat shattered to arrive around 10:30 P.M. and to be shown by Tom James to the house, where the safe was in the bedroom next to his wife, Doris James, who was sound asleep. The courier was quite uncertain that he wanted to leave classified material under such circumstances, but it was really the safest way. We were able to guard all the material personally, at all times. As I say, we operated very informally: the breakfast dishes would come off the table and the typewriter would go on. We would work until noontime, and then the secretary would go out--that is Doris James--and supervise the cooking. Then when lunch was ready, the typewriters would come off, the dishes would go on, and then we reversed that process after lunch. We got an amazing amount of things done. I find from my letters to my wife that I was able to cover the entire industrial reporting for the country--all five of the industries--in one report very early on, as I happened to run into the American representative of the Mobil Oil Company, which was supplying fuel oil to all five of the industries.

My supervising ambassador was in Brazzaville some 1,500 miles to the south. An ambassador for Chad had not been appointed, and it took several months.

THAILAND (1976-1977)

JOHN RICHARD BURKE was deputy chief of mission in Thailand, 1976-1977, and in the absence of the ambassador was the chargé when there was a coup. The presence of experienced army and naval attaches with good contacts within the Thai military proved invaluable.

Burke: What you do at the time of a coup is you try to gather as much information as possible about the contending forces. I was really fortunate in that I had an extremely good army colonel who had been in Thailand for at least a couple of years at that point, and he had excellent connections within the Thai military. So he was able to get first-class information on the situation as it developed. And there was also a naval attaché, a captain, who had a social relationship with the man who ultimately became head of the coup group, an admiral. And between the two of them, I'd say we had the coup pretty well taped from the beginning in terms of the people involved, what their purposes were and all the rest of it. It seemed to me that there was a great reluctance on the part of the (Thai) military to move in and take charge. They didn't really want to, it seemed to me. I think that's a fair judgment. They did because they felt the situation was beginning to unravel so badly. They did take over and did restore order and things calmed down. The monarchy was never threatened, and, of course, the monarchy in Thailand in recent history at least provided the great stabilizing force in terms of the society.

COSTA RICA (1954-1958)

ROBERT FORBES WOODWARD stresses the necessity for the ambassador to be completely informed of all CIA operations and reporting at an embassy.

He had been kept in the dark about a planned attempt to overthrow the government of Costa Rica of which the CIA had knowledge.

Woodward: My most serious concern was the so-called action operations of the CIA. I can't mention anything other than the Costa Rican incident, which might have been prevented if the CIA had wanted to be more forthcoming. I can't think of any specific instance in which they've caused me a great problem.

I made a comment to Senator Frank Church, after he had had his investigation and made his report, that I was sorry he hadn't included in his investigation [of the CIA] an appraisal of benefits the CIA had brought to the United States. In the first place, it would be useful to have an impartial appraisal of the significance of the "intelligence" information they had provided, at least in Latin America, and in other countries where we were not at war, and to form an opinion as to whether it was of great assistance to the United States in any way, whether the information was in any way significantly of a type that would not normally be reported by an embassy or a consulate. Perhaps more important would be a systematic effort to try to measure the accomplishments of action programs the CIA has carried out, whether they were necessary, and whether they were more dangerous and potentially embarrassing than any benefits they have yielded; in other words, to make a really studious appraisal of their whole operation.

Frank Church said he agreed. Of course, this was just an off-the-cuff conversation. He said he agreed that that might have been a very useful thing to do, but it was too late then. He was a member of a group that was listening to foreign affairs lectures that we both went to, and it was at one of these lectures that I was talking with him. I just made this comment to him, which is neither here nor there, but I wished that such an analysis could be carried out, that somebody would undertake such an analytical study. At least I might find out whether I'm nutty in thinking that the CIA is a menace and wondering whether they do enough good to warrant their existence.

During the brief time I was assistant secretary, one of the things that I argued for in an interdepartmental committee for support coordination with the CIA, was that there should be some method by which the embassies would be certain to be aware of what their station chiefs were reporting. I was convinced that we were never aware of that in any post where I was assigned--in Costa Rica, Uruguay, Chile, or Spain. They went through the motions, I think, of showing certain reports to somebody in the political section of the embassy, but it was clear to me that we weren't getting all they were reporting on subjects which they knew were of interest to us. For example, we were reporting on a presidential election campaign in Uruguay, and one of the CIA officers lightly commented to me, after it was over, and after the Foreign Service officers had guessed wrong, "Of course, we [the CIA] knew who was going to win, and we told headquarters who was going to win."

I thought, "Well, you 'expletive.' Why didn't you tell me?"

Anyhow, that's the sort of thing that's enough to give you the willies when somebody says, after the event, that they knew the answers, and they reported it correctly, and you didn't.

BOLIVIA (1973-1977)

WILLIAM PERRY STEDMAN, Jr. was ambassador to La Paz, Bolivia from 1973 to 1977. He found that at a hardship post such as La Paz the senior staff is younger than in other posts. They perform well, and esprit is high.

Stedman: The staffing of our embassy in Bolivia is complicated because it's a hardship post. You're operating at 12,500 feet above sea level. You have to recognize that this has a bearing on the officer, as well as his family. If anybody has any kind of physical weakness at all, you'd want to be very careful of sending him into that altitude. Most healthy people do perfectly fine, but you still have some concern. As a consequence, I would suspect that occasionally we get somebody who's quite good, but who will opt out or won't get himself in line for assignment there.

We have a tendency in Bolivia, generally, to get younger people in senior positions. The political officer, the economic officer, the administrative officer are generally a little younger than you would find at a comparably sized post if you didn't have that altitude hardship. They all do a good job. In fact, they may do a heck of a good job because they're energetic and they know full well that they have an opportunity to show their stuff at a somewhat higher-ranking job.

We have had pressure to cut back senior-officer positions, and I tried one experiment which probably may have worked with one individual, but didn't work subsequently. That is to combine the political and economic sections. I had one chief of the combined section. It seemed to me that we were making some gross mistakes. We would send a political officer into the foreign ministry, and the fellow you talked with there, since they're a relatively small establishment, would want to talk both political and economic subjects, and our fellow would only be able to talk the political side. It seemed to be rather silly. Also it seemed to me that the economic officers ought to know more about the political situation. So the notion of breaking the barrier and bringing them together appealed to me. I did it under pressure, I must admit, to cut back. It worked well with one or two people, but then I think it generally has disintegrated.

So I think we get good people, in general, in the hemisphere. We had a good band of junior folks in La Paz. They were enthusiastic. Probably like most hardship posts, when people leave there, they have established fraternal ties that continue to exist. There's a kind of *esprit* among people who have served in Bolivia.

IVORY COAST (1974-1976)

ROBERT SOLWIN SMITH, ambassador to the Ivory Coast, 1974-1976, discusses the regional role certain embassies play.

Smith: We had an embassy of about 17 Americans in the embassy itself and probably 150 Americans in the U.S. government offices in the country as a whole, including an AID regional office, dating back to what I had helped bring into being 8 or 10 years earlier. Therefore, a large AID presence, a USIS staff, a regional military attachés office, a regional CIA office, a regional budget office for the State Department; a whole lot of people who had regional responsibilities not directly under my authority. So it was an odd kind of governing, negotiating and dealing sutuation. When they were doing something in relation to the Ivory Coast, they came under the embassy and under the ambassador. When they were doing something else, traveling elsewhere, or working on programs elsewhere, I had absolutely no say. We worked this out I think reasonably well.

I think the embassy officers felt that they were oddly in a kind of minority status in all of this. I'm sorry to say there was a little too much segregation of the embassy people on the one hand and the AID people, who were the largest other group on the other hand, with Defense and CIA people, a few of them fitting in kind of in between and mixing fairly easily.

I tried to keep some balance in this. Again, my own orientation helped, my own background in having been both in State and AID. The AID mission director and I, the regional mission director and I, had worked together in the AID Bureau of African Affairs at an earlier stage. The junior economic officer in the embassy and I had worked together on some debt negotiations in the time I was in the State Department, so I had old friends and acquaintances and colleagues in both areas.

There were a few times when I really had to say to one side or the other I just think you are being unreasonably isolated or separatist or prejudiced or whatever. There was that kind of thing.

ZAIRE (1975-1979)

WALTER LEON CUTLER served as ambassador to Zaire from 1975 to 1979. It had an undeserved reputation as a hardship post.

Cutler: Kinshasa was not a popular post from the standpoint of people volunteering to go and serve there. We always had trouble recruiting people, but once they arrived, they found the substantive issues challenging, and they found personal life much better than they thought it would be.

In other words, I think it's one of those posts (and there are many in our service) that have a reputation which is not altogether positive. It's probably because of all of the stereotypes and images which we acquired earlier. And, here again, I'm talking about the blood and anarchy of the old Congo, the Civil War and so on. It was a hellhole for quite some years. I think that we remember those images, and then when an assignment is suggested to Zaire, we tend to resist. So one arrives with low expectations. And, because those expectations were so low, I think one tends to be pleasantly surprised. We had a lot of people who asked to extend. The Peace Corps (we had a very large Peace Corps contingent in Zaire) had one of the highest extension rates of any country in Africa. And life was tough on those volunteers, because conditions in the countryside were not very good.

HUNGARY (1961-1962)

When HORACE GATES TORBERT arrived as chargé d'affaires at Budapest in 1961 he found a very small staff plus a Roman Catholic cardinal (Mindszenty), who was living as "guest-prisoner" at the legation.

Torbert: Budapest was a very small post. We didn't have any ambassador there. It was a legation at that time. But they had Cardinal Mindszenty living in the legation, and this was a very difficult thing. We still had almost no relations with the Hungarian Government. We were constantly harassed by security people. For example, there were always three cars full of goons poised outside the legation offices, which is where Mindszenty was, to be sure that he never escaped. Actually, the last thing Mindszenty wanted to do was escape. He believed that he belonged in Hungary, and he had been a member of the Council of Regents, and he was the only surviving member, the only one left in Hungary. He felt that he was the symbol of the *ancien régime* in Hungary.

I got there about the first of February of that year [1961], I think, roughly. I might say as a preface that when I arrived there, it was very interesting, because at that time, the power of the United States and the influence was such that I found that the entire Western diplomatic community was waiting with bated breath for my arrival, because I was the leader. I was a chargé. Everybody else was a minister. In other words, they ranked above me diplomatically. Nonetheless, I found that immediately when I got there, I was expected to sort of take charge of morale and everything. The contrast, when I went to Bulgaria [as ambassador] ten years later, more or less, our influence had eroded where nobody gave a damn when I arrived; everybody was on their own by that time.

6

Conducting Business
with Heads of State

*Our ambassador to Great Britain presents credentials to the Queen as Head
of State. Embassy business, however, is conducted with the prime minister, the
foreign minister, and other officials of the British government.   In most
countries the ambassador deals with both the head of state and the head of
government.   Often they are the same person. Whatever the country, the
establishment of harmonious working relationships with the host government
officials on a timely basis is important.*

   *Not all chiefs of state or heads of government are easy to get along with.
While most are intelligent individuals who simply wish for friendly cooperation
with the U.S. government and its representatives, others are not and are highly
suspicious of U.S. intentions. A few are simply cantankerous.*

ROMANIA (1981-1985)

*Dealing with Romania's Nicolae Ceausescu was unpleasant.   DAVID B.
FUNDERBURK describes that former communist dictator and tells how it was
to carry on relations with him during Funderburk's tenure as ambassador to
Romania, 1981-1985. The interview was conducted prior to the dictator's fall
and execution in 1989.*

Funderburk: Well, Ceausescu is a man who thinks that he's God--he
doesn't want to hear criticism. So an American official, secretary of state,
vice president, whoever, comes over and visits Ceausescu; they are being
advised by the State Department, obviously, to bring good news to this
man and to congratulate him and to praise him, because that's what he

wants to hear. No one wants to be the bearer of ill will or bad tidings to Nicolae Ceausescu, because if you are, if you even try to subtly slip in some criticism of this guy and the way he's running his fiefdom, he goes virtually berserk right before your eyes.

He gives the impression of a very ordinary person, very short. I noticed a picture of him yesterday, with the other Warsaw Pact leaders. He was the shortest of them. He's probably about 5'5". Perhaps he has a Napoleonic complex, because of his shortness. So he's very ordinary in that sense, probably even bordering on ugly, I think I've described him. A very stern face, very serious demeanor. Otherwise, nothing really very distinctive about him, except his mannerisms.

He was one of the, probably 400, indigenous members of the Communist Party in Romania prior to World War II. When there were almost no communists of Romanian origin in Romania, he was one of the handful. He was also very astute in terms of grabbing and maintaining power, which is something communists excel at. They go through a process of purges and killing off enemies or opposition within the party, and then by the time they've made it to the top leadership, they're in pretty good shape for wielding power and manipulating people. And there's no question that Ceausescu instills fear in people. He is shrewd. He is intelligent in a lot of ways. He is a power monger, and one who certainly knows how to, I would say, psychologically punch the buttons of people that he is dealing with and talking with. He does, or at least his aides, do their research in terms of whomever they're dealing with, far more deeply than I think our people do. Thus when he's sitting down with Al Haig, he knows far more about Al Haig than Haig knows about him. He knows what button to push to get the support or the sympathy or empathy of Al Haig. And so in this sense, he's very shrewd, very astute. The Romanians laugh at him on the one hand. Yet they're very fearful; they're very intimidated. But at the same time, they say, "Well, he's a graduate of the third grade. He's virtually illiterate. He stutters when he speaks. He can't pronounce Romanian properly." And so they rather laugh behind his back about this. But at the same time he's overcome whatever problems he had in that regard, in terms of his ability to maintain power. Maybe because of his background, he's always been anti-intellectual. So he's purged and been very tough on the cultural and intellectual Romanians.

CHAD (1972-1974)

Despite its remoteness, Chad has had a special place in American relations in that part of Africa, in part because of its long territorial struggle with Libya. EDWARD WILLIAM MULCAHY was fortunate when he was chief of mission, 1972-1974, to have an easy, informal relationship with Chad's then president, Tombalbaye.

Mulcahy: [The president of Chad, Tombalbaye] liked Americans. I had the good luck to follow Terry Todman as ambassador there. Terry had been my assistant desk officer when I had Trusteeship Affairs almost 20 years before, but he had become ambassador long before I did. Terry was a native of the Virgin Islands and a very, very personable, sweet guy with an excellent command of French. He and the president had really become very close. I told the president, when I presented my letters of credence, that I hoped I'd become just as good a friend as my old buddy, Terry Todman. He took me up on it. He'd have me over without any protocol on ten minutes notice.

When I'd want a formal talk with him about something, he'd always say, "Well, do you want to come with your flags flying at 10:00 tomorrow morning or do you want to come this afternoon without flags flying?"

I'd always go without flags flying and just drive my personal car. He didn't live in the presidential palace. It was really not safe. It was in a bad location downtown. He lived in a camp surrounded by military that had been built as a village for a Pan African Conference, where there was a small villa for each head of state. He used one villa for his office and another for his living quarters--he lived very austerely. He was very nice, very congenial and you could talk to him, and you could explain matters to him when the "no" would come back from Washington to almost everything he asked for except drought aid.

YEMEN (1972-1974)

WILLIAM REX CRAWFORD, Jr. was the first American ambassador to live in San'a, the Yemen Arab Republic, 1972-1974. He had developed close relations with the foreign minister when he had been a junior officer in the post in the 1950s. This made for a good working relationship with the government throughout his tour as ambassador.

Crawford: I traveled all over the country. Ambassadors should never get stuck in the capital. I resisted the efforts of the Department of State to send me a Chrysler Imperial, which would have been operable on only 11 miles of road in the capital. Instead, I managed to get a Range Rover, so that I was able to travel over the entire country, to call on tribal leaders and villagers, to see irrigation projects and water drilling projects, to see the Peace Corps volunteers in their villages, and to take them in hand on weekends. With those stationed in San'a, I went out on tours all over the surrounding areas looking for archeological remains. I had a wonderful relationship with the government. My best friend there had become the foreign minister, and he'd call at five minutes to 1:00 and say, "Where are the corn flakes?" He had a terrible ulcer, so he'd drop in in five minutes, driving my wife up the wall, for literally Wheaties or corn flakes for lunch, which was the only thing his stomach would take. We would talk about anything and everything going on in the country.   It was still a very fragmented country and a lot of problems remaining from the civil war. But he was passionately devoted to its development and new-fangled techniques as satellite photography for economic development projects and so on.   It was a very special relationship.

MALAWI (1974-1978)

ROBERT AYER STEVENSON was ambassador to Malawi from 1974 to 1978, where to be effective it was necessary to develop good relations with the chief of state.   In this case it was President Hastings Kamuzu Banda, an American-educated dictator with an abiding hatred for Jehovah's Witnesses. The good personal relationship he cultivated with Banda made solving some sticky problems easier.

Stevenson: Of course, Malawi is of very little substantive interest to the United States.   We had about 300 missionaries in the country, and that was largely the American presence, plus British American Tobacco Company, who had a few people, because Malawi is a big producer of Bright Leaf dark fired cigarette tobacco.

When I got there President Banda was in full control.   He is a benevolent dictator for the majority of Malawians,   but for some, he's a cruel, cruel dictator.   He hates the Jehovah's Witnesses with a passion, and they get very rough treatment.   My relations with President Banda were very good, as a matter of fact.   We hit it off fine.   He loved to talk about the States.   He had been educated here at Wilberforce Academy in Ohio, and then he'd gone to Indiana for two years, and he would have finished in Indiana, but a professor at the University of Chicago was looking for somebody who knew Chinyanza, the language of that area.   He was doing a study of it, and a professor friend of his at Indiana had said, "We have a student here, Hastings Kamuzu Banda.   Maybe he could come over to Chicago and help you."   So he transferred to Chicago for his junior and senior years, and he helped this professor with Chenyanza.   He's an interesting old man.   He runs the country efficiently.   Malawi is one of the best run African countries, not any question.   But he can be cruel.

One time they had picked up one of our staff members, a Malawian, and they'd put him in jail.   He was a rather naive young man who worked for our library.   We had two libraries there in Malawi that were very heavily patronized by the Malawian students.   This young fellow had been approached by a South African white communist and asked if he had certain books.   He'd met him at a meeting of librarians.   He said, "Do you have such and such a book?"   And he'd said, "Yes, I have it.   I'll mail you a copy."   He didn't know anything about this white South African.   So he mailed him a copy of the book, and that got him into correspondence. The Malawian police were watching. From South African intelligence, they knew that this guy to whom he had written was a communist. So they arrested him.

It took me a while to figure all this out, but I went to see the old man. We were under some heat from USIA to get our man out. I said, "You know, I'm going back on consultation, and I want to try to get some help for Malawi. I have a problem, because you're holding this fellow." I went over the story with him. I thought I was doing a good job of it, but the old man drew back in his chair. He always received you, one on one, in this nice office that he had. He said, "What? Don't try to blackmail me! I don't need your aid. You can take your aid and stuff it! No way will I take action based on what you've told me."

Well, I was, naturally, quite taken aback, but I said, "Well, Your Excellency, you know, I'm really on the spot on this matter. If you can't do it for any other reason, would you do it for me personally?"

He looked at me. "All right. For you I'll do it." That was it. He runs the place like an old-fashioned African chief. Fear and respect is what he wants. But if you work with him, you can [get what you want].

CENTRAL AFRICAN REPUBLIC (1973-1976)

WILLIAM NORRIS DALE was ambassador to the Central African Republic, 1973-1976. He describes the ceremony when he presented his credentials to the chief of state, President Bokassa, a most unusual dictator.

Dale: I read the prepared remarks, and then afterwards he (Bokassa) invited me for an apéritif. I had the idea that an apéritif was a little drink in the bottom of a small glass, but the apéritif that we had was a tumbler full of whiskey, and he drank lots of them. I couldn't keep up. I didn't try, but one of those was about enough to knock me out.

During the course of our conversation, he said, "There is one thing you should know. My grandfather was a cannibal."

I said, "Really?"

He said, "Yes, and I have tendencies in that direction."

Well, I thought he was joking. But you know that later on he was found to have been a cannibal, that he ate children, whose parents would not, or could not, afford proper uniforms for school. It's absolutely true. That's why he was tried for murder. He is in prison now in the Central African Republic. He has been sentenced to death. They did not call it cannibalism; they called it murder.

He looked like a grasshopper. Rather small, very tough physically. A man who thought of himself as a combination of great general, tribal chief, emperor, and millionaire. He thought it was quite proper, for instance, to siphon off a large part of the revenues of the state for his private use. He bought estates in France; he bought very expensive cars. At his country place, in Bangui, he kept the supplies that he bought, dozens of television sets, for instance. What are you going to do with dozens of television sets? Dozens of heaters, dozens of refrigerators, all kinds of things you could never possibly use. He just bought them, one after the other.

If there is such a thing as evil, a positive evil force rather than evil as an absence of good, that man is evil.   Some of the punishments he told me he meted out were just dreadful. For instance, if one of his aides did not do as Bokassa thought he should have done, he would send him abroad for "education" for a term. But when he got back, he would invariably find his wife pregnant, and Bokassa said, "I always let him know who was responsible." That was one of his more favorite punishments.

INDONESIA (1977-1981)

EDWARD EUGENE MASTERS was ambassador to Indonesia, 1977-1981. The president was Suharto, who never said "no"; but his "yeses" could mean four different things. Learning what the "yes" meant took some practice.

Masters: [Speaking of President Suharto] A reserved person, as Javanese tend to be. But whenever I wanted to see him, I could see him; he was always responsive. He was always helpful, when it wasn't against his interests to be helpful. So I felt that we had a very good professional relationship. I saw a lot more, of course, of some of his staff people. In Indonesia you quite often have to do things indirectly, because Indonesians don't like public dissent, difficulty, and bad news. So I did a lot of work through intermediaries, some at the cabinet level, and some below the cabinet level; which again, I think shows the advantage of knowing the society before you get there--knowing who those intermediaries are, and how to use them.

In some cases I would seek an appointment with the president, and put it up to him directly--or the foreign minister. But in other cases, I might still want an appointment, but I might want to pave the way for the appointment, so as not to surprise him. So there were a number of people in different areas that I knew were close to the president, or to this minister, or to that minister. And I would talk with them, and say, "This is what I want to do. Do you have any guidance on how we can work this out? What's the best way to handle it? etc. etc."

And he'd say, "Well,"--in some cases he'd say, do this, do that. In some cases he'd say, "Well, let me think about it." You'd know he was going to go talk to the guy that you wanted to see.

We used to joke in Djakarta that President Suharto had four ways of saying "yes." He never said "no"--there were four yeses. One really meant yes. One meant "maybe." One meant "I hear what you're saying." This would be, kind of, as you're talking, he's saying "yes, yes." That doesn't mean he agrees with you. And the final yes means "it's a dumb idea, forget it", but he says "yes". So from the context, and the body language, and maybe knowing how the guy thinks, you've got to figure out which "yes" you're getting. And that, sometimes, I found--even knowing the Indonesians as well as I did--sometimes is tricky, but usually you can tell.

Where I had any doubt, I would go to an intermediary, and say, "What did the President really mean?"

And he would say, "He means it's the stupidest thing he ever heard of." But if I had doubt, I'd double check it that way.

BRAZIL (1966-1969)

JOHN WILLS TUTHILL was ambassador to Brazil, 1966-1969. He had difficulties with the military dictatorship because he insisted on seeing those who were in opposition to military rule.

Tuthill: I had a lot of trouble with Costa y Silva [the president], because Frank Carlucci [his political officer, later secretary of defense] and I saw a fellow named [Carlos] Lacerda who was the editor of a newspaper in Brazil. He and Linc Gordon [former American ambassador] disliked each other, and it was not much of a newspaper. But he was one of the real intellectuals. He was part of the political opposition but not of the terrorist stripe. He made a lot of charges. The main vehicle he had was a newspaper, and he made constant attacks. Frank and I agreed that the time had come that we ought to see him, so I had two meetings with him. Of course, I didn't try to hide it, because, you know, Brazilians were listening to telephone conversations. Costa y Silva raised this with me. At that stage, I had been there about two years, and I felt my time was about up anyway. Costa y Silva was furious about it, because he felt it was being "disloyal" to him, and he gave me a lecture on this. After he got through with this lecture, he said, "Mr. Ambassador, I would appreciate, therefore, if you would not see Lacerda any more."

I said, "Well, Mr. President, I'm very sorry to disappoint you. Your ambassador in Washington is free to see the opposition party in the United States as much as he wants--although not the terrorists. And I'm not going to see the terrorists in Brazil. I have to maintain my own freedom to see people in Brazil, whether or not they agree with the government."

Well, then the papers started to have headlines saying, "Will Tuthill Be *Persona non Grata?*" And at one stage, Frank Carlucci said to me, "Jack, I know you don't give a damn whether you're a *persona non grata* or not, but I've been PNG'd [declared persona non grata] twice aleady. Once in Tanzania and then some other place in Africa." And he said, "If I have three PNGs against me, people start to think Carlucci doesn't get along with anybody."

Washington was fully supportive, both the Department and the press at home, because then it got into the press. I remember one editorial in the

New York Times or *The Washington Post* that called it "The silly season in Brazil," referring to the Costa y Silva position.

ECUADOR (1960-1965)

MAURICE MARSHALL BERNBAUM was the United States ambassador to Eucador, 1960-1965. He found President Arosmena a particularly difficult man with whom to deal. Arosmena had a severe drinking problem, which affected his relations with the American ambassador and contributed directly to his fall from power.

Bernbaum: He was a really complicated individual. His father had been president of Ecuador.   He came from one of the first families in Guayaquil.   He was more or less a maverick in his community.   He was addicted to drinking, a dipsomaniac.   And somehow or other he always seemed to be interested in stirring things up.

Arosemena had been involved in various incidents due to drunkenness. One of them was when he met the Chilean president at the airport in Guayaquil and was drunk. It was said that if it hadn't been at Christmas he would have been overthrown then.

Later, Admiral McNeil, president of the Grace Line, visited Ecuador with his wife. The president gave a banquet for them, because the Grace Line had participated in the inauguration of a new vessel. The president's wife had been invited to visit the United States.

His apartment was above the presidential office, so I showed up there, where I expected the party to take place. He was there with a few of his ministers, including the foreign minister. He was already half gone. As I walked in he said, "Ambassador, have a drink." I said, "Well, Mr. President, let's go downstairs, we'll have the drinks down there." We got him down there, and he made a speech decorating the admiral. He neglected to mention my presence. Whenever he was annoyed with the United States for one reason or other, he'd neglect to recognize my presence. So I knew something was up.

During the soup course at dinner, he rose--by that time he was really pretty much under the influence of liquor--and made a long rambling speech in which he attacked the U.S. government for exploiting Ecuador without mercy. Well, of course, you can imagine the reaction at the table.

He turned to me and said, "You agree with me, don't you, Mr. Ambassador?" I didn't know whether to laugh or cry, so I said, "No, Mr. President. When you're speaking of the government, you're speaking of the American people." He had spoken highly of the American people as being distinct from the government.

Then he turned to one of his ministers at the other side of the table, and said, "Paco, you agree with me, don't you?" Well, this minister at that point was studying the molding on the ceiling. Finally he said, "No, Señor President."

Arosemena got up, and staggered out of the dining room. Dinner continued, and finally we finished. The various ministers came along and said, "You're not going to make anything of this, are you?" And I said, "No, under those conditions. I don't know what brought it on, but I'm sure he wouldn't have done it if he were sober." I remember that a sub-secretary of foreign affairs came along and said, "It makes no difference what you say." He said, "The three chiefs of the armed forces who were at that dinner have just decided that this is it. This man's gone too far." And they just threw him out of power.

IRAQ (1978-1980)

EDWARD LIONEL PECK was the head of the U.S. Interests Section in Baghdad, Iraq (1978-1980) during a period when there were no official diplomatic relations between the two countries. In an interview months prior to the Iraqi takeover of Kuwait in 1990, Peck describes his impression of Saddam Hussein.

Peck: Saddam Hussein was a village thug who wore Pierre Cardin suits and has lovely bridgework and a nice mustache and all that. When I got there he was the number two man to a fellow named Ahmed Hassan El-Bakreh. And Saddam Hussein had been number two for about ten years.

He resigned and the expected took place, Saddam Hussein's smooth transition to leadership. Two weeks later he machine-gunned twenty-five of his closest associates, who, I think, felt that now rule would be a little more collegial, and Hussein wanted to make sure that they understood that it wasn't going to be collegial. He ruled Iraq with what can only be described as an iron hand.

HAITI (1967-1969)

CLAUDE GEORGE ANTHONY ROSS found that living in Haiti as U.S. ambassador was a bit like living in a goldfish bowl. Dictator Papa Doc Duvalier kept close watch on everything that went on in the country, including the ambassador's every move. Ross served in that country from 1967 to 1969.

Ross: Morale was bad when I got there. We worked on it. Papa Doc, for some reason, decided he liked me, and I always used to say, "God, I wonder what I'm doing wrong?" But this was on a purely personal level, because I avoided, as much as possible, official contact--that is to say, any one-on-one meetings, because I knew that any of those was going to be the occasion of his asking me for something that we weren't going to give him. So normally I would go only when I was instructed by my government, which wasn't all that often, for the same reasons, or when he called me in.

It was in these sessions that I learned early on how closely he kept watch on everything that was going on in the country.   I mean literally. Nothing could happen that he didn't know about.   Somebody could be washed ashore or landed ashore anywhere, and within a matter of hours, Papa Doc would know about it. The bush telegraph would start operating, and the first thing you know, it would get back to the president.   I'd go in, and he would always ask me about my wife.   Her first name is Antigone, and old Papa Doc fancied himself as a great scholar and classicist, and he loved this name Antigone. "Eh, Antigone, comment va-t-elle?"   Sometimes he'd reach in the drawer and pull out a series of photographs taken at some party we'd been at the night before, you know, dancing up a storm at the Dominican Embassy or whatever. So he really knew what was going on there. As I say, nothing happened that he didn't know about.

Of course, one of the consequences of this was that personal security was great. Our secretaries could have walked home at midnight without any fear of molestation.

7

Coping with Policy
and Washington Bureaucracy

Dealing with Washington is sometimes more frustrating than dealing with the host country. An ambassador can often resolve disagreements through face-to-face discussions with local officials. Problems with Washington are another matter. To ask guidance of the Department of State is to invite long delays while views of its offices and bureaus or those of other departments and agencies are reconciled and the particular interests and sensitivities of members of congress and of the American public are considered.

Sometimes the views of Washington and those of the ambassador as to what should or can be done are in conflict. The instructions may appear unwise or unrealistic to the ambassador and difficult if not impossible to carry out. Washington and the ambassador may have different views as to the seriousness of an issue at hand and they may have a different view entirely of the overall importance of the country concerned.

One must also recognize that there is always present in all officials in Washington a natural desire to be "on top" of the situation as well as to "cover themselves"--never to make a wrong decision, never to be uninformed, never to be caught short by an unpleasant surprise--for someone, be it the press, the president, Congress, or a ranking official is most assuredly looking over their shoulders. Speedy, explicit instructions of a kind welcomed by an ambassador are difficult to come by. Thus there is in diplomacy as in business a built-in tension between the field and the home office.

SUDAN (1973-1977)

"Don't ask Washington what you should do--tell them what you intend to do unless instructed otherwise" advises *WILLIAM DODD BREWER (Mauritius, Sudan).*

Brewer: In this age communication seems to be downgraded. We all of us get these printout letters which appear to have been sent by the charwoman in the middle of the night without any indication that human eye has ever seen any of this stuff. It is important to bear in mind what can be done with communications, and the Foreign Service, during my period of years with it, was above anything else an organ of communication. You had to be able to communicate in writing, both from the field to Washington, and in Washington to the secretary and the president, and if you couldn't get your ideas on paper concisely and clearly, and speedily, you were not going to be around very long. And in addition to being concise and clear and fast, one also learned that communication can be turned to one's advantage. For example--there are many examples--but people don't realize that how one phrases something is extremely important. If an ambassador sends a message saying, "I would like to be instructed to do so and so, please advise," he is then stopped from any action on that issue until he gets a reply to his message. Whereas, if he sends a message saying, "I am planning to see the foreign minister the day after tomorrow and will make to him the following points--l, 2, 3, 4, 5-- unless the Department objects," you have then in effect written your own instructions, and if you have not had a reply--you allow time, of course, for a reply--if you've had no reply, you've had your instructions and you go ahead. And, of course, you will get a reply. You usually, in my experience, get a very short reply saying, "Department approves line you propose taking." Because the man in Washington, who is very busy and very harried, has just had some of his work done for him by your writing your own instructions. But you haven't done it in a way which then leaves the ball in Washington's court. Washington has got to respond, and got to respond very promptly because you have said you were going to take this line in 48 hours, with the foreign minister.

ETHIOPIA (1977-1978)

RICHARD CAVINS MATHERON (later ambassador to Swaziland, 1979-1982) was deputy chief of mission at our embassy in Addis Ababa, 1977-1978. After a military takeover of the Ethiopian government of Emperor Haile Selassie in 1974 relations with the United States were close to being severed. Matheron, who several years later was in charge, had a plan to avert such a break and, in effect wrote his own instructions, which did the trick.

Matheron: We got word in the morning that they [the Ethiopian military council] were going to break diplomatic relations in the afternoon. I sent a flash to Washington and told them what I proposed to say, because I was sure that Washington couldn't get a coordinated position back in time. I got an answer back within about half an hour, saying words to the effect, "Use your approach and good luck." I always felt that if you could present a position to Washington that didn't require a lot of coordinating between all of the agencies, which was based on a common-sense approach, you usually got the go-ahead. So much has been talked about, whether diplomats are just messengers for Washington, or whether they actually have influence on diplomatic relations. I think a good diplomat can often lead the superiors in Washington to come to a position much faster if he or she takes the lead. One of the sources of my personal pride was that relations were not broken at that time, and continued on. It's always been touch and go, but at least there was not a complete break that day.

BARBADOS (1969-1974)

EILEEN ROBERTA DONOVAN (Barbados, 1969-1974) felt that her views and assessments of developments in Barbados were not given much consideration in Washington and realized later that she could have had more influence if she had telephoned the department and asked for what she wanted.

Donovan: One of the mistakes I made was in not giving myself more clout in Washington. I never called them on the telephone to ask them for anything. I took them at their word when they said only a flash telegram will go to the secretary of state, you know, a real emergency. When I think back, I realize that I didn't throw my weight around enough as far as Washington was concerned. After I wrote those masterpieces of polished prose that were my political and economic assessments for a year, and I spent hours on them as you can well imagine, I should have gotten myself on a commercial flight and gone up to Washington and said, hey, what about this? What are you going to do? What do you think? In that respect, I didn't realize that I could have had more clout. I didn't realize that I was not just a poor forgotten orphan down there.

IRAQ (1978-1980)

Occasionally, instructions to a chief of mission are patently impossible to implement. EDWARD LIONEL PECK, later ambassador to Mauritania, was chief of the American interests section in Baghdad, 1978-1980, when we did not have full diplomatic relations with Iraq.

Peck: The Americans have an exercise that they use with their embassies abroad called "goals and objectives." I received mine for Iraq, and I had to laugh. The number one objective, sent to a man in a country with which we did not have diplomatic relations and which we had in fact very, very, very limited low-level official relations, my number one objective was to get the Iraq government to abandon its hostility to Israel. This was, I thought, a worthwhile objective but somewhat unrealistic under the circumstances. The very number one pinnacle on which this whole Iraqi government effort is based is hostility to Israel. And I'm going to change that?

I sent a telegram back to Washington, which I wish I'd had somebody smart enough to advise me not to send. "Shouldn't my number one objective be--endeavor to open a dialogue with the Iraqi government; number two to establish some form of communication. Can I assume that my counterpart in Washington has a message which says, get the United States Government to abandon its support for Israel? And is that any more realistic than you have asked me to do?" Anyway, I wasn't quite that intemperate. But I got a message that said in effect, "Shut up and carry out your orders."

OMAN (1980)

The hostage crisis in Tehran (1979-1981) caused Washington to be terribly jumpy. When our embassy in Pakistan was attacked in 1980, Secretary of State Vance ordered the evacuation of all dependents and reduction of staffs of our embassies in the Persian Gulf area. MARSHALL WAYNE WILEY, in Oman (1978-1981), considered these instructions ill-advised and an overreaction by those far from the scene.

Wiley: Back in Washington, there is a tendency to look at all of these countries as being similar, to a much greater extent than, in fact, they are. Secretary of State Vance put out an order ordering the evacuation of all dependents, and cutting down the staffs of all the embassies in the Gulf area after this Pakistani affair; also the attack [on the Grand Mosque by religious extremists] in Mecca in Saudi Arabia came at about that time. However, for Saudi Arabia, the desk officer said we can't do it in Saudi Arabia because we have too many people there. We can't cut back the embassy, and take out dependents, and so on.

Although the attack had taken place in Saudi Arabia, Vance still ordered that all of the lower Gulf countries--he ordered this over the vehement objection of all of the ambassadors, all of us screaming back to him, "Why are you evacuating these countries? They are safer than New York or Washington for our people,"--and they were, literally. But Vance absolutely had his mind made up, and he would not listen to any of the ambassadors or anybody else. He wanted all of the dependents out of these countries, and staffs cut back. We all lost our families for a period of 3 or 4 months, and we all got very quizzical inquiries from our foreign ministers, saying, "What are you afraid of here?" It was very embarrassing to answer. I'd say, "I don't know what we're afraid of. This was done on orders from Washington."

The feelings got very tense between the ambassadors and Vance after awhile over this issue, because we could see no reason at all for evacuating these countries. There were no threats of any kind to our staffs, or our people, or our embassies. We would send in these long telegrams pointed out as logically and as rationally as we could that there is no particular threat to the embassy here, anymore than there has always been. He would say, "Yes, that is what they told me from Pakistan. Then, the next day, the embassy was burned down."

NIGERIA (1978)

There are times when the active participation of the president or the secretary of state in implementing foreign policy can make a real difference. President Jimmy Carter's swing through Africa in 1978 is an example of this. DONALD BOYD EASUM (Upper Volta, Nigeria) tells how Carter's visit to Nigeria helped turn that country from being fiercely anti-to strongly pro-American.

Easum: The visit went absolutely splendidly. And to show you how a powerful country can be turned around in a year and a half from riots in the street, death threats to me, jailings of American businessmen without our knowing it, where they'd spend the night sleeping on a table in a security chief's office with one bare light bulb up there and they'd be questioned about what they were doing and where. If you wore a camera around your neck, you were immediately arrested. American companies were being just automatically rejected on contracts. Why did this kind of change take place so fast? Well, because of a different policy on human rights. It's as simple as that; to explain it a little better, a different policy with regard to racism in South Africa.

And then the personality. Who could be more different than Kissinger on the one hand, and Carter on the other? Or Carter and Vance on the other? Here were two decent, humane individuals, willing to listen. On the other side, I won't use adjectives, but you had somebody unwilling to listen, only interested in pushing his own particular brand of policy which he would argue was in the service of the United States. I won't argue about that. The style was seen as manipulative and untrustworthy, and a style that Nigerians felt, and many other Africans felt, was derogatory to them as people. So much for that.

We had a meeting that was an extraordinary meeting. Obasanjo [Nigerian chief of state] talked about the need to support the Patriotic Front in Rhodesia, the alliance between Mugabe and his ZANU (Zimbabwe African National Union) on the one hand, and Nkomo and his ZAPU (Zimbabwe African Peoples Union) on the other. They were now fighting from safe havens in Mozambique, which was recently independent, and from Zambia. They were putting heavy pressure on the Rhodesians and you had a terrible situation. Britain had not yet come down hard in favor of getting everybody together for discussions on a new future based on majority rule. That was the situation at the time.

Obasanjo said to Carter, "I like very much what I hear you saying about the Rhodesian situation. As you know," he said, "at the moment we're at a stalemate. We can't get the ZANU and ZAPU people, the Patriotic Front people, to talk with the Smith people [members of the white Rhodesian government], and we can't get the Smith people to talk with them. What we're pushing for is what everybody then was calling All Parties Talks." That was the big issue and nobody could seem to produce it.

The Foreign Minister and I had arranged that at that very same time the Foreign Ministers of the front line countries would be in Lagos. We didn't tell Washington in advance. In fact, Mugabe really confronted me with a *fait accompli*. He simply said, about the day before Carter was going to arrive--and this was very clever of him--"Donald, I've arranged for all of the front line Foreign Ministers to be here. And I hope you can get Cy Vance to talk with them." Well, it was a genius move on his part, because that's exactly what Vance wanted to do. And after Obasanjo and Carter had sort of agreed on the approach to the Rhodesian freedom struggle issue, it was the natural thing for Vance and Mugabe to say, "Well, sir, we've got the Front Line Foreign Ministers here, why not let Cy Vance talk with them while the President is doing some other things?" And that's exactly what we did. We had side conversations that included Andy Young and Don McHenry, and Brzezinski, who wasn't really on the team philosophically. I didn't sense he was really with it. And, of course, Dick Moose, and myself, and Tony Lake, and one or two others were also there.

Those conversations, and based on the agreement Carter and Obasanjo made, we agreed a team would go to Dar-es Salaam as quickly as possible, that we would persuade David Owen from London to come down, and that we would try to get the All Parties Talks resuscitated. This all was as a result of the fact that Obasanjo found Carter attractive, philosophically speaking. And, indeed, that's what happened.

GUINEA (1961-1963)

WILLIAM ATTWOOD found that the president can be of great help in getting things done. He points out that a political ambassador often has the advantage of being able to catch the attention of the president in order to change a policy.

Attwood: I think the ambassador has a role to play, because a lot of them will react according to how you feel yourself. I'll give you an example. When I got to Guinea, the established policy--back in the Bureau of African Affairs, or the Bureau of European Affairs--was that Guinea was a French problem. The French had dealt with it. The French had pulled out--ostracized it--and the Soviet bloc had moved in. Those were the days of the cold war. We were all cold warriors in those days, and we were there to fight the enemy.

Well, the attitude of the State Department was to do nothing--they are beyond the pale; the French don't want us to do anything; therefore we take our cue from the French. Anyway, our idea was to see what we could do, and find out if these people are neutralists, and bring them around, to give them a little aid, and to show them that what we do is more practical than what the Russians do. Never mind what the French think.

Well, that created a problem. The embassy was divided. We had one officer who felt we should just let them go down the spout; but the others gradually got to feel that it was better to make an effort, and went along with my views. Then I got the president's backing on it. And of course, if you've got the president's backing, then you find that the assistant secretaries of state go along, too! But that's the only time I used my access to the White House, in order to try to change a policy. He was in favor of making an effort there; and not just kissing it off. All ambassadors have that privilege--of going to the president. It's not one that you should abuse, but now and then, when everything comes to a dead stop--and you remember what it was like in AID. If the bureaucrats didn't want something to happen, it didn't happen. Months went by--ships weren't loaded, ships weren't available. Well, one call from the White House and all of a sudden everything got moving. So sometimes you really had to do something like that.

There's where it's an advantage to be a non-career appointee.

ROMANIA (1981-1985)

DAVID B. FUNDERBURK, ambassador to Romania, expresses his disdain for the late dictator Ceausescu and criticizes elements in the State Department and the Foreign Service for their attitude toward that regime.

Funderburk: Well, the fact of the matter is policy is made in Washington. It is very seldom that any type of policy is made in the field, that I know of, or at least in the context where I was working. I certainly think that policy, as made in Washington, should factor in, and include, the views of the people in the field, whether they are an ambassador, the economic officer or the political officer. Being there first hand and working day to day with the people, they certainly ought to have a greater first-hand knowledge of what is going on, and this ought to be factored in. Why do you need as big an embassy with a policy pretention if actually all they're doing is just carrying a message? So my problem was the fact that Washington policy was made without taking into consideration information from the field, or even despite information from the field.

The guys that I observed there had a very cozy relationship with their communist counterparts, and they seemed to be much more interested in trying to please them and trying to ingratiate themselves than they were looking out for American interests. I mean, there were no two ways about it, from my point of view. I would point out that it was a source of no little satisfaction to me that in the last year and a half, most favored nation status was removed from Romania. So somebody, obviously, in the United States, some of the people, some of the congressmen, some of the religious figures, must have come to the conclusion that Funderburk wasn't totally wrong in saying that this is a monster we're dealing with. He's destroying his country's history and heritage. The people have no free immigration; the human rights record is terrible. We shouldn't be rewarding and giving favored treatment to such a character. And yet, it was [some State Department officials] and other great career diplomats, who have all knowledge, who were saying that this was a great man and we needed him, regardless of what he was doing to anybody. So he could pull a Tiananmen Square [site of opposition to China's communist rulers] every month, and we would still send the money over there to Ceausescu, because the Foreign Service people know best. But what is the problem now? I mean, obviously, the word got out about this guy. It didn't just get out from David Funderburk.

I would say that "clientitis" was rampant in the East European Bureau of the State Department, to the extent that the way up the ladder, to get rewarded in the Foreign Service was for them to figure out a way to reward the communists that they were dealing with in Eastern Europe. And so they devised these projects and these plans. They had fun sitting with these guys. They winked. They told jokes. They were like their brother or sister. In my view, they lost track of where they were from and what country they were representing, and what the views of most American people were. I didn't have the expertise bureaucratically to report everything that was going on, crafted in a State Department style, to have effect. And I had people in the embassy who saw things the way I did, or at least said that they did, and who assisted me in this process. And they're people that I admire, appreciate and consider to be very patriotic Americans.

So I don't make a blanket generalization, but there were many, the ones who seem to be in charge of our policy, who almost made it incumbent upon people who wanted to rise in the Foreign Service, to not look out for American interests, and not put them first, but put the interest of that client's state first. And this is what I witnessed, and it was very despicable to me. And in the years since that--and I'm outraged by this, by the way--I'm outraged by the fact that I get calls every day of my life from ethnic Romanians and Hungarians and Germans who say that, "We tried to get through to the American Embassy and the American Embassy told us to go to hell." This was because there were KGB agents working throughout the American Embassy. The Romanian national employees all work for the KGB. Everybody knows that. And that person remembers that for the rest of his life, that here is America, the symbol of freedom. Yet when he walks in they've got one of Ceausescu's thugs working at the gate, telling him where he can go. This is the way our embassies operated in Eastern Europe. And it's gotten us into great difficulty in the minds and hearts of the people. I resent that, as an American concerned about our image abroad. I have an entirely different perspective on how we should project that image.

I don't say we should close an embassy off and have fortress America. I'm just as much for open America as anybody. I travelled through the country as often as I could to see people, to show the flag, to show them that America is different. But at the same time, we have to look out for our security interest and our national interest. And I don't think most of these guys, in the department that we were dealing with, did that, and they're the ones running the show today. And so I deeply resent that as an American concerned about the future of freedom.

ZAIRE (1975-1979)

When Congress and the administration are at odds on policy matters, problems arise. Certain Congressmen disagreed with the administration's policy of providing economic aid to Mobutu's government in Zaire in the 1970s. WALTER LEON CUTLER tells of this tug of war over policy as seen from his embassy.

Cutler: Steve Solarz [Dem. N.Y.], who at the time was the Chairman of the Africa Subcommittee of the House Foreign Affairs Committee, was very concerned about the nature of the government in Zaire, primarily from the standpoint of human rights. He felt that much more could have been done and should have been done by the government for the people there, that this was a country which is far from destitute--a country with tremendous resources. That the country, basically, was being mismanaged by the government, and that there was corruption at the top. This was his view of it, that there was corruption and mismanagement of resources, a lack of concern for the individual.

I knew that he was one of a number in the Congress who were skeptical (to put in mildly) of the utility and the advisability of our continuing to support the Mobutu government with an aid program. So, in other words, there was a very definite and discernible political dimension to our aid program to Zaire. The Administration looked at it in a different way. While recognizing deficiencies in the way the country, and particularly the economy, was being managed, the Administration tended to look at the hard options involved.

One option would have been to cut off aid, as recommended by certain members of the Congress and other critics of the Mobutu regime. This option was rejected. Is this the way to induce political, as well as economic and fiscal, reform? Do you threaten to cut off aid? Or do you actually cut off aid in order to get something more out of a government which feels that, while it's not perfect, it's nevertheless doing better than we think it is? Thus this option was not adopted.

I, as ambassador, recommended against consideration of that option. I could not see how American interests could be served. In the first place, our aid program was not that significant. So if we cut it off, it wasn't going to really hurt the people that much, and it wasn't going to hurt the government that much.

There were other sources of aid. The Belgians and the French and so on had programs, which, I imagine, were larger than ours. But, beyond that, the political signal, which a cutoff of aid would have sent, I don't believe would have been heeded in a helpful way. Mobutu certainly cared about his image in the United States. Certainly, some of the opponents of that regime within Zaire would have seized upon a cutoff of aid, and this might actually have increased the amount of opposition. But, basically, I could not see anything but negative results of such a move. There were other ways to encourage and try to induce reform, which I though should be tried first, and that the cutoff of aid should be left as the ultimate and last step if all else failed. So I argued against that. I did not agree with Congressman Solarz on this point. I saw it in a different way, and so did the administration.

The administration really has the responsibility for carrying on relations over the long term with a country and for looking after U.S. interests. I think some members of Congress fully realize that they can advocate this or that step, but they don't really take responsibility for carrying it out. It was an easy thing to say in those days, "We disapprove of the way the country is being run. We disapprove of our money being used to contribute to the running of the country in that wrongful way. Therefore, let's put it someplace else where it's more useful."

You can say that and take your seat, and you know it's not going to happen, because that's not the administration's view. But you've made your point. You've gone on record as having stood up for what's right, as against what's wrong. And life goes on.

PORTUGAL (1979)

Early in 1979 at the time of the Soviet invasion of Afghanistan we began sending several squadrons of U.S. aircraft to Egypt from our base in the Azores, to show the flag, without seeking permission from the Portuguese government. For their own political reasons the Portuguese objected, insisting that we must first ask their permission. RICHARD JOSEPH BLOOMFIELD tells of the difficulty he had in persuading our Defense Department that asking for permission was the best solution.

Bloomfield: It was probably the Afghanistan invasion that touched it off. The Russian occupation took place in December of 1979. We were using the Azores to periodically send a couple of squadrons of aircraft to Egypt to show the flag, in effect, and for other things. The Portuguese came to us and said, "Hey, wait a minute, what's going on here? First of all, its our base, its not your base. We, in effect, don't rent, we give you . . .have conceded certain facilities to you." Which technically was true. "And secondly, our understanding is that it's to be used in connection with NATO. We're a NATO country, and you're a NATO country, but if you want to use it for any out-of-NATO operations, you have to get our permission." And the Defense Department immediately said, "No, we're not going to do that." Of course, we'd been used to having our own way there because we had it pretty much that way under Salazar, and during the turmoil of the revolution nobody paid much attention to it. This was a new kind of situation.

The Portuguese were quite sensitive about the Middle East because during the Salazar administration in '73 in the Middle East war, we tried to send . . .we were ferrying, I believe, supplies to the Israeli Army, when the French and all of our other stalwart allies wouldn't let us use their airfields. We pretty much insisted that we use the Azores. When the Arabs put on the oil embargo they cut Portugal off completely from oil. So they suffered for that. So when this thing started repeating itself, you see, six years later, even though it was a different government, they remembered all of that.

So there was a period in which the Defense Department kept insisting that we insist on our rights. I mean they sent me telegrams that were drafted by some lawyers in Defense which were cockamamie stuff. I just pointed out to them, I said, "Look, this is a sovereign government and there is nothing in our agreement with them that says that we can use the base for anything we see fit." And I said, "If you really want to get down to it, if you want to insist on your rights, then they can just drive a bunch of firetrucks out on the airstrip and you're not going to get your planes in there. So why make trouble for yourself? Why not just tell us to go in and request it through a diplomatic note?" And I said, "I'm sure they will give permission every time. But why make trouble for yourself by insisting on principle when in fact it's a very dubious principle to begin with?" So eventually they caved in and we did that. We would do what every other embassy does everywhere else in the world, and go in and give them a note, and they'd reply almost immediately and say, "Yes, go ahead."

ITALY (1981-1989)

MAXWELL M. RABB was ambassador to Italy from 1981 to 1989, the longest stay of any American ambassador. Early on he met one of the challenges that come to ambassadors in major European countries, trying to persuade governments to support initiatives which are unpopular with their public, but which the United States sees as vital to its interests. His tactic for getting the answer he needed was novel and successful.

Rabb: The big question, and I met it only eight or ten days after I came there--I came into Italy full of good will and the rest of it. I was met with a cable that, in a sense, made me swallow hard. It came from the secretary of state. It said, not in gentle terms, but in very rough terms, that I had a task to perform. They didn't say that it is important that you consult with the leadership of Italy and try to get the 1979 understanding put into effect as it was to be in 1981--namely, the building of a base for the cruise missile of the INF (Intermediate Nuclear Force).

But the cable said, "It is imperative that you persuade the leadership to do this."

Now, it so happens that I have now been here in Italy eight full years which, as I indicated earlier, is the longest term any American ambassador has ever had in the history of Italy. Believe me, at that moment, I didn't think I was going to last out the month. It was my first assignment. There was Germany with the Green Party turning their thumbs down on this thing. So did Great Britain with the women throwing themselves across the Commons, not letting our personnel in military vehicles get through. They said no. Denmark completely signed off on this. So did Holland. Belgium was almost as bad. It was a complete mess. All that was left was Italy, which was certainly not the strongest one when it came to this type of thing. It had not really ventured far from its own soil on any matters that were international.

The situation was desperate. Of course, it was the Italians in the end who did this. But the American influence and the diplomatic pressure, properly applied in a way that did not rub them the wrong way, was very, very good, I think. At least, the result was good.

And so, upon receiving this cable, I asked for an appointment. I saw the prime minister, who was Spadolini at the time. He had several members of his team around him--ministers. I gave them my arguments. I had rehearsed them. Everything--I had worked on it, and I thought I was doing pretty well because I was getting marvelous attention.

I said, "Gee, it can't be. They are really listening."

At the end of it, I concluded, and the prime minister said, "Mr. Ambassador, look at the other Allies. Look at what they are doing. They are all moving away from this thing. Why don't you wait one year."

And I remember his hands flurrying to the sky. "Better still, wait two years."

In other words, "n-o, no." He didn't say it that way, but that is the effect of it in gentle language. Then he added, probably to stroke me because I was the United States ambassador, "Let me say, of course, if you have another major argument to make, by all means, let's have it. We will give it some consideration."

But he knew I didn't have anything. I surprised him. I said, "Gentlemen, but I do have another argument."

They said, "What is it?"

And if you think they wanted to know, I wanted to know also. I had a complete blank. I didn't know what I was going to say, but I didn't like the idea of going back home in 30 days.

So they said, "What is it?"

I said, "Well, the argument I'm going to give you is not the argument that I expect you to accept. You can forget about that. I'm just presenting it. It is that the United States of America and Italy have been good friends, but there is still plenty of room all the way up to the top with results and benefits in the field of commerce, of finance, of trade, of military activity, of culture. But," I said, "that's not the reason. You are not to accept it."

You bet it wasn't, because that was a bribe. So I passed that one by.

They said, "Well, what is the reason?"

I said, "The reason I'm going to give you is not the reason you are to accept."

Of course, I was trying desperately to think of what I could present which would not put me in a rough position. I was stalling.

They said, "But what have you got in mind?"

I said, "Well, this reason you are not to accept also, but it is interesting. President Reagan, everybody knows, is a very good friend to his personal friends, and he is a very good friend to those nations that befriend his country. But that's not the reason."

That was another bribe, so I pushed that out.

They said, "What is the reason?"

I was licked. Anyway I said, "The reason is simply this. If you will do this, you will make me a big man in Washington."

Fine. Eight days later, we got it and everyone was surprised. Italy was the first. It wasn't I who did it. It was the Italians, and I want to make it very clear, of course. The Italians had to be the courageous ones, and they did it. It was a very unusual thing. But, of course, they don't want to give the feeling that it went that way. But I daresay--and this is not really almost put in with the rest of it--but I think they must also have been influenced by what I had said were the non-reasons.

EGYPT (1974-1979), SAUDI ARABIA (1966-1970)

Dealing with Washington often means dealing directly with the secretary of state. HERMANN FREDERICK EILTS, ambassador to Saudi Arabia and Egypt, worked well with Secretary of State Henry Kissinger, but it was by no means easy.

Eilts: I have great admiration for Kissinger. I had my encounters with him. I twice resigned on him, once almost at the beginning on one of his early missions, and once later during Sinai II, because I disliked the way he was doing things. I guess I'm one of the few ambassadors who did stand up to him, and somehow he did not resent my doing so. He seemed to respect it and I was then one of the few ambassadors whom he never criticized.   He was utterly merciless, however, in talking to other ambassadors, some very senior ambassadors. His handling, his treatment of them publicly, was very often shameful, but that never happened with me. Somehow my two resignations seemed to have had some effect on him.

Working with Kissinger was intellectual fun. He had a quick mind. He could come up with ideas. He was a conceptualizer, which was very important. He looked down the road in terms of where we should be going. Whether we got to that point is something else, but it was fun working with him, in an intellectual and a policy sense. Also, in that context, when suggestions, proposals, were made to him--when I made them to him for example--I had a great many of them accepted. We've all been in the Foreign Service long enough that you know you don't win them all, but I found I could have an influence on Kissinger.

UGANDA (1963-1966)

OLCOTT HAWTHORNE DEMING left for Uganda with specific instructions to encourage the continuation and strengthening of the East African Federation. He describes the reaction of the Ugandan prime minister to his efforts. Deming was the first American ambassador to Uganda from 1963 to 1966.

Deming: It was during this period, between 1962 and 1966. The British had taken measures to tie Uganda, Kenya, and Tanzania together into an East African Federation. They had built a railway line which ran from Mombasa on the Indian Ocean up over the Kenya Mountains to Kampala. The purpose was to make the colonies self supporting or profitable. Coffee, tea, cotton, industrial diamonds and other products were shipped out of Uganda and British goods in.   The federation also had common postal, telegraph, monetary systems.   The British and we were hopeful that this cooperation would be continued after independence.

I was under some pressure from the Department to do what I could as the representative of the United States to encourage the continuation of this federation. I was instructed by Averell Harriman, then undersecretary in charge of African affairs, to go to the prime minister and urge him to take steps strengthening or continuing the federation.   I was to tell him that if he could do that the United States could see its way to providing larger economic assistance to a federation of states than it could to individual ones trying to go on their own.   I recall informing the Department that I expected to have a negative reaction because Obote and the Ugandans had always felt inferior to Tanzania and Kenya because they were both on the Indian Ocean and Uganda was landlocked.   Also the British base of operations and policy for East Africa was in Nairobi, Kenya. So I carried out my mission and the prime minister heard me out. Then he said, "Is your government trying to bribe me?" I said, "No, we're talking economics and we're talking about steps which we would be willing to take which we think would be helpful to all three of your countries." Obote replied, "I am not interested in strengthening the Federation." I asked him if this was for political, economic or psychological reasons? He looked at me and said, "Mostly psychological. You know, in a Federation before long there would be only one representative at the United Nations for the East African Federation; he would not come from Uganda."

GUATEMALA (1974-1979)

DAVIS EUGENE BOSTER found that the draft of the U.S. government's report on human rights angered the government of Guatemala, which considered it an intrusion in their internal affairs. While this policy caused discomfort in our relations with Guatemala, in the long run it worked.

Boster: One problem we had to resolve during my tour there dealt with the draft of the U.S. government's report on human rights, as mandated by Congress. They were very upset about our preparing a report on another country's human rights record. They felt this was an intrusion in their internal affairs, that no one had a right to such intrusion, except maybe the United Nations. Certainly that no single country had that right. As far as the Guatemalans were concerned, we could keep our aid if it was conditioned on passage of a human rights test. Brazil took that same line with us later. Frankly, in my own mind, I thought the Guatemalans may have had a reasonable position.

I reported the Guatemalan reaction but not my own view. I remember that some people in the Foreign Service, including me, felt in the beginning that this was some kind of unnecessary complication of our relationships with other governments, that human rights in foreign lands may not have been our business, and that in any case, our pursuit of them was to the detriment of our relationships with other countries. They would have been happier to shove the whole issue under the rug and felt that if the human rights proponents, particularly in the State Department, could be kept under control, matters would be far better.

Of course, since 1976, U.S. interests in human rights around the world have strengthened and have become a basic part of our approach to foreign policy. In some relationships--with Romania, for example--it is key. I was wrong to think of it as mere meddling. In fact, the U.S. support for human rights has worked and we no longer think it is anything strange.

8

Troubles in Asia:
Korea and Laos

The defeat of Japan in 1945 ended one war but it did not usher in a period of tranquillity in Asia. Five years later, on June 25, 1950, North Korea invaded the south from along the 38th parallel, and the Korean War began. Twenty-five years later came the fall of Saigon, which had instant repercussions throughout the entire Southeast Asia, and Laos in particular. South Korea was repeatedly under threat of attack from the north.

In this chapter we include recollections of a deputy chief of mission and a chargé d'affaires in South Korea and the chargé in Laos at these crucial times. First, Everett Drumright (then the DCM) tells how he and Ambassador Muccio conducted the embassy in Seoul at the time of the North Korean attack in 1950. Chargé Thomas Stern recounts an incident in 1976 in the demilitarized zone of Korea that almost lead to a resumption of the war; and Christian Chapman recalls the tense days of 1975 in Vientiane after the debacle in South Vietnam when the continued U.S. presence in Laos hung by a thread.

EVERETT FRANCIS DRUMRIGHT was Ambassador John Muccio's deputy in 1950 when the North Korean army invaded the south. He tells of the embassy's hurried evacuation of 2000 people, accomplished with the full support of General MacArthur's headquarters and of his difficulty in keeping track of South Korea's president, Sighman Rhee.

Drumright: So then came the invasion. That occurred early in the morning of June 25, 1950. I was awakened on that misty Sunday morning by our military attaché, who informed me that there was heavy fighting going on up on the border. Of course, we'd had incursions on quite a few occasions, back and forth stabs across the line. So I wasn't taking that one report all too seriously. I asked my aide to continue to follow that closely and to keep us informed. He called back within an hour, about 7 o'clock, and reported that the action was continuing in building up and was extending all along the 38th parallel. That meant something serious. So I rang up Ambassador Muccio. By that time it was getting on toward 8 o'clock. His houseboy told me he had left word not to be disturbed; he'd been out somewhere the night before. I said, "Well, don't mind that. You go and get him out of bed. I want to talk to him urgently." So he got him and I said, "John, we're in trouble. We have an invasion here all along the 38th parallel." He was calm about it. He said, "Okay, let's go to the office and get going there."

We met at the office and continued to assess the situation for an hour or so. We called our people in. This was Sunday; it was not a working day. It was quite evident by 9 o'clock that it was an invasion so Ambassador Muccio told me to draft a telegram to Washington telling the facts of the situation, which I did. It was Saturday night in Washington, and I gather it caused quite a commotion.

Anyway, the situation grew worse and worse. The North Koreans were highly prepared against our unprepared couple of divisions up there on the front facing them where they were crossing the line. And so our forces were forced back. Mind you, this was only 50 miles north of us. So we didn't have much time.

We called in our evacuation committee. We had a good one. We met about once a month. We set that in motion and by that afternoon we had decided to ship out about 600 women and children on a merchant ship that was at the port, only about 25 miles to the southwest. The captain agreed to take our people and put them off in Japan. So that was the first order of business.

And with that being done, we had to assess the situation continuously, and it was getting worse all the time. We had burned our papers on Monday morning, 24 hours after things started, and got the mission in position to be evacuated. When the situation worsened, we got in touch with General MacArthur's headquarters and asked for aerial help. He had the aircraft. And by Monday evening we were beginning to evacuate 2000 people--women, children, dependents, all Americans and some foreigners. We evacuated the United Nations Commission that was there working on a solution to that problem, and some of the diplomats and their families, and anyone who seemed to qualify for immediate evacuation. A lot of credit is due to the MacArthur organization for getting the planes over there, and also for sending over some planes to protect those planes, because the North Korean Air Force was active. And that pretty well took up much of our time. By Tuesday morning the evacuation was well in hand, and it was completed by early Tuesday afternoon.

We were in touch, I think, with [South Korean] President Rhee once or twice. But President Rhee evacuated by train early Tuesday morning. Things started on Sunday, so early Tuesday morning he and his entourage evacuated south on a train, which was good enough, but they didn't tell us.

Then the situation grew worse and worse. We didn't have much time. I was instructed by Ambassador Muccio to proceed south to make contact with President Rhee; so I took Stewart, McDonald, Prendergast, and another secretary, and we went south. We did locate President Rhee in a town about a hundred miles south. I went over to see Rhee immediately and found him to be extraordinarily bitter about the invasion, the evacuation, and, what he saw as a lack of help by the United States in this critical juncture. We didn't know what was going on in Washington.

Meantime, Ambassador Muccio had stayed with the U.S. advisors in the south end of Seoul, near the river, where they could evacuate. They had their headquarters there. But they had to evacuate Tuesday night or early Wednesday morning and went about 30 miles south where they set up headquarters.

The North Koreans began moving in on Seoul on Tuesday afternoon. I left Tuesday afternoon and I could hear the bombardment by that time. They came in Tuesday night.

Seoul was in their hands until after the landing made by MacArthur [at Inchon]. That was October 20. He landed and cut the North Koreans off. Their main line of communications came through this whole area, and his objective was to cut that and recapture Seoul. So his landing put us back there about the 20th.

I went up there myself while there was still desultory fighting around some of the streets and checked in at the embassy. I found that it was still there, but a hole had been blown in one end of it by our own Navy aviators. But, otherwise, it was in good shape. I found our residences okay, basically. I moved into the ambassador's residence for a day or two. We eventually moved back [into the Embassy] and were in there by November 1. We had set up shop again. President Rhee had come back and was in his quarters.

Twenty-six years later, shortly after THOMAS STERN arrived in Seoul as deputy chief of mission in 1976, the ambassador left for a summer leave in the United States after assuring him that all was tranquil. The murder by North Korean soldiers of two American officers in the demilitarized zone [DMZ], however, sparked what threatened to be a second Korean war. Action was quickly taken out of the hands of the embassy and Washington conducted the show.

Stern: I arrived on July 1, 1976, brand-new, having known relatively little about Korea. I was introduced to the Koreans on July 4, in that usual mass-gathering on the ambassador's lawn. It was also the bicentennial, so it was even larger than usual, and I had to remember all the Kim, Parks and Lees around in a very brief time. A week later, the ambassador left for his annual vacation; this is Dick Sneider, and his last words to me as he got on the plane were: "Don't worry Tom, nothing happens here in the summertime. Just relax and take it easy." A few weeks later, August 17, two of our officers were brutally attacked and killed in the DMZ.

The DMZ is an area that separates the North and South Korean forces, averaging a mile in width, some places very narrow and quite wide in some other places. When you get toward the east coast the separation is considerably broader than two kilometers because of the mountain ranges. The joint security area, which is a part of the DMZ, is a small area in which the few and far between dialogues between the signers of the armistice take place. In 1977, this area was patrolled by both U.S. and North Korean troops, which gave rise to periodic confrontations. The area consists of a watch-tower--I'm now describing the south side of the joint security area--a couple of other small buildings, and half of three buildings which were used by the conferees for their periodical meetings. On the other side was the other half of those three buildings, plus a large facade of an alleged office building which we were quite certain, however, was only a facade and had nothing behind the front. There were also two watchtowers on the north side from which the North Koreans took pictures of every American going into the joint security area, so that I'm sure all of our pictures are on file in Pyongyang. The famous tree lay on the south side of the joint security area, approximately 200 yards from what was called "the bridge of no return," which had been used during the Korean War for exchange of prisoners. We wanted to prune the tree. The North Koreans insisted that this was a holy tree. That is, it was sacred in their minds, and therefore they were unwilling to have it touched at all. Our insistence was that we could prune it because the tree had grown so big it was obscuring our guards' vision of North Korea and the bridge. There were some other buildings, some observation towers in that area. In any case, one Sunday morning a small detail of American troops, headed by a captain and a lieutenant, decided, after having negotiated, or attempted to negotiate with the North, the right to prune that tree. They finally decided that as no agreement seemed possible, they would take it upon themselves to go ahead and prune the tree.

We [at the embassy] knew nothing about it. It is still unclear today how far up in the chain of command that action had been approved. It was certainly not an issue of a nature which prevented the commanding general at that time, Dick Stilwell, from leaving the country for a well-earned rest in Japan. So, what you had in the American presence in Korea was a three-star air force officer who had been the deputy and a green, untried, untested DCM, who certainly knew nothing about tree-pruning and only a little more about Korea. As I recall, the American detail went ahead and started pruning the tree and were fallen upon by a squad of North Korean troops carrying bats and axes. In the melee the two officers were brutally beaten and finally died. For some reason or other, the alarm was not given so that the reenforcement troops did not arrive until much later, by which time the North Koreans had taken off and gone back to their side of the DMZ.

Immediately, of course, a major uproar was raised, because obviously this is not the way we'd like the world to behave. Cable traffic increased by leaps and bounds, and all of them NIACT--"night action, top-priority, wake everybody up, don't let anybody rest, we've got to get an answer to this." The first messages, of course, were in the military channels. It was a couple, if not several hours later that the embassy found out what in fact had happened. The commanding general was called back from Tokyo; no action was taken to bring back our ambassador, at least until the situation had become a little clearer. We were faced with a very difficult issue; namely, was this a provoked attack which had been ordered by higher authorities, or was this just the act of a sergeant who was in charge of the North Korean detail who had been so attached to that tree, and felt so strongly about it that he decided to murder a couple of Americans in order to defend it?

In a society like North Korea, which was completely closed, the answer to that question was not easily available. The interesting part of the episode, to me at least, was the tight control that the Pentagon and Henry Kissinger had on the situation. They immediately put monitors in the DMZ overlooking this particular area and the pictures were then relayed back to Washington so that Washington could move the troops as it wished with the American general in Seoul essentially being only an intermediary to pass whatever orders he had from Washington to the commander out in the field. The communication system was something fantastic. It was immediate, and live, and in real time. But the interesting aspect of this, and the one that really grated on General Stilwell's soul, and I'm sure it would grate on any general's soul, was that he became a messenger boy. In fact, Washington had as complete a picture of the scenario as he had. They had maps of the area, they knew exactly the distances and where our troops were, and they knew where the South Koreans and the North Koreans were. Washington was able, when the time finally came to complete the pruning of that tree, to move our troops as well as General Stilwell could. They had just as much information. This was the Joint Chiefs of Staff, it was in the War Room of the Joint-Chiefs, and they had a twenty-four hour watch on duty, headed of course by a senior officer. When the time came to move the troops, I'm sure all the chiefs were there. [Secretary of State] Kissinger, who was not, as far as I know, in the Pentagon War Room, was in the White House War Room.

The other memory I have of this incident was also of concern to some in Washington. I got a very nasty note, also NIACT [Night Action telegram] from Phil Habib asking me whether I'd seen the president. My answer was no. General Stilwell went to see him, and I felt that this was essentially a military issue, and therefore I did not go along, although General Stilwell did invite me to go with him. This is the other, I think, mystifying part of this whole story. Where, in a situation like Korea, does the political arm end and the military arm begin? I have never been a great proponent of civilian generals, as I've never been a proponent of military ambassadors. But to draw the line becomes a very fine and delicate point. And I, perhaps, drew the line incorrectly.

I perhaps should have accepted Stilwell's invitation and gone to see President Park [Chung Hee]. But my decision had been that the situation had turned to be essentially a military one and one therefore that General Stilwell ought to handle. It perhaps should not be confused by the presence of the American chargé. That obviously wasn't Kissinger's view because he would have wanted me to be present on the front lines, if we had front lines at that time. Nowhere, that I know of, in the training of DCMs, was there anything that would have taught me how to react in a situation of that kind. Perhaps had I been in Vietnam I would have had a better understanding of that kind of situation. But nowhere in my experience or training was I able to pick up anything that would have given me some guidance on whether I should have gone to see the president with General Stilwell or not.

It would not have made any difference, because the issue was so controlled by Washington. Nothing [happened between Park Chung Hee and Stilwell], I think, because Stilwell was in no better position than I was in telling him what Washington was thinking. I guess General Stilwell just briefed him on what had happened in the DMZ. Remember, all the troops in the DMZ were under Stilwell's control, even the Korean troops that were there. I guess he just briefed him, and then Park probably asked "What are you going to do next?" and Stilwell probably said "I'm waiting for orders, sir."

I was too new on the scene. I had heard something about the rivalry [between Stilwell and the ambassador, Sneider], but I didn't know how intense it was. I learned that a while later. But I was impressed by the fact that Stilwell asked me if I wanted to go. That suggested to me that, if there were a rivalry, at least it had not been applied to me yet and I could have some confidence in his telling me afterwards what went on. In fact, as I recall, very little went on, so it didn't make a difference.

After going through all the options, which could have ranged from bombarding Pyongyang to doing nothing, the decision was finally made that we would reassert our rights to cut that tree down, and we sent in a sizeable squad of American troops and a couple of chainsaws.   Sure enough, the tree was pruned.   Not cut down, pruned.   The tree is still there for all to see.

Embassy input in this whole episode was minimal.   The embassy was headed by a green DCM.   The State Department was run by a very strong secretary of state.   We were never asked for our opinions.   We kept submitting reports, of course, of what was going on in the streets, and what we could find out in the military.   In fact, Paul Cleveland (then political counsellor), later ambassador to New Zealand, was sent to sit in with Stilwell in the War Room at his headquarters.   And I went over there periodically myself.   But, it was a one-way street.   We reported whatever we could pick up, sent it back, usually as an urgent NIACT message.   But not once, except for that message that Habib sent on my inaction, did we ever hear from Washington.

I think there were B-52's and we brought the navy, the Sixth Fleet carriers off the shore.   There was no hysteria.   I don't think there was anybody in either the embassy or the military who foresaw this as beginning a World War III.   I was so engrossed in my own problems I don't know what the rest of the embassy was thinking, but I didn't feel there was any great concern.   People weren't packing up and going home.

This raises an interesting question of whether we were much too relaxed about this.   One of the reasons I did not feel any sense of panic or urgency was that we did not see any signs on the North Korean side of any mobilization.   The military activity was primarily on our part.   Our intelligence collection capability on North Korea was relatively limited.   Nevertheless, we could have detected some movements had they been taking place.   And they were not taking place, so that I don't think anybody--either the command or in the embassy--felt very threatened at that point in time.

CHRISTIAN ADDISON CHAPMAN returned to Laos as deputy chief of mission in 1974 after a fifteen year absence. On April 15, 1975, Phnom Penh fell to the Khmer Rouge; on April 30, Saigon fell. In both cases the U.S. embassies were evacuated in haste by helicopter. Laos appeard to be next on the list. In July 1975 Chapman was chargé, with the task of trying to prop up the non-communist leadership and finally to keep an American presence in the country after the communist takeover.

Chapman: I returned to Laos as DCM in June, 1974.   The ambassador was Charlie Whitehouse.   The situation was that we had a very large AID mission, and we had a very large military assistance program although it was not called that.   The situation was very, very tense and uncertain. There was a national government which included the Pathet Lao under Souvanna Phouma. I had been in Laos fifteen years before, and Vientiane had grown.   It was a much more tense situation. You couldn't travel around the country.   You were pretty well confined to Vientiane.   We could fly up to the northeast, to the Meo country, the Hmung Muongs, the tribes that lived on top of the mountains between Vientiane and Vietnam, and fought the Vietnamese all those years.   We were supplying them and the question of supplies was a very major subject. The AID mission was very active, road building, providing medical supplies and education.   We developed textbooks in Lao and a whole educational system.   We built schools.   We trained agriculturalists. We sought to help the Lao raise their food supply by improving and diversifying their crops. The effort put into that little country by the United States over thirty years was really enormous.

It is a very small, fragile society, and not very energetic.   There were some very real accomplishments;   schools had been built, hospitals had been built.   There was one Western-trained doctor in 1958-1959.   There were a hundred by the time I got back.   That was real progress.   The young people were better educated, coming back from abroad and taking senior positions in the administration. However, significantly, at one of the first dinner parties that Ambassador Whitehouse gave for me, attended by military officers, I knew all the guests from about fifteen years before. They hadn't changed, the colonels or the generals.   The great families had remained in power.   It was the same cast of characters. Things didn't change even within the Pathet Lao. Some of the great families were represented.

It was very clear that an independent Laos was dependent upon the support and active involvement of the United States; that the day we weakened that support the Vietnamese, who were in the eastern part of Laos in force, would just take over through the Pathet Lao.   Indeed this is what happened.

Charlie Whitehouse left for reassignment at the beginning of April. On April 15, Phnom Penh fell to the Khmer Rouge, on April 30, Saigon fell, and the following day there were large demonstrations in Vientiane against the nationalist ministers and generals in the government, demanding they be thrown out. I immediately got the country team to fan out all over town to try and keep the nationalist leadership steady.   We pointed out that we were continuing to support them, we had large AID and other programs that we were maintaining.   But fear swept the city.   Within ten days the entire nationalist leadership, except for Souvanna Phouma, crossed the Mekong and fled into Thailand.

The problem between the United States and Laos under these circumstances was that we had played such a large role that any indication of our being concerned that things were going badly, that maybe we should retrench in some way, would have absolutely panicked the situation. Any chance of maintaining this dual government of the Pathet Lao and the nationalists would have been finished. We would have been held responsible for the end of the independence of Laos. So we were caught in this situation, particularly after May 1, when I was trying to encourage the non-communist leadership to stay on, by assuring them that we would continue to support them. I told everyone in the American community to stay steady and calm and not to panic. When the leadership left, the situation turned more and more sour. We started evacuating our people, first the families. There were about 800 Americans there, wives and children included, but I wanted to maintain at least the principal officers, who might be able to give a degree of stability to the situation. I thought it would be very bad if we just pulled up stakes and left, which would be viewed as the abandonment of Southeast Asia. So by the third week of May we brought in some specially chartered planes and started getting families out. At the same time we were continuing to have discussions with the Pathet Lao and Souvanna Phouma, trying to encourage them to work with us, to continue these programs. The Pathet Lao had just come down from the hills and were, in retrospect just as anxious as we were, not knowing just what would happen. This was their first real meeting with Americans. May, June and July were very tense.

We had met several of the ministers who were there. But after May, while we continued to deal with Souvanna, we worked mainly with the Pathet Lao, who had taken over the government. As a community, we were terribly vulnerable, and I think that one of the things that helped us get out of this terrible situation in which we found ourselves was that we were in constant touch, morning, noon, afternoon, evening and night with the Pathet Lao leadership, and most particularly, Phoumi Vonvichit who was Minister of Foreign Affairs. There was sustained, continuing communication. One lesson I brought out of that period was that in a tense situation it is essential to keep communications open. What is dangerous is the fear that's built up over time to the point where the least incident can be misunderstood, misinterpreted and create a very serious crisis.

[We had very little in the way of instructions from the State Department], and I was very grateful. This was an essentially tactical situation, and I was grateful to the State Department for not telling me how to suck eggs on the spot. I could have sent a telegram to Washington that said, "Situation deteriorating fast, we should evacuate all personnel and close the embassy." And Washington would have said "okay."

I felt that it was important to maintain a presence in Laos. I felt that given the role the United States had played in Asia and Southeast Asia, we could not abandon ship and scurry away like a small frightened country.

We were too important. And if there is an embassy today in Vientiane, it is because we made that decision at that time.   We were under a lot of pressure to get Americans out. I wanted to retreat on an orderly basis. I did not want to appear that we were turning tail and fleeing.   We managed to get out . . . planes came in and we got out many of our people by air and many simply drove their cars out. All on a more or less orderly basis.   To me, that was important.

The staff were pretty steady on the whole. In fact, I was very proud of the way the Americans reacted. There was no hysteria, and all remained on the job. There was understandably a lot of bitterness among the AID people who had worked very hard to help the Lao and, many felt that we were being treated very poorly. [Some of them] felt that they had worked very hard to help the Lao and now they were being thrown out of the country, with the Pathet Lao showing no interest in pursuing programs that we had developed over years. There were some nasty reactions, but by and large the American community stayed very steady and disciplined.

We were in continuous discussions with the Pathet Lao leadership to see if the aid programs that had been elaborated over the years, at great cost, could not be salvaged for the benefit of Laos. For instance, we had an entire warehouse full of medicine. There was a very large depot of earth moving and road building equipment. There were programs in progress. It was to no avail. The Pathet Lao held to the philosophy that politics primes all and that all these matters were technical and   of secondary interest.   In the end, after a dramatic capture of our aid compound by so called students and a fourteen-hour confrontation between myself escorted by Stephen Johnson, a young political officer who spoke Lao, and a mob of several hundred "students," and after other varied happenings, we decided that the Pathet Lao were simply not willing to pursue normal relations. Finally, one morning in June I went to the office of the minister of economic affairs with whom we had been negotiating over aid, and just put down on his table a box full of keys--all the keys we had of the AID compound. He had wanted to have a big, symbolic ceremony of turning over all our assets to the government, but given their unwillingness to enter into any meaningful dialogue or to recognize that we had laws prescribing the disposition of assets, we left it all, noting that our laws were being violated.

From the beginning of May I had a country team meeting every morning to make certain there was complete communication and coordination among ourselves. There was General Round, who was the senior military officer, head of the MAAG and senior attaché. All told we were half a dozen, including representatives of AID, CIA and USIA. We met every morning at 9:00 A.M. to go over exactly where we were. Everything was going so fast.   Then each would carry out the decisions in his own mission. It was mainly a question of phasing down our operations and coordinating our actions. Washington's concern was for the safety of Americans, and that's why we accelerated the evacuation by air and by car. Washington put a lot of pressure on me to get my wife and three children out. They were wonderfully steady. We did not feel that as the senior family we could leave before all others had left safely. They finally left, the last family to leave, at the beginning of June, following a particularly nasty rocket from Washington.

At the beginning of June, June 2, Phil Habib, who was then assistant secretary for East Asia and Pacific affairs, came to take a look at the situation. I told him that we had to stay calm, withdraw to the extent necessary, try to maintain working relations with the government, and avoid aggravating fears. His response was, "Don't be a cowboy." He came away sensing that we could maintain relations with the Pathet Lao government and that it was useful to keep an embassy there.   I spent four years in World War II as a fighter pilot and I have never been so steadily frightened as in those three months, May, June and July. We were absolutely defenseless as a community. With all the arms lying around Southeast Asia, one kook tossing a grenade could have created a very ugly situation. In the event, we got away more or less whole.

[The difference between this situation and that in Vietnam is] the Pathet Lao had been in the government with the nationalists; there was not a war situation, as in Cambodia and as in Vietnam. Vietnam was conquered militarily. Phnom Penh was conquered militarily. In Vientiane the Pathet Lao were there already and simply took over completely when the nationalist leadership left. There was no fighting, there was no battle. It was a completely different situation.

We were just maintaining a presence. We were down to a dozen people from eight hundred. Then, at the beginning of August, Tom Corcoran came, to relieve me. He arrived one morning and I left the same afternoon. Nothing illustrates better the tensions of the moment than this change of chargé. We didn't know what the reaction would be. We thought that they might try to keep me. So we made the relief in the most expeditious and quiet manner possible. But it was a very tense time.

The experience of dismantling the American mission in Vientiane was very illuminating. I must say, one felt that the Pathet Lao had a point when they said that the United States was a state within a state in Laos. We had a police force of about 500 or 600 men, with night sticks to protect the Americans in the compounds. We had a fire department with a couple of fire trucks. We had an infirmary, with a doctor and nurse. We had an independent telephone system connecting all houses and offices. We had an independent power generation capability all over town. We had all the elements of a government for our community. When you take that apart, you measure the extent of the effort. We had [a total of about] 800 people.

I don't like to speak too much about [CIA efforts] because it was a very highly classified subject. Let's say it was a very large effort, to the point that you looked at events and you wondered whether it was authentically generated by the society or whether it was a CIA-generated operation.

To this day I find it difficult to pass a judgment. In 1958-1959 most of us felt that the effort being put in was not related to the strength and absorptive capabilities of the society. We were putting much too much weight on these fragile societies. At the same time the reason for this effort was the Sino-Soviet bloc, which was indeed threatening, and there were Communist insurgencies in Thailand and in Malaysia and in the Philippines. North Vietnam was very vigorous and Communist. Adding everything up it was a very threatening situation. If we could have made a lesser effort, and if we had let the Communists take over earlier, what the impact would have been on Thailand and Malaysia is uncertain. I thought the domino theory was justified. I still think so today. So once we became involved in that kind of effort, I don't know a time when we could have reduced it without seeming to abandon these countries, with consequences that would have been felt worldwide. When we left Saigon under those dramatic circumstances in 1975, there was a shudder around the world. There was real concern. In fact European attitudes changed after that.

It was a bitter moment, I confess. I came back after three months when I thought that I had accomplished a good deal, maybe in a negative sense, but at least had kept the American flag planted in Southeast Asia, and to a degree had contributed to reassuring the Asians that we were not abandoning them. As it was, I could have come back from anywhere. Only two people went out of their way to welcome me back to the department. Two lawyers took me to lunch. I went around the department just to say thank you for having supported us, for not sending detailed instructions, and giving me a free hand. I called on everyone. No one asked me to see them.

9

The Six-Day War, June 1967:
Egypt, Jordan, and Israel

The mood in the Middle East in the spring of 1967 was one of war. Egypt's President Nasser announced the closing of the Straits of Tiran to Israeli shipping, a direct challenge to Israel. Israel began mobilizing, preparing for attacks on Syria or Sinai or both. King Hussein feared that Israel was determined to attack Jordan and seize the West Bank. The question was not will there be war, but when will it start. The answer came on June 5 when Israel made what it called a preemptive attack on Egypt, effectively destroying the Egyptian air force on the ground and capturing the Sinai Peninsula. Jordan made good on King Hussein's hasty commitment to Nasser to come to Egypt's aid if the latter were attacked by Israel. He suffered a humiliating defeat and the loss of the West Bank to Israel. Syria suffered the loss of much of its airforce and the strategic Golan Heights bordering Israel.

When such war situations arise, our embassies must think immediately of the welfare of Americans in the area, plan for their safety, and possible evacuation to safehavens. They must take measures to secure the protection of U.S. private and government property. They must keep themselves informed of what is going on and advise Washington, using their most reliable information and best judgment. Our embassies in Amman, Tel Aviv, and Cairo were doing just that in June of 1967.

The chapter begins with the comments of Findley Burns concerning events just prior to and during the Six-Day War as seen from Amman, Jordan, where he was ambassador. William Dale, who was then deputy chief of mission at our embassy at Tel Aviv recalls the war as seen from Tel Aviv, Israel. An account of developments as viewed from Cairo, Egypt, is given by David Nes, who was chargé d'affaires at the embassy in Cairo at the time.

AMMAN (1967)

FINDLEY BURNS, Jr. U.S. ambassador to Jordan less than a year when in June 1967 the Middle East exploded into what became known as the "Six-Day War." The ambassador describes events preceding, during and immediately after the war, including the fatal miscalculation by King Hussein which lost him the West Bank to Israel.

Burns: I was in Amman. A momentous event for Jordan happened about a week before the war began. It took all of us totally by surprise, including the CIA, which had very close relations with the Jordanians. The event was that the King got on a plane and flew to Cairo. This was after Nasser had closed the Straits of Tiran. As a result of this visit, an alliance was made between Egypt and Jordan, which required Jordan to come to the defense of Egypt if the latter were attacked by Israel, and Egypt to the aid of Jordan in the event of similar attack. Furthermore, as a result of his visit, Hussein embraced the PLO (Palestine Liberation Organization).   This really shook everyone, because it was totally unexpected. We had received no inkling from any source whatsoever. I can only conclude Hussein made a sudden decision to do what he did, maybe only 24 or 48 hours beforehand.

I now understand the rationale of why he did it. He was convinced that war was coming. By the way, in that particular conviction, I totally agreed with him, and so did the officers of the embassy. It wasn't at all certain, however, as to who would begin it. Hussein was convinced that the Israelis were going to attack him.

During the week before the war began, I saw him every day, sometimes even three times a day. These visits would be held either during normal office hours, or I'd be called over at 11:00 at night to his house.   I say "house," because his daytime office was in the palace, but he lived in a house. Or I'd be called in to see the prime minister, but never the foreign minister. The foreign minister in Jordan at that time was a figurehead.

Hussein was convinced that the Israelis were going to attack him. I argued with him at length that he was wrong. I always took the chief of our political section with me to these meetings, and both of us argued that in the event of war the Israelis would have their hands full. We didn't argue with Hussein in his thesis that it was conceivable Israel would attack Egypt and even possibly Syria, but we flatly disagreed Israel would attack Jordan. Israel was interested in keeping a moderate government in Jordan, and an attack on Jordan could undoubtedly end up unseating the king. And furthermore, Jordan's relationship with the U.S.A. should certainly give Israel much pause.

Hussein replied: "They want the West Bank. They've been waiting for a chance to get it, and they're going to take advantage of us and they're going to attack." I might say that this difference of opinion between Hussein and me existed right up until the time the war started. [He wanted] to find out what we knew and to press for an assurance that if Israel attacked, we would defend them. I replied that we don't give hypothetical answers to hypothetical questions. I informed the State Department, and they never suggested a different response. I knew what was possible for the U.S. Government. We could not make a formal alliance. We had refused the request from Israel for a formal alliance. We hardly could turn around and give one to Jordan. Our failure to do so later caused Hussein to say, "If you'd done it, I wouldn't have attacked Israel." But I still believe to this day, that if Hussein had sat tight, he'd have gotten through without being attacked.

He had another reason for his pact with Nasser, he said. He was convinced the Israelis were going to attack him, and knowing he'd never get a defense pact from the United States, he wanted to bind Egypt to come to his defense. He thought it not at all unlikely that Israel would not attack Egypt but only Jordan. By the way, he did not make a similar arrangement with the Syrians, with whom he had extremely bad relations right up until the day the war started.

As you know, the Israelis attacked the Egyptians, Egypt then cashed in its chips with Hussein, and said, "Now honor your pledge. You attack." He did, and it was a disaster.

One of the problems was that the Jordanians only had defensive military equipment. All their training under Glubb Pasha and his successor was for a defensive war, retreating slowly and making the Israelis pay dearly-- but never, never an offense. When they in fact went on the offensive, for which they were utterly untrained, utterly unprepared, utterly ill-equipped, it was a catastrophe. Tanks ran out of gas, to give you one example, because fuel reserves were positioned to the rear, not forward. They were extremely well-trained soldiers, but basically trained for defensive operations, not offensive ones. The Israelis said afterwards the best-trained soldiers they encountered were the Syrians, with the Jordanians next, and the Egyptians last.

Telephone lines were open all during the Six-Day War, and Washington called me frequently. What preoccupied Washington was the safety of the embassy staff and American residents and tourists.   When the mutual assistance pact between Hussein and Nasser was signed in May, we were absolutely convinced not only that there were going to be hostilities, but that quite possibly Jordan was going to be involved. Our concern was that, in case law and order should break down in Amman, which, by the way, it nearly did, what could we do to insure that the embassy survived?

One of the things we did was to get in work crews to shore up everything so that the embassy couldn't be broken into and to insure that we had a large supply of gasoline, food, bedding, etc. We didn't know how long we might be in a siege situation.

It was not possible to reduce the American staff of the embassy (about 100) before hostilities started. We only had a week between the time Hussein signed the pact with Nasser and the start of the war. To move staff out publicly at that time would have been misread all the way around by everybody. Washington certainly was not in favor of it, and neither was I.

[We had an evacuation plan] but it proved to be utterly useless, as so often happens with plans you make up that far in advance for hypothetical situations. Since we had a fairly accurate idea of exactly what the situation might be, we made up our plan from scratch. The plan basically was to get all but key embassy Americans and all other Americans (tourists, etc.) out of Jordan. But the third day of the war, the night before Jordan's total collapse, I got a telephone call at about 8:00 in the evening from the minister of the interior. He said, "Mr. Ambassador, I think I ought to tell you that in my opinion, by tomorrow morning, Amman will be in chaos. There will be no law and order. If I were you, I'd get every American out of town tonight." Two hours later, we received a cable from CIA, stating it was reported that Hussein, by private plane, had landed in Rome. However, those of us who knew Hussein doubted very much the report. It was *not* in character!

As for getting the Americans out of Jordan on the night in question, it was quite impossible. We concluded it would be less dangerous for them to remain in Amman than to try to evacuate them and probably get them shot in the process.

The "decision group" consisted, in addition to Richard Murphy [acting DCM], of a very bright assistant defense attaché, the CIA station chief, and the director of AID--all of them as sharp as they could be. When evacuation matters were involved, we brought in the chief of the consular section, who was responsible for keeping track of the Americans (about 400 of them) and the administrative officer. I'd simply say, "Get the boys in. We've got a problem." They were reading the cables as fast as I was, and they'd be knocking on my door, saying, "What are we going to do about this?" It was very informal, but it worked. We were almost continuously in session, night and day, by the way. We just worked around the clock.

Of the embassy staff, which numbered perhaps 100 Americans, we had only 25 in the embassy during the war itself, and ten of those were marine guards. The rest we asked to stay home. They were bundled together--4 or 5 to a house. Our great worry was the hoards of Americans who had fled to Amman from the West Bank before the invading Israeli forces.

There were at least 300 tourists, clergy, archaeologists, etc. The chief of our consular section did a wonderful job of getting them all to move into the largest hotel in Amman, which made guarding them much easier.

We were lucky to have good people. You never knew what you had to do next. We had a supply of gold sovereigns which we'd gotten just before the war broke out. I'd asked the king before the war actually started for a royal guard. It was part of Hussein's personal Bedouin guard staff. They set up camp all around the embassy, with fires going at night, boiling tea and coffee. Every now and then we'd go out and pass gold around to keep their "loyalty" undiminished.

On the fourth day, the army began straggling back to Amman, all armed, and under little or no officer or non-com discipline. But the Jordanians are personally well disciplined. I could only attribute the order that prevailed to that. Also, any time a crowd formed the government would sound an air raid siren, and everybody would scatter. The people never caught on. We only had one air raid during that war, and that was on the first day. The prime minister [thought of that gimmick]. It was his major contribution to the war. After the king himself the person who had the most power was Wasfi Tel. The prime minister at the time was a gentleman who wasn't terribly strong. Tel was Chief of the Royal Diwan, or the equivalent of our White House Chief of Staff. You know what Wasfi Tel told me after the war? He said, "Well, any schoolboy cadet could have done better in that war than we did."

About a week after the end of the war, we were able to evacuate the American staff who were not key, plus the 300 or 400 Americans who had fled to Amman. We convinced Washington to send the planes in from the east, and to paint out U.S. Air Force insignia and substitute large red crosses. The Jordanian air force was still convinced the United States had helped Israel militarily. There was real danger that the Jordanian anti-aircraft gunners would open fire on our planes. The day before our air lift was to leave, I got a call from the British ambassador saying that he had tried to convince Whitehall to do what we were doing. Nonetheless, London insisted on flying in directly over Israel, with RAF insignia showing. The ambassador thought they'd all be shot down long before they got to Amman. So we agreed to take the British, and before long, everyone else. I think there were 1,200 people evacuated in that air lift, including Russians.

At the airport, it was so dicey with the Jordanian Air Force that the king sent his royal Bedouin guards to set up machine gun posts at the airport to protect our planes and the evacuees. Until those planes got off the ground, I admit I was nervous. They got out, however, without anything happening.

I think that had Hussein been willing and/or able to make formal peace with Israel directly after the Six-Day War, he could have gotten the West

Bank back. But, he didn't, and probably couldn't, without his dynasty's falling.

In reorganizing an embassy for a crisis there are two things an ambassador would think about in a situation like that. The first is you want the people there whose functions most directly relate to the crisis that will confront you. For example, you want the chief of the political section, the CIA station chief, and the administrative officer (because you've got the problem of keeping the embassy--the guards, the security, the communications--all running). You also want competent people. The conclusion you might draw is that six people is enough to run an embassy, and you don't really need 70. Two comments on that. Number one, you are working under intense pressure, and you're not working eight hours a day; you're working 24 hours a day. You can't keep that up for a long period of time, obviously.

Secondly, while there are a great many functions which are important to perform, normal economic reporting or agricultural research are not relevant to getting through a war that is going to last less than a week. You need the economists back right afterwards to ascertain what the economic effects of the war will be, but during the actual hostilities, they aren't necessary. One of the officers I had there, one of the six, was an economic officer (the AID mission director), but basically he was there because he was a very able officer and could do all sorts of the things that were necessary to do.

TEL AVIV (1967)

WILLIAM NORRIS DALE was the deputy chief of mission at the American embassy in Tel Aviv, Israel, during the "Six-Day War." He describes events as seen from his vantage point. He touches on our embassy's dealings with the Israeli government officials before and during the hostilities and speculates on the Israeli reason for attacking the U.S. naval ship, U.S.S. Liberty. He also discusses such matters as the conduct of embassy operations with a reduced staff and the process of assembling and evacuating Americans to Cyprus.

Dale: The United States had thought they had extracted a promise from the Israeli Government that they wouldn't go to war. The Israelis did not consider they had made that promise, and they had no intention of putting off going to war. They didn't think that our plan for what they called the "Red Sea Regatta," (warships going up the Red Sea to test Nassar's claim that he had closed the Straits of Tiran), was correct. The Israelis didn't think that would work, and they intended to go to war. Once they made up their minds to this, they called Dayan back as minister of defense. That was the signal they were going to war. The only question left was when Dayan would order it to begin.

We knew they were mobilizing. Our consul general, Cliff English, saw all kinds of people mobilizing in a vacant field beside his house. We were able to put together many such indications and concluded that the war could start at any time, but we couldn't tell from the evidence that we had that it would start as soon as it did. As to the reporting, the ambassador wanted to give the impression that we thought it wouldn't start, as long as he could possibly get away with it, because he knew we thought we had a promise from the Israelis [not to go to war]. It was arranged in Washington, I think, between the U.S. government at a high level and Abba Eban. Or at least they thought they had the promise from Abba Eban, and had arranged [it] with Eshkol. It came as something of a surprise to us, but Ambassador Barbour didn't want to undercut that until it was absolutely necessary. I'd set up a command post there, where we monitored the Israeli broadcasts. The morning of the fifth came, and planes were breaking the sound barrier, coming and going. They often did that in the past, because they'd been practicing for months. It was just more intense. Finally, the ambassador called and said, "My cook says a war is on. What does the embassy say?". . . . "Well, my cook says that the Israeli Air Force has destroyed the Egyptian Air Force on the ground," which was entirely correct. When I called up my contact in the foreign ministry, Shlomo Argov, and asked him if Israel had attacked, he said, "Well, there was provocation. "I said, "What was it?" He said, "I don't know yet. I'll try to find out." But that was a delaying action. There wasn't any. They attacked when they were ready.

[Initially the ambassador did not feel betrayed by the Israelis at the time] but he did later before the war ended. His main contact was the American desk officer, Moshe Bitan. Moshe Bitan had told Wally Barbour that Israel realized there was a United Nations resolution for a cease-fire, and Israel intended to obey it, but he said, "We had just a little matter we wanted to clear up on the Syrian front." I was there. Now, the Syrians had not attacked in the Six-Day War, as you probably know. I think they fired a few shots and that's all, not participating. But he said it would only take an hour or two and not to worry about it. So Barbour sent some kind of telegram to that effect.

Instead of that, Israel moved all its troops from the Eygptian front who weren't involved, and from the central front, because they were beating the dickens out of Jordan by this time, up to the northern front. The Golani brigade went up to the Golan Heights and led a major attack, which was not what Bitan had said. This was also the time of the *Liberty* [U.S. Navy vessel attacked by Israeli Air Force], which may very well have been attacked because they didn't want us to hear all the orders that were necessary to transfer thousands of men. I don't know that; that's speculation on my part.

Later on, the ambassador got a hold of Bitan and said, "You deceived me." He was, for him, quite angry. He was always very careful, because he always had President Johnson looking over his shoulder, so he never got really angry. But he was as angry as he ever got. Bitan said, "Yeah, I deceived you, but the Arabs deceive you more than we do."

The Israelis as soon as they had finished their attack on [the *U.S.S. Liberty*], called the naval attache, Ernie Castle, and told him that an American ship had been hit by mistake by Israeli forces, because they thought it was an Egyptian ship. It had a similar silhouette, a Liberty ship. They said, "Don't you want to go out and see if they need any help?"

So Ernie got his lunch, which he had brought to the office--we were more or less living in the office--which was a paper bag, an orange, a sandwich, took out the sandwich, left the orange, and put in a note, "Do you want any help?" And flew over the *Liberty*, which I think was sort of listing out there. I'm not sure it was listing; it was almost unguided in the water, smoking like everything. He dropped it on the deck from the helicopter. The personnel of the *Liberty* waved him away. So Ernie came back a little disconsolate, and said, "They need help like everything, but they won't take it from the Israelis." He didn't realize, nor did the Israelis tell us at the time, that there was a big American flag on that ship. So we didn't know that, and we thought it was a genuine error.

[Ambassador Barbour did not become irate about that, or] if he did, he didn't show it. He had to be very careful not to show emotion like that which might set the staff, you see, to thinking things. So he was very, very quiet about what personal thoughts he might have had.

He was deceived; they fooled him. The *Liberty* was not an accident, and he must have known it. Well, he put it this way to me once. He said, "You know, Bill, Israel's relations with the United States is the way of the future. I don't care if the Arabs have all the oil reserves in the world. Our relationship is going to be with Israel, and I'm going to promote it." This was shortly after the Six-Day War. That's all he ever said. I think he saw the strength of the bond between Israel and the United States, which became clear about that time. We did send an awful lot of war material towards the end of that war.

Crisis situations arise--I wouldn't say gradually--but they do not arise all at once. You have perhaps a week, perhaps two weeks in which the crisis gradually becomes worse. During that time you begin, I think, almost casually, to change your organization to fit the requirements of the growing crisis.

In this case, one of the first things we had to do was limit our telegraphic traffic so that no routine or administrative type telegrams would be sent and the wires would be reserved for crisis type messages. We kept a telephone line but that was of uncertain usefulness, depending on the situation. We also used ham radios at one point. That's how I got in touch with my children. They were in different places in the United States.

So we had first the messages to do, then we had the evacuation plan to put into operation. This became the responsibility of the consular section. They kept in touch with all American citizens. And the consular people implemented the evacuation plan when it became advisable to do so. We gave advice to American citizens to leave well before the fighting started.

As far as embassy personnel were concerned, they went out, as I recall, in two batches. The first batch were wives and children for whom it was quite easy to leave. Then when the fighting actually started, we organized an airlift, with a plane which had just been repaired in Israel. The plane actually had trouble with one wing and they had just finished re-securing the wing to the body of the plane. The Air Force officer who offered the plane, knowing we needed one, said he hoped it was all right and he thought it would get as far as Cyprus. So I called our ambassador in Cyprus, Toby Belcher, and told him we were coming in on a wing and a prayer, and to prepare quarters and food and whatnot for the people who would be coming over. Toby did a splendid job of it, as always.

The person in charge of actually loading the personnel into the buses to go to the plane was Tazie Currey. This was her first post, and she was said to be the youngest Foreign Service officer. She spoke something like six languages. The organization itself began to develop about a week before the fighting started. We transformed the conference room into an operations center and the senior staff was organized into a crisis management team. The officers who had no regular duties at this point, like economic officers, were converted into operations officers and it was their job to keep the operations room up to date, to keep all the telegrams that were pertinent, easily available, to let us know when new information came in, to keep the map up to date to show us where the fighting was and other such tasks. We had shifts so that the embassy was always manned with enough people so we could handle anything that came up, day or night. Some people slept at the embassy, to begin with, and during the entire crisis there were at least a couple of people staying overnight. Bit by bit as the crisis began to resolve itself and the fighting grew less, people were allowed to go home at night. I went home at night after the first couple of nights.

The ambassador had been invited by the Israelis to go to their war room in the Department of Defense, which was still located in Tel Aviv, not in Jerusalem where the bulk of the government was located by that time. And Wally Barbour, therefore, spent almost all his time in the Israeli war room. He never explained to me exactly what he did there.

As far as I know, he did not [have a link of communication with Washington from the war room]. He might have been able to telephone, using Israeli-controlled circuits. But eventually it became difficult to use the phone. When I wanted to get in touch with my three sons and tell them what to do and what was happening to us, I did it by ham radio, and it worked splendidly.

We never really doubted the outcome of the war. There were two factors here. One was the attachés, who knew pretty much what the opposing forces consisted of, and had a high respect for the Israeli military, which was well deserved. They sent in a prediction, which, as I recall, was that if war should break out, the Israelis would have it won at the end of a week, more or less.

Also, I had, myself, been fortunate enough to be taken around the central front by the commander of the front, General Narkiss, about three weeks before the fighting started. This had nothing to do with, as far as I know, the fact that the war was imminent. We weren't even thinking about that. It was a long-standing invitation which finally came to fruition at that point. I went up and down the whole central area and he explained what his troops would do, where they would give a little ground, where they would advance, where there reserves were. In fact, you could see them all along that central front area and he explained what they would do to retake Jerusalem, if the Jordanians were silly enough to attack the Israelis. He explained that they would go along the hilltops on either side of the city and pinch it off and that East Jerusalem, with its holy sites, the Wailing Wall and so on, would fall into Israeli hands. But he did not anticipate that King Hussein would actually attack Israel.

As the war started   the Israelis did send a message by way of General Bull of the United Nations, to King Hussein, saying, in substance, "If you do not attack, we will not attack you." They also let it be known that they wouldn't consider a few stray shells being landed by the Jordanians for the sake of appearances to be an attack. But the Jordanians attacked at Government House. That was the U.N. headquarters at that point, the old British headquarters. There may not have been a tremendous attack, but it was significant enough so that it gave the Israelis the opportunity, quite justifiably, to repel the attack and take the West Bank.

There is one thing I would have done differently. When I had heard that the fighting had started, I called my contact, Slomo Argov, in the foreign ministry and asked him whether it was really true that Israel had attacked. And he said, "Oh, the Arabs must have done something. I think I heard that they fired at us." I took that more seriously than I should have. I reported it, when actually, Slomo, I think, was making it up as a bit of justification. Later on there was no record of any provocation at all.

CAIRO (1967)

Following is an account of the Six-Day War as viewed from Cairo, Egypt, by DAVID GULICK NES, who was chargé d'affaires ad interim at the time.

Ambassador-designate Richard Nolte had arrived in Cairo on May 21 but was unable to present his credentials owing to the crisis culminating in the so-called June "Six-Day War." David G. Nes, chargé d'affaires, continued to conduct the affairs of the embassy during this period until Egypt broke diplomatic relations with the United States and the embassy was closed. Nes recalls the events immediately preceding the war, including unsuccessful attempts by the United States to prevent a war by allaying Nasser's fears of an Israeli attack. He also describes the Embassy's organization during that period and how the Americans were evacuated to safehavens.

Nes: Tensions between the "front line" Arab states and Israel had been increasing during the past year--engendered by guerilla attacks across Israel's eastern border and Israeli reaction such as its raid on the Jordanian town of Samu and its later destruction of six Syrian Migs on the outskirts of Damascus. A reported statement by Israeli Chief of Staff, General Rabin, on May 12 to the effect that his forces would occupy Damascus and overthrow the regime set the stage for the subsequent events leading up to the "June War." Meanwhile, Arab criticism of Nasser and demands that he do something intensified.

The next day, the fuse was lit when Soviet Ambassador Pojidaev informed the Egyptian Foreign Office Under Secretary Al-Fiki that Israeli troops were moving for attack on the Syrian border. On instructions from the Department, I called on al-Fiki May 16 and informed him our intelligence reported no unusual troop movements in Israel. This was passed on to Nasser, who is reported to have considered this demarche as merely the cover for an Israeli attack. By this time, relations between the United States and Egypt had sunk so low that Nasser seemed to believe that we were in collusion with the Israelis to destroy his regime. The origin of this belief stems from the history of U.S.-Egyptian relations over several previous years which is beyond the scope of this discussion. In brief, Nasser seemed to be reaching a degree of frustration bordering on irrationality.

From May 13, the events moved quickly to crisis proportions. During the 14th and 15th, Egyptian troops ostentatiously paraded through the Cairo streets en route to the Sinai. In my conversation with al-Fiki on the 16th, he explained this move as purely defensive and only designed to respond if Israel attacked Syria massively.

Ambassador-designate Nolte arrived the evening of May 21 and in remarks to the press discounted any possibility of war or of a crisis situation. The next day Nasser, in a speech to an officer group, announced that he was closing the Straits of Aqaba to Israeli shipping. Such a move had always been considered a *casus belli* by the Israeli government.

On the 23rd, President Johnson sent Nasser a personal letter expressing friendship with a plea for avoiding hostilities and offering to send Vice President Humphrey over to discuss the crisis. On May 26, the provocative editor of *al-Ahram*, Mohamed Heikal, had published an editorial to the effect that war was inevitable. In the embassy, we had already begun preparations to evacuate dependents and non-essential personnel, and accomplished their departure easily by chartered aircraft from Cairo to Athens, May 26-29. My wife and two younger daughters left on home leave orders on the latter date. (We had been planning to leave July 10 in any event). On the eve of their departure, Mrs. Anwar Sadat, wife of the future president, telephoned my wife to express sorrow at this distressing turn of events. She had invited my wife to come to her house once a week to help her with her English for the past year.

Needless to say, the week preceding June 5 was one of frenzied diplomatic activity, and the cable traffic between the embassy and Washington kept our communications and secretarial staff working 24 hours a day.

While Nasser was obviously endeavoring to soften his provocative moves of the previous week, the embassy had no reason to believe from the cable traffic that Israel would long delay a military strike so as to permit diplomacy or an international naval presence in the straits to deescalate the crisis. We began discussing the possibility of a break in diplomatic relations and the further evacuation of both official and non-official Americans should war come. The embassy, meanwhile, was not kept fully informed of our contacts with the Israeli government, but gained the impression that we had neither requested nor obtained a "no first strike assurance" such as we had asked for and gotten from Egypt. There was some belief that the Israelis had given us several weeks of grace to "open" the straits by diplomatic or military means; that is, until June 11 or thereabouts.

As the first days of June approached, plans initiated by the Egyptian government were set in motion to send a delegation to Washington on June 6 headed by their vice president Zakaria Muhieddin.

In the embassy, we established a sort of crisis center headed by our very able Arabic speaking political counselor, Dick Parker, assisted by the CIA station chief Bill Bromell, PAO [public affairs officer] Bob Bauer, the administrative counselor, Martin Armstrong, and the consul general. With dependents and non-essential personnel out of the way, we concentrated on our relations with the key Egyptian ministries, namely foreign and interior, and on the exact location of all American residents, including many distant from Cairo or in the Suez oil fields.

By Sunday, June 4, we seemed to have reached a day of quiet and some moderate optimism. We had a "no first strike" pledge from Nasser. The Muhieddin Mission was going to Washington, and 11:30 A.M. the next day had been set for our ambassador designate to present his credentials. There seemed a chance, albeit slim, of a peaceful outcome.

During the morning I attended services at the Anglican cathedral and then lunched with Ashraf Ghorbal from the foreign office (later ambassador to Washington) who was organizing the Muhieddin Mission; and after checking the embassy, went out for nine holes of golf with dinner thereafter at the John Dormans (American Research Center) on their Nile river boat. In fact, we were in the eye of the hurricane. Cairo that night was a dead city, the streets deserted, building blacked out and car lights blue.

On Monday, June 5 the chancery began the day routinely with the 8:00 A.M. staff meeting. We discussed continuing the evacuation of remaining Americans to Alexandria, the Muhieddin Mission, Nolte's presentation of credentials--who would accompany him and what he could appropriately say to Nasser. As the meeting broke up shortly before 9:00 A.M., Radio Cairo reported Israeli air attacks throughout the country. Outside we could hear explosions in the direction of Cairo West airfield and some anti-aircraft fire, but no Israeli planes were visible over Cairo. I immediately called Judge and Mrs. Brinton (an elderly American couple retired in Cairo) who awaited an embassy car to take them to the airport for an Athens flight and told them to sit tight. Shortly thereafter, the Foreign Office called canceling Nolte's presentation of credentials. The next day, John Dorman arranged for the Brintons to reach Alexandria.

Throughout the day Cairo Radio and TV reported gigantic Egyptian air and land victories. The mood throughout the city was euphoric amid periodic air raid sirens which just seemed to stimulate greater enthusiasm. From the BBC we were getting another story. That evening I attended a small garden cocktail party at the Bauers in the midst of which all hell broke loose overhead. While no Israeli planes could be seen or heard, anti-aircraft fire was intense and showered us with shrapnel, forcing all the guests indoors for the rest of the evening. A modified diplomatic and intra-Embassy social life continued through the week, but all official Egyptian contacts seemed to disappear.

The following morning, June 6, the early morning Cairo Radio broadcast reported that U.S. and U.K. planes had participated in the air attacks of the previous day, and the mood on the streets of Cairo became ugly. The big lie was obviously orchestrated to explain why Israel alone never could have defeated the Egyptian air force--i.e. shades of Suez. We advised all Americans except those needed in the embassy crisis center and communications to stay at home. Our communications were switched from commercial channels to our emergency radio links through the Sixth Fleet.

Later that morning, our consul general in Alexandria, David Fritzlan, called on the emergency radio to report his offices were under attack; and that he and the staff had retreated and were barricaded in the communications center on the second floor. Within a few minutes he reported the mob had set fire to the building and his radio went dead. Very shortly thereafter, a similar distress call was received from our consul in Port Said, whose offices were also under siege. Happily, within the hour, the British consul in Alexandria called to say that Fritzlan and staff had been evacuated safely and taken to the police station for safety. The situation in Port Said was similarly resolved. Our buildings in both cities were virtually destroyed, but no one, miraculously, was injured.

In Cairo, we asked the minister of interior for full protection, which was quickly forthcoming and involved a paratroop company around the embassy and small military units at the embassy residence and my residence on Sharia Wilcox in Zamalek.

Early that evening, Nolte was called to the foreign office and handed a note breaking diplomatic relations. I followed up with the chief of protocol requesting that we be permitted to retain under a protecting power twenty-four officers and an adequate support staff, the same complement permitted Britain following the Suez War. This was refused, and further talks were agreed to for the next day.

We had strongly recommended to Washington that Spain be requested to handle our interests. The Spanish ambassador in Cairo, Angel Sagaz, had exceptionally good relations with the Egyptian government and was a very personable, competent career diplomat. The Department reluctantly agreed because they were not enthusiastic about asking the Franco government for anything and feared media and political criticism.

At 9:00 P.M. representatives from the interior ministry called at the chancery and demanded that all Americans in Egypt be immediately concentrated in the Cairo Hilton Hotel--an impossible and impractical order based on out-of-date lists, which our consular staff corrected for them.

Wednesday, June 7, I spent much of the day in frustration shuttling between the Foreign Office and Spanish embassy seeking agreement on the embassy staff we could leave behind. Back at the chancery, talks were underway with embassy Athens to charter a ship for evacuation from Alexandria. The Egyptian government had demanded that all Americans, except the agreed number, leave by Saturday, June 10. This involved about 550 all together including those already in Alexandria and Port Said. Those in the Suez Gulf oil fields were being exempted. The mood in Cairo was becoming increasingly threatening as reports of Egyptian defeats filtered in from the BBC and other foreign stations.

We had already destroyed classified files and code machines. These were equipped with chemical destruction kits. The Marine sergeant in charge apparently misread the directions, and considerable fire ensued on the chancery roof where the machines and files had been taken. This resulted in consternation among the Egyptian troops "protecting" us who assumed it was a bomb, and the equivalent of five to six alarms were sent in to the neighborhood fire houses. The resulting confusion and noise was awesome! The fire was quickly put out without Egyptian assistance. When things calmed down, we officially turned over the embassy to the Spanish ambassador, lowering the stars and stripes and raising the Spanish flag. Ambassador Sagaz seemed a little overwhelmed by the size and complexity of our compound, which was many times the size of his establishment.

Thursday, June 8, we learned from the BBC that Israeli forces were approaching the Suez Canal and had taken Sharm el Sheikh. Egypt, however, refused a U.N. sponsored cease-fire. About mid afternoon, we received an "immediate" message reporting that the U.S. Navy ship *Liberty* was under attack, presumably by the Egyptians, and planes were being launched from the Sixth Fleet carrier *Saratoga* for a retaliatory strike against Egyptian targets. All of us thought, "Well, this will certainly destroy any further Egyptian cooperation for our safety." An hour or two later, a second "immediate" arrived reporting that the attackers were Israelis.

The next day, June 9, we had good news. Embassy Athens had succeeded in chartering a recently renovated cruise ship, the 3,000 ton *Carina* built in Glasgow in 1930. She had accommodations for 150, and we would be 550 minimum. Also, the Egyptians had laid on a special train from Cairo to Alexandria for 9:00 A.M. Saturday morning, the 10th. All seemed in order for a non-eventful departure. The foreign office had finally agreed to our leaving under Spanish protection four officers headed by Dick Parker and some dozen support personnel. They specifically requested that Bill Bromell stay. Since they had read the *Invisible Government* [a book about the CIA], this CIA contact was considered as providing a direct channel to the White House if ever needed. [Bromell had been "declared" to the Egyptian government].

In the course of the day, I paid courtesy farewell calls on six Western ambassadors who had been particularly helpful to me as chargé and on the provost at the Anglican cathedral.

In the early afternoon, Cairo Radio announced that President Nasser would deliver an important address to the nation that evening. Parker, Bromell, Bauer and I repaired to the ambassador's residence for dinner. In the 25 minutes of "Mea Culpa" Nasser assumed all responsibility for the defeat and said he was resigning the presidency. It was perfect theater, as within minutes the streets were thronged with mobs chanting "Nasser, Nasser." During the dinner Ambassador Sagaz called to report that Parker had been declared *persona non grata;* and so Bromell would be left as senior officer to manage the packing of several hundred households and location for shipment of as many cars left on Cairo streets. What a fate for a senior CIA Officer!   From the chancery we could hear numerous explosions throughout the city only to learn in due course they were intended as a sign of support for Nasser.

At 10:30 P.M., we were called by the interior ministry and informed that our security could not be guaranteed in the daylight on the next morning, and we would have to board our boat train at 2:00 A.M. That gave us three-and-a-half hours to round up some four hundred Americans and arrange to get them safely to the station. Leaving Parker in charge, I returned to the Sharia Wilcox residence in an unmarked car with an embassy driver and a marine, both of us carrying several hand grenades. Hopefully, this would give us a chance to escape from a mob were we to be surrounded and attacked. At the house, I grabbed two bags already packed, embraced in farewell our tearful cook, Goma, and proceeded back to the chancery, picking up the Pan American Airline representative George Angelis and his wife, Katy, en route. We encountered one street blocked by demonstrators, we stopped and they passed around us without incident. Back at the chancery, the crisis team had done a magnificent job in contacting all known Americans, arranging for them to reach the embassy compound.

As there was still conflicting advice from the foreign office and interior ministry as to the security situation for a 2:00 A.M. train departure, I sent Bromell out to talk with the director of Intelligence at Heliopolis--also to try to reverse the decision on Parker. He returned with an affirmative on the first, a negative on the second, and a request that I stay as senior U.S. diplomat. We replied, without reference to the Department, that I would stay if we could retain the complement of officers and staff originally requested. This was refused.

On Saturday, June 10, between 1 and 2 A.M. we began shuttling our people in six embassy cars and a NAMRU [Naval Medical Research Unit] bus to the station accompanied by Egyptian military guards. I sent the Cadillac with two marines around to the residence for Nolte. Finally, as the last to leave, I closed the chancery door for the final time and affixed the Spanish seal.

Aziz, our senior embassy chauffeur, drove the Angelises and me to the station without incident. There we found the train being loaded efficiently and all personnel seemingly accounted for.   Just before 2:00 A.M. Ambassador Sagaz appeared, having driven himself through still blacked-out Cairo to say farewell--a very courageous and thoughtful gesture. (He was later assigned as Spanish ambassador to Washington). The train pulled out at 3:30 A.M. with shades drawn, arriving on the dock in Alexandria at about 7:30 A.M. And then the greatest hassle of the week ensued.

All together, we had some 1500 pieces of baggage which customs insisted on opening and inspecting each and every one except Nolte's and mine. This took six hours until 3:00 P.M. during which time we were provided neither food, water nor toilet facilities. During the day, one of our AID officers became seriously ill with an internal hemorrhage. As he needed immediate surgery, the Egyptian authorities permitted his transfer to a local hospital, where he died shortly after arrival--the only American casualty in Egypt during the war.

The *Carina* docked at 3:00 P.M. Going on board to talk to the captain, I was informed we had to sail by 5:00 P.M or wait until the next morning. This involved loading those 1500 pieces of baggage now being repacked on the dock in considerable confusion. Jim Hutchins, our agricultural attaché, quickly solved the problem by forming a living conveyor belt, or bucket brigade, each piece being passed from hand to hand in a human chain to the total astonishment of the watching Egyptian authorities. By 4:45 P.M. all was aboard, and the *Carina* sailed for Piraeus.

Outside the twelve mile limit, two Sixth Fleet destroyers joined to escort us on to Greece where we reached port at 2:30 P.M. on Sunday, and were met by Ambassador Phil Talbot. The best quote of the voyage came from 89-year-old Judge Brinton, who had joined us on the dock in Alexandria. When I asked whether he and Mrs. Brinton were comfortable in a cabin I had managed to get for them, he replied, "Well, I haven't had such a nice sea voyage since we were evacuated during the Suez War!"

I think there are lessons to be learned from the embassy's involvement in the June War. Some of them are:

1. Never, ever should the White House send a politically-appointed ambassador with no diplomatic or embassy-country team management experience to his post in the middle of a developing crisis with a war near at hand.

2. As a crisis situation develops, a small--no larger than six officer-team should be established to deal with both the diplomatic and administrative requirements. Ideally, they should include the DCM, political counselor, CIA station chief, administration and consular heads. In our case, we included the PAO because of his excellent local contacts, good judgment and approach to critical problems with both equanimity and a fine sense of humor. Our senior secretary, Mary Pollock, provided office support for the crisis team and did a superb, officer-level job, working 12 hour days or more throughout without complaint.

3. It is very helpful to have a CIA station chief who is "declared" to the host government so as to establish close working relations with the intelligence and security people.

4. Pre-crisis evacuation planning is often useless and--as a practical matter is replaced by ad-hoc decisions dictated by the local situation and extent of cooperation by the host government.

5. Finally, because of understandable communications limitations, the embassy should be prepared to make hour-by-hour decisions without reference to the Department of State.

10

The Jonestown Affair:
Guyana, 1978

*On November 18, 1978, the world was shocked by the events at the Peoples'
Temple, Jonestown, Guyana, in which hundreds of the American followers of
religious cult leader Jim Jones committed suicide by drinking poison. The
Temple was located in the small tropical country of Guyana on the northern
coast of South America. It's members were almost exclusively Americans from
the San Francisco area, where Jones first had his mission and where he had
a measure of political influence. In Guyana the colony grew and seemed to
be trying for a reputation of respectability there. But rumors began to circulate
that all was not well and that dissatisfied members were prevented from
leaving. This prompted a congressional visit to Guyana to determine the true
situation and wishes of the hundreds of Americans living in the colony.*

*Despite some obstacles the delegation did visit the colony and learned that
there was dissatisfaction among some of the members. Some of them were
unhappy and wanted to leave with the delegation. Jones feared if this were to
happen, the colony's future would be in jeopardy. To prevent it a group of his
followers attacked the delegation, killing Congressman Leo Ryan, and
wounding others. Upon learning of the congressman's death and fearing the
consequences, Jim Jones ordered the mass suicide of the entire colony. A tape
recording of the grisly proceedings was found at the site.*

*JOHN RICHARD BURKE was U.S. ambassador to Guyana at the time.
He tells of the role he and his embassy played in trying to facilitate the visit
of Congressman Ryan and his staff to the Peoples' Temple; how they dealt
with the problems of evacuating the wounded in the Ryan party; the*

arrangement they made for the removal of the bodies of the suicide victims from Jonestown to the United States via U.S. military aircraft; and how they dealt with the flood of queries from the press. Finally, he comments on the seemingly endless investigations by various groups on the handling of the entire episode.

Burke: Certainly I was aware of the People's Temple situation before I arrived. I was briefed on it in the Department. I knew that Jim Jones had been a prominent political figure in California, that he had been commissioner of housing for the city of San Francisco, and that Moscone, who was then the mayor of San Francisco, acknowledged that without the assistance and support of People's Temple and its votes he probably never would have been elected mayor.

I certainly did not have a clear idea, either from the literature I read or conversations, just what the philosophy or the religious orientation of People's Temple was. It seemed a little fuzzy. In any event, I was interested in the fact that some 800 to 1,000 Americans had chosen to come down to Guyana and participate in the establishment of this community in a very remote part of the country. In fact, the area in which it was located was very close to the contested border with Venezuela, and the land on which it was situated I think Venezuela still claims, although they haven't in recent years made any effort to take it over again. But it is a very remote part of the country.

When I arrived I asked my consul whether or not he had visited the place and how often. I was able to get the Department [of State] to authorize the charter of an aircraft so that we could at least have quarterly visits to the site to talk to members. We were getting letters from time to time from next of kin in the United State expressing concern about the welfare and whereabouts of their relatives. The consul [Richard McCoy] would accumulate these letters and on his trips would ask to see and talk to the ones who were the objects of these letters. He did a very conscientious and systematic job of doing this. I think it (the Temple) was established in 1974, and they made a great PR [public relations] effort throughout Guyana. They had an office in Georgetown which handled all their shipments in and out and did their PR work with the Guyanese government and with various people who would come to visit. They made a great effort to get members of the Guyanese government, especially the minister of education and the minister of social welfare to come up and visit.

It was a remarkable establishment. It probably had a more sophisticated infrastructure than any Guyanese community in that part of Guyana. There were something like 140 permanent dwellings associated with it. They cleared over, I think, 900 acres of jungle, and had it under cultivation in the period of '77-'78. They were not self-sufficient yet. They were obliged to import a good deal of their food and the other materials and resources they needed for sustenance and whatnot, but they put on a very good show for all visitors. They had a weekly radio program that was aired on the radio in Georgetown, and all the prominent visitors would be invited to expound on the great experiment that had been undertaken by Jim Jones and his followers in the country.

There are restrictions under which an embassy operates. The embassy has no control over a private American citizen abroad until such time as he might come a cropper or be arrested by the local authorities. Then all you can do is go visit and make certain that he or she is being treated in accordance with local laws and regulations and that if a person is going to be subject to trial that they will be represented by appropriate counsel. If the individual who is arrested wants next of kin notified, the consular officer can do that. But if the individual chooses not to have next of kin notified the consular officer is restricted from independently notifying the next of kin abroad because of privacy considerations.

I had no special instructions. I certainly reported everything we were doing in terms of visitation. I had got the Department's rather grudging agreement to spend the money for chartering a plane every quarter to send the consul there. That was really about the extent of it. Every time our man came back he would file a report on what he had seen and heard, and it was duly submitted to the Department.

The Jonestown operation, the people immediately around Jim Jones, were well-educated people, some were lawyers. They were very familiar with not only the Privacy Act but also the Freedom of Information Act, and I knew that People's Temple had filed a Freedom of Information request for every report that had been made on the Temple from the embassy in Georgetown predating my arrival. They had made similar FOI (Freedom of Information) requests to the FBI [Federal Bureau of Investigation] regarding their activities in San Francisco and in the California region. So they were aware of the protections they had and they exercised them with considerable vigor.

Jim Jones did not come to [the embassy at] Georgetown during the period of my embassy before the events associated with the demise of People's Temple. Mrs. Jones did come to call on me one day with a couple of the people from the Georgetown office. It was a courtesy call. She told me all about what they were trying to do; she outlined in some detail just when they expected to be self-sufficient; ostentatiously showed me a handwritten letter that Jim had received from Mrs. Carter, the president's wife, thanking Jim Jones for having organized rallies on behalf of President Carter during the campaign of 1976. She made a great point of the political connections that they had in the state of California.   For example, then Lieutenant Governor Dymally, who is now a representative in Congress, actually had introduced Jim Jones to Forbes Burnham [Prime

Minister of Guyana]. Dymally is himself Trinidadian born and knew Burnham and actually brought Jones down when he was first looking for a place to establish his People's Temple. Burnham told me later on when we were discussing the People's Temple that--this is after the fact--that he probably would never have agreed to the establishment of People's Temple if Dymally hadn't been the one who brought Jones down and had introduced him and had vouched for him and the whole effort.

We'd received notification--I guess it must have been in September of 1978 or possibly August--that Congressman Ryan and Congressman Derwinski were planning a visit to Guyana, and they wanted to visit Jonestown. There were a series of meetings between officers of the Department and Ryan and Ryan's staff over the next several weeks organizing the visit. I informed the Department, of course, that Congressman Ryan would have to enter into direct contact with People's Temple if he expected to be received in Jonestown, because I had no authority to barge into Jonestown if the administration of Jonestown didn't want my presence or the presence of anyone else. It had been made clear to us that the government of Guyana respected their wishes in terms of how they controlled the community.

So Ryan, or his staff, did get in touch with Jones and with the people, I believe, first of all in San Francisco--there was still an office in San Francisco or representatives of People's Temple there--and the mechanics were worked out in a three-way operation. We certainly communicated to People's Temple the desire of Ryan to visit them and urged them to receive Ryan. They expressed concern because they said that Ryan had been unduly influenced by certain people in the Bay area who had defected from People's Temple and that he intended to bring these people down with him. They felt that he was essentially an unfriendly individual and would not come with an open mind, that he had already made up his mind about People's Temple.

In any event, we continued to exercise whatever influence we could on People's Temple and representatives in Georgetown. Also, my consul on his trip to Jonestown, (and my DCM, as a matter of fact) , [said] that the congressman appeared to be going ahead with his visit and that it seemed to us that he should be received. So the trip finally began to take shape, and it did come to pass. I can't remember the precise date of Leo Ryan's arrival, but I offered him hospitality, and he stayed with me while he was in Georgetown before his going up to Jonestown.

We knew about the acute suspicion on the part of Jones and the people around him regarding Ryan's motives. They hadn't finally agreed to let him in. That was communicated to Ryan and his staff before he left Washington. However, beyond that, we certainly had no inkling that the situation was likely to turn violent. I think our feeling was that the worst that might happen is that Leo Ryan might go up to Jonestown with the media people he brought with him, with the defectors from People's Temple and with the certain next of kin with him and that they'd be turned back at the gate.

It seemed as a common courtesy to send with them my DCM [Richard Dwyer]. When you have a CODEL [Congressional Delegation] visiting, of course, the Department requires that a control officer be appointed. It seemed to me that Dick Dwyer was the most suitable. He had visited the place himself as DCM along with the consul on one of the regular consular visits; he knew the people; he knew the ground, and he was a very able FSO [Foreign Service officer]. I had absolute confidence in him, in his being able to handle almost any situation that might arise. So he became the control officer. It seemed to me that Leo Ryan expected appropriate courtesies extended to him, and that's why I asked Dick to go along.

I would like to make one parenthetical remark before we move into that visit. When the Department had informed the embassy that the Ryan CODEL was coming, I was concerned because of the Privacy Act and the Freedom of Information Act and how they would relate to the relationship between Congressman Ryan and the people who were coming with him. I asked the Department to send along one of the lawyers from the legal advisor's office so that if questions arose regarding any of the embassy's records or records of conversations with People's Temple or with the representatives of Jim Jones we could get some expert legal advice as to what could and could not be shown to the congressman and those people accompanying him on the basis of the Privacy Act and how it protected the People's Temple and the representatives of the People's Temple.

The Department said that they really didn't have anyone available to send. I sent yet another telegram and slugged it for the personal attention of the assistant secretary for Latin America, Pete Vaky, and asked him to intervene with the legal advisor's office and see if he could not prevail upon them to provide this expert advice. I ultimately got a cable from Vaky reiterating the position taken by the legal advisor that they just had no one available they could provide to us.

This relates to something discussed earlier, and that is the limitations, really, on an embassy or a consulate in terms of what control or what sort of influence or what sort of responsibility they have relating to private citizens abroad, and that the embassies or U.S. missions have no real control of any sort over a private American citizen unless that citizen chooses to be responsive to advice or recommendations that a mission might provide.

With regard to the visit, Ryan was still negotiating with People's Temple on the question of access after he arrived in Georgetown. He met with representatives of People's Temple and Jim Jones and reiterated his request that he and his party be admitted to Jonestown to meet with the residents there. Jones and his representatives were still reluctant to grant him permission to enter Jonestown.

Jones brought or caused two of his lawyers from the San Francisco Bay area to come down and advise him during this visit. One of them was the rather well-known American attorney, Mark Lane, and the other--his name escapes me now--was the regular counsel for People's Temple in the Bay area. Lane was, more or less, on retainer with People's Temple. But the other lawyer was a full-time lawyer for People's Temple in the Bay area. These people did talk to Ryan. They made recommendations to Jones that he receive the Ryan CODEL, and I think they ultimately were instrumental in getting Jones' final agreement to let the Ryan party, or at least part of the Ryan party, come to People's Temple.

[The lawyers] were very protective of Jones. They had the same suspicions of Ryan and his group that Jones had. So they were actually legal counsel and in the employ of Jones and protective of his interests and interests of People's Temple as they perceived them.

When the CODEL was preparing to leave Georgetown to go to Jonestown, we did arrange for a charter aircraft to take the party up to the area. There was no airstrip in Jonestown itself, and the nearest airstrip, I believe, was something like seven miles away. The trip from the airstrip in that remote part of Guyana to Jonestown itself had to be negotiated by a vehicle provided by Jones and People's Temple. As it turned out, I believe they brought them in on a truck, but there was no public transportation of any sort that regularly went from the airstrip to Jonestown. The normal way for People's Temple to get a lot of their supplies was by river, because it was possible for coastal transports to bring supplies from Georgetown almost up to People's Temple. In any event, it's an extremely remote part of Guyana, and most of it is jungle.

The group left on Friday. They were negotiating right up until the last minute, almost up to the time of takeoff, with Mark Lane, the People's Temple lawyer, and with Jones about entry or the denial of permission to enter. As a matter of fact, the agreement to let Ryan and most of his party in was only given after the party had arrived at the airstrip in the vicinity of People's Temple.

The group did move in and were received at People's Temple. The citizens of Jonestown put on quite an entertainment for them on the Friday evening. The reception was fairly congenial as reported to me by Dick Dwyer, I believe by radio telephone. The only linkage that we had with People's Temple was through People's Temple office in Georgetown. Dwyer did report to us on Friday evening that they had gotten in, that Jones had received Ryan, and that the reception had been generally a pleasant one. The group seemed to respond to the entertainment and the hospitality provided by the People's Temple inhabitants.

The arrangement was, given the lateness of their arrival, that they would remain overnight in Jonestown and come out sometime during the course of Saturday.

Late on Friday evening, apparently some of the residents of People's Temple got a message to Ryan saying, in effect, that they'd like to leave with him the next day. He talked to Dwyer about it, and Dwyer said that he certainly would lend his influence and authority to help these people leave. The time of departure was approximately noon on Saturday. When the people who indicated that they wanted to leave with Ryan became known to Jones and to the inner group that advised Jones and were, in essence, the informal council within Jonestown, there developed a good deal of animosity between Ryan, the defectors and the loyalists, if you will, the people loyal to Jones. One of the people actually tried to stab Ryan at Jonestown. He [Ryan] had a superficial knife wound as a consequence, but several people intervened before any real damage could be done.

The group was finally packed aboard the truck and off they went back to the airstrip. It was during the boarding operation, when the party arrived at the airstrip and began to get into the chartered aircraft waiting to take them back to Georgetown that the attack occurred. The attack, again, has been well documented by television footage and also by eye-witness accounts.

A small group from People's Temple had followed the truck in from People's Temple, and while the group was boarding the aircraft, the group from People's Temple attacked the Ryan party with weapons. I believe these were shotguns and a .22 rifle and possibly a higher caliber rifle. As far as I know, there were no automatic weapons used in the attack. Congressman Ryan was killed during the initial attack, as were, I believe, two other members of his party. Several others were wounded, including Dwyer.

The larger of the two aircraft did take off when the attack occurred. The pilot revved his engine and without waiting to take any survivors or others just took off and headed back to Georgetown. The other aircraft, I believe, stayed on the ground. The remainder of the party, the survivors including the wounded, were huddled together on the airstrip, really. They were concerned about the possibility of a further attack.

As it turned out, after the attack the group just turned around and went back to Jonestown. They did not wait around to try to ambush the rest of the party. However, the group was in some fear that they would be back, and I certainly can't blame them for that at all. When the group got back to Jonestown, they reported what they had done and that they had succeeded in shooting the congressman. They conveyed this information to Jones, and it was at that point that Jones ordered the mass suicide at People's Temple.   There's a remarkable tape recording of this whole business, the last hour of Jonestown, which one of my consular officers picked up right after the whole event had taken place. I had instructed the consular officers to accumulate as much information as they could in terms of documents, in terms of files, in terms of anything that might be of use in an investigation of Jonestown. One of the consular officers did find this tape on a reel-to-reel tape recorder within the pavilion which was a central structure at Jonestown. What happened, obviously, was that the tape had been running, and the tape ran all the way to the end and ends in silence. You can hear the cry of the people as the suicides were taking place, and the people were being encouraged to come up and get their glass of fruit drink or whatever it was, laced with poison. It's a remarkable tape.

This takes us to about 7:00 on Saturday night. Now, the first word I got that something was very wrong was while we were waiting for the aircraft to come back to the airport in Georgetown. One of my consular officers was out at the airport with vehicles to pick up the people when they came back. I was at my residence and in touch with the people at the airport and with the duty officer at the embassy. We were still dependent upon communications through the office of People's Temple in Georgetown.

Then I got a call from the prime minister's office, he asked me to come see him as soon as possible. I went to his office where he had most of his cabinet present with him. The pilot of the aircraft that had taken off was also there. This was obviously the first report that they had gotten about what had happened. So I got this initial report from Prime Minister Burnham and the others present, including the pilot.

I went immediately back to the embassy and sent off a flash cable. I also got on the phone to the director of the Office of Caribbean Affairs, Ashley Hewitt, and told him on the basis of this very preliminary report that the attack on the Ryan CODEL had taken place, that in all probability Ryan was dead, and perhaps several others, that there were wounded, and that the fate of the rest of the party was still not known.

We hadn't at that stage any idea that the mass suicides were taking place at People's Temple. I then went back to the Prime Minister's office, and we discussed what could be done to rescue the survivors from the airstrip. The airstrip had no lighting of any sort for night operations. So there was no question of sending an aircraft up there until first light of Sunday. I asked him if they had any sort of military force in the area that might go to the airstrip and provide protection, and they had nothing immediately available in that part of Guyana. So there was really nothing that we could do until Sunday morning.

Now, it was recalled, of course, that Jones had threatened that if attacked or if his community were put in any sort of jeopardy that they might resort to something like mass suicide. And this was a matter of some speculation and certainly concern during the night. My immediate concern, of course, was getting the people in from the airstrip and getting them hospital treatment in Georgetown. So it wasn't until Sunday that we were able to evacuate the wounded and the survivors by charter aircraft. I believe that there were some Guyanese military who were brought up on that first day, a Sunday, and were under instructions to try to get into Jonestown and see what was going on there. I can't remember the numbers involved, but my recollection is it was a very small group, perhaps a detachment or certainly no more than a squad, really.

Now we, of course, got the information from the survivors as to what had happened. In fact, some of the people had gotten out on the aircraft that had flown out after the attack. There was even a can of television film that had gotten aboard that aircraft and was actually broadcast in the United States either Saturday night or early on Sunday. This was actually footage of the attack on Ryan and the shooting of Ryan, and, I think, done by the cameraman who was himself wounded. And I remember this particularly because Dick Dwyer's daughter, who was in college in the United States, actually saw the footage before she even knew and recognized her father as being in the party under attack. It was remarkable that that particular footage got out so quickly and was broadcast so quickly even before we ourselves had firm details.

Dwyer, to his credit, though wounded, was able to provide leadership to the group that was stuck at the airstrip. Actually, they were pretty well huddled, and there was a bar at one end of the airstrip in the tiny community up there. They all congregated there and were able to get something to eat. They spent the night, really, in great apprehension as to what their fate might be if the Jonestown group came back.

That really pretty well covers the event itself. As you can well imagine, as soon as my message got to Washington and was passed around the official community in Washington, and the director of Caribbean Affairs Ashley Hewitt had spread the word as well, we began to get all sorts of requests for amplification, for details and all the rest of it. Over the next three to four weeks our embassy, very tiny by most standards, was just about swamped, as you can well imagine. We pressed into service the USIA [United States Information Agency] team and the AID [Agency for International Development] people as well and had them all standing watches. They did a most credible job in supporting this effort.

When we had firm information that there was no one left alive in Jonestown itself and that there were all of these corpses in the tropical sun, the question of what to do with the remains became a matter of great urgency. Barbara Watson, who was then the assistant secretary for consular affairs, asked me if local interment could be arranged. I did discuss the matter with the member of Burnham's Cabinet who was placed in charge of the Guyanese task force, to deal with this great tragedy. After consultation they said that they'd prefer that the bodies be removed from Guyana. The only way that they could have been interred, really, would be by using bulldozers and creating some sort of a mass grave on the site.

Once the decision was taken by the Guyanese government that the bodies should be removed from Guyanese territory, then it became a problem for us as to how to deal with this. The U.S. military, of course, had had previous experience of this sort. There was a collision of two jumbo jets on the ground in the Azores where many hundreds were dead, and the army did move in and did take out all the bodies. This was a much more difficult task, obviously, because you were dealing with a part of Guyana where there was no strip capable of taking a large aircraft of any sort, a large transport. The only jet strip in the entire country was one at Georgetown. So what had to be done was to use the strip at Georgetown as the transfer point and bring in large helicopters and the graves registration team to prepare the bodies at Jonestown, lift them from Jonestown to Georgetown, put them aboard the C-141s and then transfer them to the air base at Dover, Delaware.

It was remarkable, really, how smoothly this whole operation went. The U.S. military did things on this particular operation they had never done operationally before, such as refueling the large helicopters when they were in transit from the United States to Guyana. Ultimately, the State Department was billed for the cost of this whole effort. In retrospect, I told the Department they should have prevailed upon the Pentagon to actually write off the cost of this operation against their training budget, because it really provided the sort of exercise that the U.S. military seldom gets in a part of the world that they knew little about.

To the credit of the military, I don't believe there was a single injury to any of the troops involved. There was no crash of any of the helicopters during their ferrying exercise. It was a remarkable performance by all hands.

Guyana, of course, became the focus of world press attention for at least 72 hours, and swarms of journalists descended upon Jonestown, or actually on Georgetown. There were, I think, at one stage 350 foreign journalists in Georgetown covering this story. It was a very difficult press relations exercise to handle because it was almost impossible for these people to get up to the scene. The Guyanese government had two briefers who were qualified to handle the press. We had a two-man USIS [United States Information Service] operation, and the strain was really enormous on them.

I don't recall any extra help that came in from USIA. The Department did send us in some consular assistance, and they also arranged for Victor Dikeos, who was the DCM in Panama, to come over and temporarily replace Dick Dwyer, who, of course, was wounded. He took a small-caliber rifle bullet in the buttocks. He was laid up for the better part of two weeks before he could return to duty.

As I say, the Department did provide a certain amount of consular help, the temporary DCM, and we did begin to get representatives of the FBI down, of course, looking into the matter. It was fortunate that when I was able to get my consular officers up to Jonestown on some of the first helicopters going in there, I had instructed them to scoop up everything they could in the way of documentary evidence relating to Jonestown, so that we could somehow piece together how all this had transpired. We ended up, I think, with about five crates of materials which ultimately were provided to the FBI for their own investigation.

There was no doubt in my mind that there would be a postmortem examination for official purposes of this whole affair. I certainly was prepared for it, and I felt that the record of my embassy in terms of our dealings with Jonestown prior to Ryan's arrival were impeccable.

I had also sent a long telegram in June of 1978 outlining the particular problems that Jonestown presented to us as the consular responsibility and asking, actually making a recommendation, that I be instructed to approach the Guyanese government and begin discussions with them about Jonestown. I asked the legal advisor's office and the assistant secretary for consular affairs to give this matter careful consideration and to advise me as to whether or not, given the privacy laws and the rights of private Americans abroad, if this could be interpreted as an intrusion, an official intrusion, if we were to talk to the Guyanese government about this community.

We already knew that there had been Freedom of Information requests for all of our files from People's Temple and that they were being processed in the Department. Certainly [these requests were] an inhibition to this extent, that you could not pass back raw gossip, rumor, innuendo, that anything reported had to be absolutely accurate in terms of factual content. Shortly after I arrived I began to talk to my then-consul, Richard McCoy, about People's Temple and his various meetings with People's Temple. He informed me that in his meetings two or three representatives would usually show up. These were people from the Georgetown office coming into the consular section to talk about this, that, and the other thing. So I instructed him that from then on he should not take on these people solo, that he should always have another consular officer present with him in such meetings. He would then have the protection of another witness so that he wouldn't be put into an exposed position of having people alleging that he had said something, with his having no witness, no separate witness, who could contradict such a story.

Everything that we filed on Jonestown was as precise as possible and did not contain material which could be construed as actionable by legal representatives of People's Temple or Jones or any of the people living there in the community.

I have always been opposed to doing much in the way of substantive reporting by telephone, primarily because you don't have a record of what's been transmitted. If you've made a note or a memorandum for the file, you know pretty much what you've said, but you can't be absolutely certain whether or not your remarks were misinterpreted at the other end or that you had been imprecise in the way that you had said it, or that the individual you were speaking with in Washington had misconstrued what you had said. Moreover, in most cases there's no record of a telephone conversation. So I really never cared for this as a means of communication except in extreme situations when that was the only thing available. So I did not do any reporting on Jonestown outside the regular telegraphic channels.

In the period prior to the Jonestown affairs, I do know that on one occasion, my consul, Richard McCoy, was going to Washington. His trip coincided with the defection of one of the female members of People's Temple, who came to us for assistance. Because he was going up for a consular meeting, I told him when he got to the Department to be sure and report. We did telegraphic reporting on her defection and what had been furnished to her in the way of support and assistance by the Assembly. But I told him to provide background to people in consular affairs about this matter.

I'm sure I must have heard [about the possibility of mass suicide], possibly in connection with this defection, but I certainly did hear of it. It seemed to me extraordinary, obviously. One of the difficulties in dealing with an institution like People's Temple is that people on both sides are oftentimes extremists. I think when one thinks about People's Temple when it was originally established, that the idea of close to 1,000 people leaving the United States, coming down to establish a community in the wilds of Guyana under the leadership of a very charismatic, religious leader, is extraordinary. And I guess my problem was or would be that I found it difficult to imagine what would cause people to do this. Certainly the charisma of the individual leader, that might have been it, or the promise of some sort of a Eden in Guyana for these people. It's just remarkable.

But most people who would associate with something like this tend to be zealots. So, therefore, they're zealous in terms of their initial support for such an enterprise, and then when, for one reason or another, they become disaffected with the enterprise, they become almost as zealous in their opposition to it. So with rumors associated with Jonestown and with Jones himself and charges against him and against the community, there was no objective witness to separate fact from fiction in terms of both stories.

Now, one thing that did not become very clear in terms of the reportage on Jonestown is that despite the fact that this was an extremely remote part of Guyana in which the People's Temple was established, People's Temple went out of its way to encourage visits by Guyanese government officials, by people from Guyana, prominent people from the diplomatic missions in Georgetown. They had a weekly radio program, for example, that was taped in Jonestown and broadcast. I think they bought time from the local radio station in Georgetown. And they would highlight on these radio broadcasts the visits that various celebrities had made to Jonestown, the minister of education, minister of culture or the representatives of various embassies that had come to visit.

They also, of course, applied for membership in the Guyana Council of Churches, and right up until the end of Jonestown and People's Temple, the People's Temple was a full member of the Guyana Council of Churches, which included every denomination in the country--Catholic, Episcopalian, Methodist. Of course, representatives of the Guyana Council of Churches did pay visits from time to time to Jonestown. So one was really forced to conclude, at least in the eyes of many, this was a responsible enterprise.

Well, certainly after the immediate problem had been dealt with and the remains evacuated, when things began to get back to some sort of normalcy, then the investigations began. The congressional investigation consisted of a visit by three staff members of the House Foreign Affairs Committee. Ryan, of course, had been a member of the House Foreign Affairs Committee and, as a matter of fact, the congressional delegation that he was authorized to conduct was under the auspices of that committee. It's interesting, in a way, that when the congressional delegation was originally announced to us, it was going to include two members-- Ryan plus a minority member, Edward Derwinski. But somewhere along the line, Derwinski dropped out and it became Ryan alone. When he arrived and we were chatting one evening in my residence, I asked him about this, and he said, "Well," he said, "the normal situation for a congressional delegation is to have representatives of both majority and minority side," and that his CODEL had been approved on the understanding that there would be a minority member. But when the minority member dropped out, he'd pressed ahead, in any event.

The first investigation was conducted by these three staffers from the House Foreign Affairs Committee. They conducted interviews. They brought along a stenographer and conducted interviews with me, with the other members of my staff who had been involved in any way with People's Temple. They attempted to take testimony from the prime minister and various other officials within the Guyanese government. But despite personal letters from Congressman Zablocki as chairman to the Guyanese government asking for their cooperation and participation, they were denied any such sessions.

The other investigation as such was one conducted by two retired Foreign Service officers. They came down sometime after the visit by the House Foreign Affairs Committee staff, and they conducted their own investigation or review of the embassy's performance. They also were looking at the performance of the Department itself and did meet, of course, with the officers in various parts of the Department connected with it; for example, those in the consular affairs and also those in the Latin American Bureau. They duly prepared a report which was issued--I can't remember when precisely, but considerably after the event.

Those were the only two investigations as such. We had several journalists who came through working on books. We briefed them, talked to them about the whole affair. We did cooperate and work with the agents of the Federal Bureau of Investigation who came down to investigate the whole Jonestown event with particular relevance to the shooting of Ryan and People's Temple and how it operated. But that was about it in terms of official investigation.

I think it was two years after that there was to be a hearing before the House Foreign Affairs Committee, and they asked my DCM Dwyer and me, plus Richard McCoy and Doug Ellis, who was McCoy's successor as consul [and was actually the consul at the time of Jonestown] to testify before a subcommittee of the House Foreign Affairs Committee. It was a subcommittee chaired by Dante Fascelle. It would have been the Latin American Subcommittee of the House Foreign Affairs Committee. I prepared a long statement, a formal statement, which I intended to give at the opening of those hearings, and I duly submitted it 72 hours in advance as you are expected to do [with any sort of formal statements that executive branch officials give before congressional committees]. The hearing was cancelled an hour or two before it was scheduled to begin, without any real explanation. I heard later that the chairman of the full committee, Zablocki, had decided that he didn't want to pursue this matter. That was it.

One thing struck me as curious about the [State Department] investigation that was conducted. It seemed to me appropriate if there were to be a departmental investigation it should have been done by the inspector general. It struck me as odd that this investigation was carried out under the counselor of the Department rather than the inspector general.

I think that the Department was particularly concerned about this whole matter of Jonestown for several reasons. Obviously the idea of losing a congressman wasn't all that attractive. There was another aspect. You may recall that right after this whole matter erupted, the connection of various important political figures with Jones began to surface. Jones was an important political figure in California at one time, and he had played a key role in the election of the then-mayor of San Francisco, Moscone, and had himself served in an official capacity as housing commissioner for the City of San Francisco. He had connections with, I believe, the speaker of the California Assembly. He also had connections with the then lieutenant governor of California, and several other political figures.

On the national level, too, he had several letters of congratulations from various politicians whom he had assisted over the years. So the whole Jonestown affair, from the point of view of the Department, was a very sticky one and way out of the norm of usual diplomatic practice. But then when people began to look at the embassy's record on this, and what we had done on the way of reporting on Jonestown and People's Temple well before the event, it was pretty clear that the embassy had done quite a responsible job and probably gone as far as it could given the natural and legal inhibitions that now confront us in dealing with consular problems.

11

Cyprus:
Preventing a Greek-Turkish War

The island of Cyprus obtained its independence from Great Britain in 1960 after a protracted and bitter struggle. Rather than solving matters, independence only intensified the struggle between the majority ethnic Greeks and the ethnic Turkish minority. Some of the former wanted Cyprus to become part of Greece (énosis), others of them wanted a Cyprus politically independent of Greece but dominated by the Greek majority. The Turkish minority insisted on a Cyprus in which their interests were well protected. A resolution satisfactory to all elements appeared impossible and the result was a civil war that resulted in a physical division of the country into Greek and Turkish enclaves with United Nations peacekeeping troops supervising a cease fire. This too proved inadequate to maintain peace.

In 1964 Turkey was prepared to invade Cyprus, precipitating what could have been a full scale Greek-Turkish war pitting two of our NATO allies against each other. U.S. diplomacy in Ankara sidetracked this.

Ten years later, in 1974, when the military junta in Greece tried to oust President Makarios (of Cyprus) and thus control Cyprus, Turkey moved in troops and annexed the Turkish enclave in the north. The island was plunged into a new frenzy of Greek-Turkish hatred with the United States, friend and ally of both parties, caught in the middle. Our embassy on Cyprus became the target of Greek Cypriot demonstrations during which our ambassador was murdered.

Our ambassador to Turkey in 1964 was Raymond Hare, whose account of his intervention with the Turks appears below. The events of 1974 are described by Lindsey Grant, deputy to the late ambassador Rodger Davies, who was assassinated during the trouble. So Davies was replaced by William R. Crawford, whose recollections of the period follow. Finally, the fierce anti-American demonstrations in Athens at the time of the Turkish invasion of Cyprus in 1974 are described by Jack Bloom Kubisch, ambassador to Greece in 1974.

ANKARA (1964)

RAYMOND ARTHUR HARE was U.S. ambassador to Turkey in 1964 when an invasion of Cyprus appeared inevitable. He describes here his interventions with the prime minister, Inonu, which persuaded the Turks to call off the invasion.

Hare: As you know, Cyprus is a small island off the southern coast of Turkey. It is actually visible from Turkey. Inonu once told me that they, the Turks, had made many concessions to the Greeks, and the only thing left in the south was Cyprus. There was violence on Cyprus because the majority of the population there was of Greek origin with a smaller Turkish population. The Greeks had tried to push their policy of *énosis*, which in effect would unite Cyprus with Greece. This had been accompanied by a terrorist campaign led by a Colonel Grivas. The British, who had been in charge in Cyprus, gave the country its independence and in a way washed their hands of the problem. Then Archbishop Makarios, whom the British had deported for his troublemaking, returned to the island and was elected president. The old problem of the two ethnic elements rose again, and real violence erupted. We became particularly interested in the problem largely because it involved two of our NATO allies, Greece and Turkey.

The Cyprus problem was typical of some situations where both parties can state their positions, but neither can go beyond a certain point without feeling that they are giving something away. This gets so crystallized, so stylized that, though you talk of negotiations and try to promote a reasonable solution, you aren't actually prepared to do so. For instance, in the case of Cyprus, if you talked about the country in terms of the "people" of Cyprus, that means that you were pro-Greek. If you talked about the country in terms of the "peoples" of Cyprus--in plural--that meant you were pro-Turk. Actually, the Turks never aspired to have the whole island. Their idea was to have full association in the government or a partition of the island.

This problem of Cyprus came to the boiling point while I was ambassador to Turkey. The situation reached a point where there was imminent danger of hostilities. We had established a sort of "watch committee" at the Embassy to keep tab of the situation, and each morning at our daily staff meeting we would go around the table reporting items of interest and views on what was going on. One day in the morning staff meeting after listening to the various reports, I said, "I feel there is something different about what you are telling me." They told me, "No, Mr. Ambassador, it's the same." I said, "I know it's the same, but it sounds different somehow." I just felt it. After you have worked with something long enough you sort of get a sixth sense in the way you feel about it. I said "Prepare a telegram" (what I called an "amber" telegram), saying that this situation should be "watched."

Later in the day I got a small piece of information that fit exactly into my suspicions. I felt that something was in the wind as far as the Turks were concerned. I telephoned the Turkish minister of foreign affairs and said, "Mr. Minister, I have a very urgent matter that I would like to discuss with you." He replied, "I'm sorry, I can't do it now. I'm going to see the Prime Minister in a few minutes". "This is really very urgent," I said. "Please!" He said, "Well, I have to see the prime minister in twenty minutes. Can you get here by then?" "Surely," I said. Getting there was made a bit easier by the fact that the foreign ministry was not far from our office, and the offices of the foreign minister and the prime minister were on the same floor in the same building. I got there and told him, "We are both acutely aware of the situation in Cyprus. We both follow it, and somehow today I had the impression that perhaps something was different which might indicate an intention on your part to take military action." He looked at me funnily and said, "Well, perhaps you are not wrong. As a matter of fact the decision on the subject is going to be taken at eight o'clock tonight; and if the American Government has anything to say about it, they should say it by that time."

This was about five o'clock or thereabouts in the afternoon. I got back to the office very fast and wrote a very urgent telegram. I got a reply right back; it was mostly boiler plate, all the obvious things. I was to tell the Turks, please don't do this; you could cause this, you could cause that, and everybody would end up in a dangerous situation. I don't remember exactly what the telegram said, but I think it said in effect, "Use you own devices."

I went around to the foreign office; it was about 7:30 or so when I got there. Anyway, it was before the meeting time. The foreign minister suggested that we should go in to see Prime Minister Inonu, which we did. I started out my plea with him, which was nothing special, mainly boiler plate. Inonu said, "Well, it's quite true that we are thinking about a military movement into Cyprus." He explained that this was a move to protect the Turkish community there, the Turkish enclave.

I had my instructions to dissuade them from military action and also, having been around in military situations a good part of my life, I felt that this was a very dangerous move for the Turks to take. First of all, I knew that they were not really set up for an amphibious operation of this kind. Such an operation takes time, and it requires all sorts of special equipment. So, if the Turks were going to try a landing, that would be serious, and things would probably get much worse. On the other hand, if they used their air force, that would be disastrous because their air force was very strong and the results would again be disaster. Either way they chose the prospect would be dangerous.

Inonu got up several times to leave, and each time I would say something to make him wait a little longer. Finally, he said, "Mr. Ambassador, all my people are waiting in the next room to discuss this matter; they are waiting for me, Mr. Ambassador. What do you want?" Well, I had no instructions to say what we specifically wanted, but I had learned--it's the old thing when in doubt, play for time. So without hesitation I said "Twenty-four hours, sir." He said, "Well, I don't know. I will see what I can do. We are supposed to go at eight o'clock tomorrow morning."

Well, they didn't go. The move had worked. Meanwhile back in Washington they had developed a letter to the Turks from President Johnson to Prime Minister Inonu. It was called the "Johnson Letter," but I've learned since that Dean Rusk and Joe Sisco had worked on it. I don't know if Johnson ever saw it or just gave perfunctory approval. It was a very tough letter, but it was reasonable in the sense that it was a warning. Here we were, joint members of NATO; we were friends of both Greece and Turkey, and if Turkey should make a movement whose end we couldn't see or predict, it might have wider and graver consequences. We could not guarantee what we would do; we couldn't guarantee our support in a situation of that kind. The letter was not well drafted, however, and there really was no necessity for its severity. After all, my play for time had worked; the move had not taken place. This was a time to act firmly but with diplomatic restraint.

I took this message to the prime minister and gave a copy to Erkin. When Erkin had read his copy of the letter he became really furious: "Mr. Ambassador, after this the relations between Turkey and the United States will never be the same," he said. Inonu on the other hand said, "Mr. Ambassador, I think I'll read the last paragraph first." The last paragraph was a very nice one asking him and his Greek counterpart to come to the United States to discuss the matter. It is very hard to understand how Inonu would think of something like that, that he could draw on such wisdom. He had had no time at all to study the message or to consider it. His reaction was instant and amazingly wise.

NICOSIA (1974)

In the early part of 1974 LINDSEY GRANT was Chargé d'affaires ad interim at our embassy in Nicosia. Upon the arrival of ambassador-designate Rodger Davies he became deputy chief of mission and served as such until he left Nicosia on transfer. A few days later, August 19, the ambassador was murdered. Grant tells of the period leading up to Turkey's invasion and annexation of the Turkish enclave and the events which followed.

Grant: There was a military junta, not a very bright one, in Athens. Archbishop Makarios despised them, but he could not be against *énosis*, union of Cyprus with Greece.   The national guard, which was made up of young Cypriot lads, was officered by Greeks from Greece itself who tried to fill them full of *énosis*.   Makarios, I suspect, would have been delighted for *énosis* to occur under himself.   He had a very broad view of his historical role.   Makarios could have done that, but he had done otherwise; and he certainly didn't like to have his own national guard officered by and being indoctrinated by Greek officers responsive to their junta.

What worried us was that somebody would get ham-handed enough to try to impose more direct control on Cyprus from Greece, that the Turks wouldn't tolerate this and would invade, which, of course, is exactly what happened [in August].   It happened because Archbishop Makarios, being a man of cunning and reason himself, assumed too much reason on the part of the junta in Athens.   He taunted them with their smallness and, in effect, said, "I am going to be the one who commissions new national guard officers."   The dictators, the junta, in Athens then turned their officered national guard loose to try to kill Makarios [July 15, 1974]. And they missed him.

The tanks came towards the front door [of the palace].   It wasn't a very wise maneuver or, I thought a very sophisticated one.   We learned later from a first-hand account of Makarios' assistant, that Makarios' military aide came through the French doors and said, "The tanks are approaching. Shall we go?"   Makarios turned and said goodbye to this guy, walked out the French doors, down the lawn, into a car waiting in the back.   They took off for the British military base.   This, of course, brought the Turks in.

I was just in the process of leaving.   I had gotten my wife out on a flight a few days before.   I was, of all things, putting our cat on the early morning flight. I decided to go to the office to see what was happening. I got there, and we could begin to hear some rumbling.   One of the officers, the administrative officer, who lived near the president's palace, reported that there were tanks moving towards the palace. That's how it started.

Having made one error, in trying to oust Makarios, they, the junta, compounded it by putting in charge the one person that was sure to bring the Turks in.   They put in as president of Cyprus [Nikos Giorgiades Sampson] a person who I think was probably certifiably psychotic, who was known for his virulent hatred of Turks and for his willingness to kill them any time he could.

This intra-Greek conflict between the pro-Makarios and the pro-Ioannides [Brigadier General Demetrios Ioannides, the Greek strong man in the military junta running Greece] factions was resolved rather swiftly in favor of the Ioannides faction which then put in this man Sampson. That led to the first Turkish invasion [July 20].   After that Turkish invasion, I went around to all the ousted Cabinet ministers and had conversations with them to find out what they were thinking. Nobody was blaming the U.S.

But then the Turks made that second move [The Turkish army made a major advance, occupying one-third of Cyprus, starting August 14] and the U.S. suddenly emerged as the scapegoat.   During one of these demonstrations against the embassy, demanding that we do something to get the Turks out, a sniper got up on a building under construction nearby and shot blind into the ambassador's office and down the hall. By just a horrible break he managed to kill Ambassador Davies and one of the local authorities. This was on August 19. The chance that the anger would turn on us had always been seen by us to be very high. We had stopped the Turks once before in 1964, and they thought we could do it again. I spent a lot of my time before this happened telling little stories about how we couldn't have stopped them, to try to get the Cypriot Greeks to be less confident that we were going to save their skins.   It had absolutely no effect on them.

Consequently, when they turned, they turned much more virulent. When the erstwhile foreign minister came in to sign the condolence book for Ambassador Davies, he started telling me down there in the lobby of the embassy how Rodger had been murdered by the CIA because he was too soft on the Greeks, and that it was all our fault that the war started--we had put the [Turks] up to it. It was just an incredible reversal in a week. A week before he had nothing to say about the U.S. role.

So there you are. The thing that shouldn't have happened did happen. The thing that kept it from being as bad as it could have been was the action by Prime Minister Constantine Karamanlis. He simply opted out of a war with Turkey. It was a belated act of statesmanship at the last minute by one leader.

Actually, in advance [of the Turkish invasion], we sent a message to Washington saying this was going to happen. I think that the agency [CIA] people in Nicosia were excellent. I think there was a great deal of candor, and I think we saw things in very much the same light. The other thing to be said is that unlike China, you didn't need the agency. Cyprus was so transparent, everybody loved to talk.

We were getting, I thought, quite adequate coverage of the physical evidence of [Turks] movement, and we knew very well that the Turks had put plans into motion; but you never knew the intentions. Were they doing this as a bluff to force the Greek hand? We had plenty of intelligence about what the Turks planned to do, but you always have enough on either side and enough uncertainty that you can never be 100% sure of any intelligence you get. In this particular case, there was one message that said, "The Turks are mobilizing and are using this Genghis Khan division. These guys are all over 6 feet tall, they all hate Greeks, they're all illiterate. They're savages." This was being sent and leaked to the Greeks to scare the Greeks. It was so obvious that my question was: Is it being used to try to scare us into making bigger efforts to get the Greeks to back up? It turned out that they went ahead.

I remember a few days beforehand in that interim, while we were waiting, we knew about the movements of troops. The military attaché said, "I'll bet four to one that they come in." I remember saying, "At four to one, I'll take the other side of it. But at five to two, I'll bet they'll come in." We were speculating, and that was the range. We all thought it more than likely. That was the level of expectation, not because of the good intelligence about Turkish intentions. We knew much more about how the Greeks felt. But even Turks like [Rauf] Denktash, didn't know what the Turks on the mainland were going to do. Denktash was the leading Turk on the island. The Turkish ambassador, I'm pretty confident, didn't know either.

At all events, Ioannides had pulled back enough to take out Sampson, the madman, and put in as president Glafkos Clerides, the most reasonable Greek he could have, the one who had negotiated with the Turks about a solution. However, that was too late to stop the machinery. We assumed, since the machinery was still rolling and the Turks were not asking for any information or beginning negotiations, that they were for serious; that they wanted a chance to get at these guys. They were mad enough, and since they weren't putting out any feelers to see what Clerides might offer them, they were probably going to roll it.

So we were pretty much on that wavelength, and we did get all the Americans out, all the dependents and all the people we could find, and this was pretty complete. In other words, we were acting on an assumption which turned out right.

NICOSIA (1974)

WILLIAM REX CRAWFORD, Jr., a former DCM in Cyprus, was hurriedly brought in to fill the gap left by the assassination of Ambassador Davies. He spent four difficult years as ambassador to Cyprus where he succeeded in establishing a working relationship with both Greek and Turkish elements on the island.

Crawford: I went off to hike in Norway sometime in August, and had hardly started when the Norwegian police found me on top of a fiord and flew me back into the capital, where I was told by our ambassador that I was to return to Washington instantly at the secretary's request. Our ambassador told me of Ambassador Davies' assassination [August 19, 1974] in Nicosia and speculated that this was the reason for the peremptory summons. On my wilderness hike, of course, I had heard nothing of what had happened in Cyprus after leaving the Department. It was August 19 that the Norwegian police tracked me down.

I flew back. I think the fact that Kissinger had seen me just a few weeks before in relation to Syria was relevant, as well as my four years previous experience in Cyprus. President Ford and the secretary prevailed on Congress to treat Senate confirmation as an emergency. From start to finish, from notification to the Senate to confirmation, took about two hours. I was sworn in, and I was off in just a few days, arriving in Cyprus as I recall on August 27. By that time the civilian airports in Cyprus were closed off because of the fighting. The only way to get into Cyprus was to fly into the British sovereign base area. So I flew to England, and the RAF took me into the British sovereign base. I came, so to speak, by the back door.   Dean Brown had been out there for a few days holding the fort after Rodger's death. I believe I arrived exactly ten days after Rodger was killed. It's curious that there really were not any instructions from Washington. I certainly never received any instructions from Dr. Kissinger, except to go out there and get there in a hurry. So I think it really was more instinct than anything how I came to conceive of what I should be doing. Nobody ever told me. I suspect that's true more often than not. On the plane crossing the Atlantic, I decided that the first thing I had to do was get back into effective communication with the leaders on both sides. Makarios was in London, and the acting president of Cyprus was Clerides. In a sense, the first policy thing I did, although I in no way thought of it as making policy, which produced immediate grumbles from Dr. Kissinger, was in my brief remarks on being sworn in by the deputy secretary. I spoke of an island whose very independence and unity were threatened unless remedial measures were taken soon to prevent a permanent division of the island, to get the communities back into negotiation, to terminate the foreign military presence, etc. Word came down through Arthur Hartman, the assistant secretary for European Affairs, that the secretary had rather blown up about his new ambassador in Cyprus making policy before he even arrived on the island. I said, "It's simply a statement of fact. The island is now divided, and unless somebody does something, it's going to stay divided. I wasn't trying to make policy, Arthur."

He said, "Well, the Secretary is angry."

So I said, "By the way, Arthur, I'm going to stop and call on Makarios in London." Arthur looked troubled. I guess he realized more than I did at that point the extent to which the secretary--this does not give credence to those who think the United States was involved in the effort to overthrow Makarios; we absolutely were not--but it was perfectly true that the secretary of state did not like Archbishop Makarios, and vice versa. I actually rather liked him [Makarios]. He was very cagey. There was no pious virtue about him despite his chosen profession. He had tremendous sagacity as a politician: very wily and very tough. However, you had to admire that. He was shrewd. As Dr. Kissinger once venomously said to him in my presence, "Your Beatitude, we don't have any problem with you, except you're too big for your island."

So when I repeated that I intended to call on the Archbishop, he said, "The Secretary would not like that."

I said, "I'm sorry, I've already been asked by the Archbishop's entourage to make sure that I stop in on my way out. Although he is not currently the president of Cyprus, he will again be. Clerides is only the acting president. I really have no choice." So I did call on Makarios. I'm very glad I did, because it helped pull back on the suspicion, which Makarios really had, that the United States had not only supported the junta, but also its effort to remove him. So it helped to get me off on a better foot. At least I didn't have Makarios and his supporters against me. Arthur shrugged and said, "I'll tell the Secretary that the horse is out of the barn door, you've already been asked by the Archbishop's entourage to make sure that you call. It would then be a clear insult not to do so." I emphasized that from my point of view, not to mention my safety, it really had to be done. And I'm glad I did, because that was a calculation.

We had just had an ambassador who got killed by ultra-Greek nationalists and who were still very, very angry over the failure of the attempted coup. Makarios already felt that we were responsible for what had happened. When I got to Cyprus, it was the ultra-nationalists, the types who were advocating union between Cyprus and mainland Greece, who were certain to be implacably hostile. It was the second such movement [the first having been back in the 1960s under Grivas]. It was they who had killed Davies. If, in addition to this group, the others, the Makarios supporters, who constituted the overwhelming majority of the Greek Cypriots and truly adored him as a leader--if they were against me, I would just be zero in effectiveness. It was not only a question of physical survival. I wanted to make sure that the word got sent back from Makarios in London to his supporters on the island that I was okay and fair and could perhaps be helpful.

Then in Cyprus, fortunately, I had a very close, friendly relationship with the acting president, Glafkos Clerides from previous service. Fortunately also, the same was true in his own-by-then sector of Cyprus, of Rauf Denktash, the Turkish Cypriot leader. The first thing I did was to insist on and gradually gain freedom of movement. By then, Northern Cyprus, one-third, or a little less, was controlled by the Turkish mainland army. They gave lip service to the idea that Rauf Denktash was the leader of

Turkish Cyprus, but in fact, he was entirely dependent on the mainland Turks and very much restricted in his own movements by them. The Turkish military wanted none of the messiness that might have gone with an independent local leader.

So I went to the Turkish ambassador. There were two or three telephone lines across the line. The first full afternoon I was there, within 18 hours of my arrival, I got on one of those lines. Ambassador Asaf Inhan had been the Turkish ambassador when I left two years before. After greetings, I told him that within 48 hours I proposed to come across the line.

He said, "Bill, I'm glad you're back, but I think that would be most inconvenient and probably not possible."

I said, "First of all, in conducting its military operation, Turkey has announced that it is not trying to destroy the unity of Cyprus, nor the independence of Cyprus. As far as I'm concerned, I am the American ambassador to Cyprus in all of its parts, and I must have freedom of movement. There's an additional reason beyond policy. I have a lot of American citizens in the north whose welfare, under American law, is my responsibility. They have just been through a war and many of them are in trouble. I must be free to visit them." So he sighed.

I called him later again to say that we would be arriving at the checkpoint two days hence at 4:00 in the afternoon. I knew he had to check it out with the controlling Turkish mainland military.

The next message from the Turkish ambassador was that I had to have a visa. I said, "A visa to go to all parts of a single country to which I am accredited?" So I got them to drop that.

When we got to the checkpoint as we had said we would two days later, there was an escort. I said, "I don't have to be escorted. I know my way." The Turkish military said, "Call it an interpreter." So I had a jeep full of "interpreters" with machine guns at 16 checkpoints from there out to the northern coast. The Turks were still very much on a wartime footing; they shoved guns in your face and so on.

I did establish the principle of freedom of movement, although it was very limited at first. I was able to drive out to the northern coastal city of Kyrenia; I called on my American citizens there, which is where most of them happened to be, and bit by bit I was able to extend it every weekend, to expand the area along the coast the military would allow me to visit.

I was able to convince the leadership on both sides that my freedom of movement was in their interest. To the Greek Cypriot government, which is the only one we recognized, and is still, I was able to say, "Surely, for the sake of the ultimate reunification of the island, it is useful for you to have me insist on this principle of freedom of movement in all parts of the island. Furthermore, I can perhaps see things going on of which you're unaware that may be of interest." Remembering that we were accused by Greeks of having caused the attempt on Makarios and subsequent Turkish invasion, they swallowed and said, "All right, we trust you. We understand why you're doing it, and we'll try to explain to people why you're going to cross that line. We'll try to explain it so you don't get shot when you come back."

Then the rest of the diplomatic corps, the British, French, and Germans in Nicosia, who had in truth been cowering on the Greek side for fear of incurring the government's anger, not knowing how to deal with the situation, followed suit. It became the established way for all missions to deal with the confused situation in which there were two declared administrations, only one of which was recognized.

It was not very pleasant living. There were no dependents. Early on, we had to make changes in the embassy staff, because people were pretty demoralized. They'd seen their ambassador killed, gone through a war, and had a very rough time. We removed some and brought back others who had previous Cyprus experience.

We had no dependents, and I flew in with two American bodyguards who stayed with me the whole first year. They lived in the residence. Because Rodger Davies had been killed by shooting through a window, I was never allowed near an open window. The windows were blocked off with sheets of steel, so it was very hard to tell when it was daytime or nighttime. I got out very little. When I did, it was always accompanied by two extra cars of Cypriot police, all armed fore and aft. In the car there was so much bulletproofing, I couldn't see out of my own window. And a great deal of hostility. Of the Greek Cypriots, by and large, people I had known socially in the earlier period, few of them came forward to offer anything. Those who did knew they were risking their lives or, at minimum, violent criticism. I was enormously grateful to the brave few who did.

There was a very long history of Greek Cypriot maltreatment of the Turks, so this has antecedents going way, way back. After arrival, I set about trying to help the whole process of U.N.-sponsored negotiations between the two, to help the special representative of the United Nations, who is now, by the way, the Secretary General of the United Nations, Perez de Cuellar. In reality, the United States had more authority than the Secretary General's special representative, because we had more influence with Greek and Turkey and with the two communities in Cyprus.

Over the four years that I was there, we tried in countless different ways to nibble away at the intractable situation, intractable because Turkey had achieved, in 1974, what it had long wanted, and that was to move Cyprus out of a waffley area of Greek-Turkish influence and irrevocably into a zone of Turkish military hegemony. They just never liked the idea that this island thirty miles off their shores might suddenly become hostile and cut them off to the south. The Turkish ambassador expressed it to me in just those terms. He said, "Turkey is an imperial power and a continental power. That we are unnaturally prevented from breathing to the north and the east by the presence of the Soviet Union makes it all the more important that we be able to breathe to the south and to the west. 1974 solved the southern dimension. It remains to solve the western dimension."

I got solid support from the Department of State, all the way up to Secretary Kissinger, about whom Cyprus stories are legion. I'd like to think that I got along with him quite well. I could deal with him, with humor, and he seriously wanted a Cyprus solution, no question about that. He felt the whole Cyprus thing threatened to be a real blot on his reputation in history, and he really did want it resolved, if it possibly could be, in his time as secretary. So he gave me every possible support.

The enmity between Makarios and Kissinger was very real. Though Makarios dealt fairly with me, he kept letting his newspapers blame and continue to blame Kissinger for everything that happened. I reported all this. Kissinger finally, quite rightly, could accept this no longer, saying, on the one hand, to the archbishop/president of Cyprus, who had by that time returned, "You ask for our help in solving this. You ask for aid. On the other hand, you are against us in every one of your controlled newspapers. You can't have it both ways." So after the worst of these, I was recalled. This was maybe in the middle of 1975, 1976, and it was really at my own suggestion. It was the only way we could show Makarios we were serious about not accepting continued insults. So I was recalled very quickly and sat in Washington for two or three weeks.

Then I said, "We've made the point. I think we should find some way of getting me back to Cyprus." The then under secretary, Philip Habib, asked if I had any ideas.

I suggested that I draft a strong letter from the secretary to the archbishop, and that to the letter be added an oral message from the secretary that I would be charged with carrying back, to say, "You can't have it both ways. If there's any more of this violence and insults to the United States and criticism of the American role, we will terminate that role and let the Cyprus situation stew in its own juices." I went back; the dual messages worked, the inspired insults stopped; and I picked up my job again.

By that time, we had established full freedom of movement. For another, we had a massive aid program. This, of course, gets into the whole business of the friends of Greece in Congress and out of Congress.

Here I digress a bit. The day I was approved by the Senate Foreign Relations Committee, I went down with Secretary Kissinger, who was giving classified testimony to the Senate Foreign Relations Committee. This would have been sometime before I left, the 26th or something like that, of August 1974. I went with Secretary Kissinger, who told the Senate Foreign Relations Committee how we saw the situation, what he intended to do, and he introduced me and asked for the committee's earliest possible approval.

After the secretary had spoken, Senator Jacob Javits of New York spoke. He was a truly remarkable man, I might say. I am paraphrasing somewhat, but he said something like this: "Mr. Secretary, everything that you've said to us this morning sounds appropriate to the circumstances, and we think you're on the right course. We support you. But just a word of advice. Rightly or wrongly, I am regarded by some as the leader of what is known as the Jewish lobby in Congress with which you have occasionally taken issue over policy. Whether that is or is not correct, let me just talk to you for a minute about some realities of American politics. Jewish influence in the United States is concentrated in a few key cities-- New York, Los Angeles, Chicago. Greek influence in this country is everywhere. There isn't a sheriff, a small town mayor, a state governor, highway commissioner, who hasn't to some extent become indebted to Greek American support, financial support and votes, whether Republican or Democratic. Greeks in the United States have an organization which links them, called AHEPA [American Hellenic Educational and Protective Association], the society for the preservation of Hellenic culture. It has never been a political organization; it's essentially cultural to preserve the sense of Hellenism and so on. Greek-Americans have never exercised national political influence. Their interest is in the liquor licenses, the highway contracts, the restaurant licenses, and so on, to protect their own local position. They've never before exercised this essentially tremendous weight on a national level."

"But the Cyprus issue has galvanized them as they have never been galvanized before, and they have a structure through which to bring political influence to bear on the national level. If from time to time, Dr. Kissinger, you have had reason in your mind to take issue with the Jewish lobby, just wait til the Greek lobby hits you."

Indeed, it hit him. When the Greeks got behind Carter's campaign, as an alternative to Ford-Kissinger, as you recall, leaders of the Greek community in this country passed the word to the leaders of Greek Cyprus that, "When our man Carter gets in, we will make sure that anybody who has had anything to do with Cyprus during this disastrous period is eliminated." They specifically said there would be a clean sweep of our ambassadors in Athens, Ankara, and Cyprus. The secretary of state, of course, would be changed. They said that first. And the assistant secretary for European Affairs, Arthur Hartman. "We will promise you there will be a complete change of characters." Indeed, within weeks of Carter coming in, they got the change in Athens, got the change in Ankara. Arthur Hartman went off with dignity to be ambassador to

France, but they got him out. They did fulfill their promise on that. A couple of other semi-subordinate officials, the director for Southern European Affairs and so on, were moved. I was, in effect, told by my Greek Cypriot friends that the "Greek lobby" had assured the Cypriot leadership: "Crawford's next."

Then an interesting, wonderful thing happened, which was reported back to me by the Greek Cypriots, particularly the Greek Cypriot foreign minister, an old friend. He reported these conversations with the constant flow of American-Greek principals to the island. So the foreign minister said, "Bill, they've told us that they're going to get rid of you. What would you like to do?" I replied that, "If there's something useful I can do here, I'd like to do it, to help put this island back together again." So the Greek Cypriots, including, by the way, Archbishop Makarios, went back to their Greek-American friends and said, "If you insist on this, as condition for aid to Cyprus, if you think it's got to be done, fine. But we think that Crawford knows the island, is fair, and we'd just as soon have him stay." When I got back, for instance, with that angry message from Kissinger, that was just before Carter came in, Makarios spoke to me. He had this benign, lovely look, with his big tall hat. He said, "Mr. Ambassador, isn't it true that under your system, ambassadors submit their resignations when a new president comes in?"

I said, "Yes, Your Beatitude, it is."

He said, "Wouldn't that be in your case, also, as a career officer, that you would submit your resignation?"

I said, "Yes, Your Beatitude."

He said, "What are your wishes?" Meaning he was angry at Kissinger, furious, too, at my bearing this angry message; in a word, seething.

I said, "Your Beatitude, if the time has come when I can no longer serve the cause of peace in Cyprus, I'll be happy to go. If there's still some way to be of use based on my knowledge of the island and experience here, I would prefer to stay." He just smiled very faintly, having made the point that he could remove Kissinger's envoy at will. I stayed for another three years.

On one of Makarios' visits to Washington after all of these events, I think he was coming in from London, I was called back for the visit. I went up to talk to the secretary before Makarios' arrival, and Dr. Kissinger said, "Bill, what do I call him?"

I said, "Your Beatitude."

So we went downstairs to the front entrance. Dripping with cynicism and dislike, Dr. Kissinger greeted the Archbishop when the limousine pulled up at the door. "Your Beatitude, I'm so glad to welcome you to Washington, Your Beatitude." We went upstairs, and Makarios was sitting there resting his hands on his scepter symbol of office and his lovely hat and all the rest, and that's when Kissinger just started right off saying,

"Your Beatitude, I want you to know that we have great respect for you, Your Beatitude. It is only, Your Beatitude, that we feel you're too big for your island. Of course, if you chose, you could, I suppose, be president or prime minister of Greece whenever it suited you. I suppose the one thing that would unify all those Greek politicians, Your Beatitude, would be the prospect that you would come in to be president of Greece or prime minister. Now, on the other hand, if, Your Beatitude, you were General Secretary of the Soviet Union, that would give us real problems to have such an adversary, Your Beatitude." The meeting got nowhere, obviously.

Then as we were going down the elevator, all crushed in there with the archbishop and his bodyguard, Secretary Kissinger and his bodyguard, me, into an elevator that ordinarily holds five, the secretary said to the archbishop, "Your Beatitude, when I'm with you, I really quite feel that I like you."

The Archbishop looked at him benignly and said, "Dr. Kissinger, it lasts for just about five minutes after we've parted, doesn't it?"

[As to accomplishments] first of all, we were able to establish freedom of movement in a situation in which the United States was excluded from dealing with one-third of the island and its leadership. The aid money, though it was excessive, was spent as wisely as could possibly have been the case. A lot was done for displaced persons, but, at our insistence, for basic economic development and improvement on both sides of the line. We got Greek Cypriot approval, believe it or not, for spending money on depressed Turkish communities, as well, because Turkish Cypriots had been displaced in the whole process of population transfer. So we spent money in proportion to the population ratio, 80-20, on the Turkish side, with Greek Cypriot approval. The aid money was spent fairly and effectively on doing a lot of good things that needed doing, more than probably needed doing in some cases. We established a role for the United States as the effective communicator and purveyor of ideas which might lead toward a solution of the problem, any aspect of the problem or its entirety. We made it clear that our role would be more behind the scenes; it was our preference and certainly in the interest of the parties to keep the U.N. peacemaking presence out in front. Everybody came to see that that was a logical way of approaching it, because we were so neurotically identified in different ways by our two allies, that we couldn't play the neutral role. You have only to witness the Greek influence in the American political process by that time.

We were able, on arrival, to establish effective working relationships with leaders on both sides, despite grievances and hatreds and all the rest, largely buffered by the friendships that we'd carried over from previous experience. Over time, the extent of animosity began to ebb, and more and more of a genuine friendship began to be restored to replace this real hatred which had existed certainly from 1974. It was palpable. Several attempts were reported to have been made on my life, and there was no question about it, it was a very unpleasant atmosphere. We were regarded as the betrayer of Greek Cyprus. By 1978, that was no longer true. We were looked to as the power *de facto*, and the only power that could really do anything in a final sense to develop a solution. So it was a very different atmosphere when I left.

Immodestly or modestly, whichever, I think I was the right choice to go back in, because I had a documented record of friendship with both communities, an impartiality, and was able to build on that. I had had four years of recent experience on the island, and many friendships, and built on those. If it had been somebody else who didn't have that kind of relationship, it would have been a far harder task.

Talking to our military attaché about a month after I arrived, he said, "If you don't mind my saying so, Mr. Ambassador, I thought you were out of your mind when, within 24 hours after arrival, you started wanting to cross the line, wanting to talk to the Turkish Cypriot leadership. I just couldn't understand what you were up to, but now I see it. It worked. You established working relationships within a few days at all levels, on both sides."

ATHENS (1974)

The fall of the junta in Greece as a consequence of their disastrous policy that led to the Turkish takeover of part of Cyprus, brought in a new democratic government. For the first time many of those with anti-American feelings were able to vent them on our embassy. JACK BLOOM KUBISCH [ambassador to Greece] had arrived just in time to bear the brunt of this in the latter part of 1974.

Kubisch: On demonstrations I would just say that I've seen many demonstrations in my life. I saw the demonstrations in the 60s in Washington where 50,000 or 100,000 people would demonstrate. I saw them in Brazil in the early 60s when there were 100,000 people in the streets of Sao Paulo and Rio and Brasilia. And even during the Vietnam Peace Accords, our embassy in Paris was attacked several times by 10,000, 20,000 or 30,000 people in the Place de la Concorde. We were well protected by the French authorities, fortunately. But I had never seen demonstrations of the kind that took place in Athens. There were demonstrations of 200,000, 300,000 or 400,000 people that gathered in the center of town all day long and then marched on the American Embassy, 200 to 300 abreast, marching by, using the worst, most obscene epithets in language, and trying to break into the embassy. They did succeed in breaking into the embassy once, tried to set it on fire and did over

$100,000 worth of damage. It was really a period of great turbulence in Greece and deep, bitter anti-American feelings.

The Greek authorities tried to protect the embassy. For example, on the day the mob broke in, or the evening they broke in, we knew there was going to be a big gathering downtown and a march against the embassy. So about 4:00 in the afternoon I sent everybody home, and I left the embassy with the American security officer and the marine guards, and several others. And as the groups came by, they marched by, they got to the embassy at about 8:00 in the evening. By prearrangement they burned an American flag as a signal and then stormed the embassy. There were a couple of hundred Greek police surrounding the embassy as a barricade, and I had given the marines instructions not to draw a pistol and shoot anyone because they were looking for a martyr, the demonstrators, the leaders of the demonstration, to try and bring on even more anti-American sentiment in the country.

I had told the marines not to draw their pistols or shoot anyone unless, as we used to say in the navy in World War II, you were in the last extremity where they had you down, they were about to do you terrible damage, then you could draw your pistol and shoot. And those marines, we had twelve at the time in the marine security guard, did a wonderful job. They fought off the people breaking into the embassy with brooms and fire extinguishers and chairs and so on. A lot of people were hurt. There were a lot of broken bones, broken arms, broken clavicles and so on. A lot of police were badly injured, but no one was killed.

12

The Fall of Saigon: Spring 1975

The war in Vietnam dominated American political lives throughout the presidencies of Lyndon Johnson and Richard Nixon and into that of Gerald Ford. Finally, in the spring of 1975, North Vietnamese forces swept southward, and in April it was all over, the war was lost. Our ambassador in Saigon during that period was A. Graham Martin. He had as his deputy Wolf Lehmann, who held the title of deputy ambassador, a unique title created because of the size of our mission and the importance of the U.S. commitment to South Vietnam.

The eyes of the entire nation were on Vietnam as the government in Washington wrestled with the problem of what to do so as to end the war with the minimum cost in lives, money, and prestige. Events moved swiftly in Vietnam and involved not only U.S. military forces but large civilian contingents including our embassy. The president and the entire U.S. government were frantically trying to bring order out of the chaos that was developing, which resulted finally in a complete withdrawal.

Ambassador Martin and his staff were dealing with the situation in Saigon. Events were moving faster than those in Washington could appreciate or accomodate in their planning. Unexpected situations arose requiring the ambassador and his deputy to make critical decisions without awaiting approval from Washington. Many of these concerned the safety and evacuation of Americans and allied persons.

Deputy ambassador WOLFGANG J. LEHMANN was charged with organizing and supervising the evacuation of Americans and Vietnamese from South Vietnam. Coordination with the U.S. military was constant and effective, and the evacuations were carried out successfully under the most chaotic and frightening circumstances. Lehmann's comprehensive description of the critical period commencing with the evacuation of American personnel from Hue on March 18, 1975, and culminating in the final evacuation by helicopter from the Embassy roof in Saigon on April 30 gives us a vivid picture of the enormity and complexity of the operation.

Lehmann: The evacuation plans are normally kept under more or less constant review. That review was intensified in our case early in 1975. As early as February 20 we had a couple of Marine colonels come in from the military side, which was to support the evacuation, in order to review the details for evacuation planning right on the ground and make any necessary adjustments. Of course, at that stage of the game, we kept this very, very quiet. We did not tell anybody, for reasons which are obvious. As early as the latter part of February the military began to review their role in the plans right on the ground.

With regard to the consulates, the plans were also constantly reviewed. In one case, that of the consulate general in Can Tho, the plan was rather drastically changed. [It was to the south] in the Delta where I had been previous to coming to Saigon as deputy ambassador. As a result of one of the reviews, Terry McNamara, who had replaced me, came up to Saigon in March with a recommendation that in Can Tho in the Delta we switch from an air evacuation plan to a boat evacuation plan from Can Tho down the Hau Giang River into the South China Sea. After a review by us at the embassy, the change was approved, and that is the way it eventually went in April when Can Tho had to be evacuated.

The situation we faced beginning with the resumption of large-scale North Vietnamese operations had several components. One of these was evacuation planning for Americans. A related one was evacuation planning for some third country [those other than Vietnamese or American] nationals whose potential evacuation we would support. A third element was our role in dealing with the massive refugee situation that was created by the resumption of North Vietnamese military operations.

Basically, I organized the embassy in the following way. I designated the deputy AID director, John Bennett to be the principal focal point in the embassy for supporting Vietnamese efforts to deal with the refugee situation. I designated George Jacobson to be the principal focal point for supporting evacuation planning by the consulates in our field operations. I designated the defense attaché, General Homer Smith, to begin planning support operations for an eventual overall evacuation of South Vietnam. That was done by establishing an evacuation control center in the defense attaché compound out at Tan Son Nhut, Saigon's main airfield. We ostensibly set up that control center initially to support the Vietnamese refugee problem, but we did it with full knowledge and intent that that control center would be immediately convertible into a center for controlling the evacuation of Americans and others from the country as a whole. It was on April 1 that we activated the evacuation control center at the defense attaché compound.

To set the stage, on March 16 ARVN [Army of the Republic of Vietnam] evacuated Quang Tri in the far north. We had no one in Quang Tri. Immediately after the evacuation of Quang Tri, of course, the situation became critical in Hué, just a little bit to the south. At that time Theresa Tull was acting principal officer in Da Nang. The initial step we took in Hué is that we removed our people overnight only and brought them back into Hué during the daytime. We did that for several days until the situation had clearly reached the point where we could no longer do so if we didn't want to risk them. There were not many involved in this. There were only a few Americans and maybe a small number of Vietnamese employees. In that short interim period, in order to keep up appearances, we would bring them in in the morning to their offices, bring them back to Da Nang by helicopter at night--until March 18. On March 18 I instructed Tull to move the people completely out of Hué and keep them in Da Nang.

On March 20 the ARVN organized their perimeter defense of Da Nang. The situation in Da Nang was, undoubtedly, the most critical one in the entire story. The ARVN on their part made a strong effort to evacuate the most effective combat units by sea down to the south and the Saigon area so that the units could be employed elsewhere in the war. As usual, the situation was complicated by the presence of large numbers of families that were simply part of the picture of the Vietnamese military. Then, too, it was complicated by massive flows of panicky civilian refugees.

So the situation in Da Nang rather quickly got out of hand. The Vietnamese military lost control of the Da Nang airfield, which was simply overrun by refugees and by some troops that had left their units. That of course, eventually complicated our own evacuation problem. Bear in mind now, overland evacuation to the south was no longer feasible. It either had to be by air or by sea.

In consultation with Consul General Albert A. Francis, with whom I continued to have good communications until the very last moment and with whom I was regularly on the phone during the day and late into the night, I considered the possibility of asking for support from the American military to assist us in evacuation of not only Americans but others from Da Nang. The specific proposal we had in mind was for the Pacific command to furnish helicopters to be based at Cam Ranh Bay to, in effect, assist with a rotary airlift from the Da Nang area. I raised that with the Pacific command but it was turned down. The reason cited was that all their assets were standing by and had to stand by for the evacuation of Phnom Penh--"Operation Eagle Pull" as it was called--and they could not divert it to assist us in our problem. So that one fell by the wayside. We had earlier augmented the consulate general in Da Nang with several younger active officers to help Francis. By the evening of March 26 and early March 27, the situation was pretty well out of hand in Da Nang. The airfield was no longer operational because it was just overrun by mobs. On the evening of Thursday, March 27 I met with the prime minister regarding the situation. He communicated with General Trung in my presence--although it was in Vietnamese and I did not follow it--to explore the possibility of using what remained of functioning military units, primarily ranger battalions, up in Da Nang to reassert control of the airfield so that some sort of airlift out of Vietnam could be continued. It became evident during the night and in the early morning that this could not be done.

[The staff of the Da Nang consulate managed to escape on a barge and were then in Da Nang harbor. Consul General Francis was aboard a Vietnamese frigate loaded with soldiers and refugees.]

Francis stayed on that other ship which eventually came down to the south, either to Saigon or Vung Tau. The people on the barge also made it out and came down, a few of them with nothing more than the shirts on their backs. Nha Trang was, of course, the next place to be threatened. It was farther south, just midway down the coast between Quang Tri and the so-called DMZ [De-militarized zone] and Saigon. Again, in Nha Trang it was a question of moving in time but not before time in order not to aggravate the situation and make it even worse.

Within days the situation had reached the point where Nha Trang had to be evacuated. The evacuation was, if fact, carried out and completed on April 1 both by helicopter lift and some assistance from a Philippine ship offshore that took off some refugees. During all this time the only air assets we had available to use were our own Air America planes, both small fixed-wing aircraft and the helicopters. There were no U.S. military involved in any of these operations. We had both helicopters, Hueys [general purpose helicopters], and some fixed-wing aircraft, in all about 30 aircraft available to us in Air America. Of course, under the arrangement George Jacobson was the one with overall supervisory responsibility for allocating those aircraft when we needed them to support the evacuation operations as well as other ongoing operations at the time.

The Bien Hoa evacuation was basically handled through Saigon because Bien Hoa was rather close to Saigon. At some point in the game--it was rather late [and] must have been around April 19--we had, in effect, closed down Bien Hoa consulate and moved into Saigon the people to be evacuated. We had them evacuated through the Saigon operation, which was already in progress at the time. The consul general was Dick Peters, and I do not recall exactly when we had Dick actually leave. But, we designated Dick to go to Guam to assist in Guam with the handling of the Vietnamese evacuees, many of whom we were temporarily parking in Guam. We didn't have any authority to move them to the United States.

It is important to note here that the ARVN and the Vietnamese governmental structure kept control of the delta right to the end. So the evacuation of Can Tho took place concurrently with the evacuation of the embassy in Saigon. They were given the word early on April 29 when we began execution of option four of "Frequent Winds" to complete their evacuation. We had previously thinned out the staff in Can Tho during the preceding weeks.

The remainder of the evacuation was carried out by sea with the remainder of the staff, Americans and Vietnamese, going down the Hau Giang River and out into the South China Sea where they were picked up by the navy. We had, of course, various categories of Vietnamese whose evacuation we wanted to support-in some cases were obligated to support. The principal categories were: our employees, people who had worked closely with us, people who were at very high risk if they were captured by the North Vietnamese, and the large numbers of Vietnamese who had established, with the many years of our involvement, some sort of relationship with Americans, either through marriage legalized by civil authority or clergy, or through common law relationships. The Vietnamese extended family system--which translates immediately into fathers, mothers, brothers, sisters, and cousins--created a massive potential problem of evacuating Vietnamese.

At the same time, we had a situation where our authority to formally admit people to the United States was extremely limited and subject to the normal consular procedures. We did not receive until April 25, three days before the final evacuation, formal authority to exceed those normal procedures and, in fact, to evacuate Vietnamese to the United States under the Attorney General's parole program. Yet we had these other problems on our hands.

On April 17, for example, we already evacuated all Vietnamese employees of the defense attaché system who were in sensitive jobs and who had to be gotten out. There were others in those categories. One of the main problems, of course, was where do you put some of these people that you had no authority for sending to the United States? Guam was, of course, a territory, and so Guam was used extensively as a temporary holding area while Washington sorted out some of the legal and political problems that were involved. Shortly after we began really evacuating large numbers of people, largely by C-130 from the military to Guam, it turned out that some of them wanted to come back because they had left their families behind.

Somewhat earlier, when we were still in Saigon those last remaining ten days or so, the guidance that we gave to our people in Guam was, "If any Vietnamese wanted to go back, make that a matter of record and back-load them on the empty C-130s that were going back to Vietnam to pick up more."

I think there were basically three factors in considering the final evacuation and the process of getting ready for the final evacuation. The first was that we had to avoid at all cost a repetition, on a much larger scale, of the kind of mob panic that we had in Da Nang, in more serious and much more complicated circumstances [in the Saigon area]. We were able in the end to extract all our people out of Da Nang including our Vietnamese employees because we were able to get them off on the ships, on the barges. We couldn't have done that in Saigon. We couldn't have gotten them on the ships down the Saigon River. In fact, we looked at that option in some detail. Hank [Henry] Boudreau, an administrative counselor, and I went over that possible option in considerable detail, including surveying an area in Newport in Saigon as a possible holding area right next to the port. We dismissed that one as not being practical. We had to avoid mass panic in the city of Saigon because a mass panic in the city would have made shambles out of the whole process. It would have made it impossible to do what we finally did when we put into effect option four of "Frequent Winds", which was the final helicopter airlift out of the city and nearby area.

Secondly and related to the first consideration was the fact that we had some intelligence indicating that there were at least some senior ARVN people who were seriously considering taking action to prevent us from evacuating, thus having us go down with them.   "If we're going to go down, you are going to go down with us."

Having this whole American experience in Vietnam end in some sort of a violent conflict between us and the South Vietnamese was, frankly, just too horrible a thing to contemplate. The most serious consideration was the possibility of things simply getting out of hand in Saigon.

The third consideration was a political one. We did want to keep open, as long as we possibly could, the option of retaining some sort of official presence in the area in the event there would be some sort of negotiated settlement. This was a possibility that would have served the North Vietnamese interests very well had they decided to go through with it. It would have set up tremendous pressures in the United States to make good on what they've always alleged were commitments that Nixon and Kissinger made to them for assistance to Vietnam.

On the first of April we activated the evacuation control center at the defense attaché compound, ostensibly at the time to monitor the refugee flow situation. However, it was with full recognition and with the intention of getting this facility ready to control the evacuation of Americans and Vietnamese in the end. We began to draw down people in the first two weeks of April by encouraging contractors to depart by sending out a number of dependents, family members, and some non-essential personnel under various pretexts. In fact, we began in a sense ordering the evacuation on about April 3 or 4. One of the things that was done--it was not the only one--was that we had the so called "orphan lift" beginning at that time. We designated large numbers of women and non-essential personnel as escorts for the orphans, far in excess of what was really needed. That was just a subterfuge to get them out. Of course, one of the great tragedies of that particular situation was that one of the very first flights crashed on April 4, 1975, with substantial casualties of both the orphans and the so-called escorts. It was a very sad thing and one of the saddest moments of my life.

With regard to official American personnel, I had already requested earlier in March two things from the Department. One was not to have any additional family members of people being transferred come into the country. You must remember that we had an American staff country-wide of all U. S. agencies of about 2,000 people. That was approved, and there was no trouble on that one. But the other authority asked for was for us in Saigon to determine who should go out immediately without further reference to Washington. I never got that. That apparently doesn't fit the bureaucratic system, but it was the kind of leeway that we needed.   In Washington they kept insisting they had to approve each thing, which was a nuisance, to put it mildly.

However, to get back to the main point. We used the subterfuges such as I've mentioned. We tried to encourage people to leave and reduce the number of Americans in the country. On April 15 our evacuee holding facility at the defense attaché compound went operational. As I mentioned earlier, on April 17 a number of sensitive local employees--most of those with intelligence agencies and related operations including the defense attaché--were evacuated. On April 21 we began round-the-clock C-141 and C-130 flights in and out of Tan Son Nhut going mostly to the Philippines and to some other destinations. Between April 4 and April 27 about 27,000 people were actually moved out of Vietnam. Most of these were moved by military flights to either Guam or the Philippines.

These were a mixture of Americans and Vietnamese, and this is an important point.   One of the greatest difficulties we had was the considerable reluctance of many Americans to leave, especially American contractor personnel. There were a lot of military retirees who had settled down with Vietnamese "families" over the years. All of these people were extremely reluctant to leave without their families. Now, in many cases these family relationships were not legally blessed. They were simply common law relationships, but still very strong. But, there was no legal authority under which we could evacuate or take these people into the United States. Moreover, the family relationships were extended ones because they not only involved the common-law wife and the common-law children but also the mother, the father, the brothers, the sisters, and often cousins. Nobody wanted to leave without the other. Yet, we had no way by which we had any authority to bring these people into the United States and, of course, none to bring them into the Philippines. This was the kind of problem we were faced with. When we're talking about an average family here, we're probably talking of a family of at least a dozen.

That was only part of the problem. The additional problem was that, while we wanted to send Americans out, Americans kept coming in, and there was no way to stop them. Americans kept coming in including, incidentally, some official Americans and some Foreign Service officers. They kept coming in and looking for their friends and acquaintances or their relations. In many of these cases they had Vietnamese wives, and now they were coming in because they wanted to do something to get their wives' parents, brothers, sisters, etc., out under some sort of expedited procedures. So we were having a situation where we were keeping track of the number of Americans in country, and we were moving out Americans, but the total number at any given day wouldn't really go down because others would come in. This was a situation which is probably of somewhat unparalleled difficulty. At least, I don't know a precedent for it. The Cambodian evacuation, I think, consisted of less than 400 people.

Most of the [third country nationals, Koreans, Filipinos, Japanese, etc.] were making arrangements for themselves. However, they were in very close touch with us daily during those last weeks. I had either DCMs or charges or ambassadors of the diplomatic missions contacting me wanting to know what our view was and getting our appraisal so that they could decide what they would do. The British moved out on their own at that time. So did the Australians as well as the Israelis, the Belgians, the Dutch and the Germans. They moved out on their own.

There were a few left that we took out with us on the last day including the Italian ambassador, a very fine fellow. We were good friends. We brought him out along with some U.N. [United Nations] people and nationals of a couple of other countries. The Japanese made a decision to remain although they cut their staff down very much. They remained, which turned out to be rather helpful. The Chinese--that's the Taiwan Chinese--left on their own. The Koreans left, and it was a problem because there were a number of South Koreans that were left in the country on April 29. We evacuated some of them. Unfortunately, a number of Koreans were in that very last batch of evacuees along with some Vietnamese that we had in the embassy compound when the [pipeline] was shut down, and they remained behind. That is something that made me feel very bad, but we were simply told that we had no more, and that was it. Eventually, that problem was solved with the help of the Japanese who had remained. The French remained. There were a number of problems [with Washington] that arose. Some were of lesser significance than others. One of the early problems was when, on March

25, I requested authority from Washington to move dependents to safe havens in Manila, Bangkok, and other places on our own authority as I saw fit in Saigon. Well, that was never granted. The Department insisted on bureaucratic review back in Washington. That kind of thing is not suitable to this sort of situation. However, we managed to live with it.

I suppose a more serious problem arose during the latter part of April because of tremendous pressures, political pressures in Washington for us to speed things up and to do things which we on the ground knew would have catastrophic results if we did them. Obviously, the Department and the rest of the executive branch was under considerable pressure from politicians up on the Hill and others. We felt that pressure, but we just simply had to resist it. Nevertheless, it was a rather serious problem.

A third problem, of course, was one I mentioned earlier regarding the evacuation of Vietnamese. We did not receive authority to move any Vietnamese under extraordinary procedures to the United States until April 25 or 26. Up until that time we were theoretically constrained to those who were eligible for visas which, of course, meant wives and children of American citizens, and that was all.

Another category of problems arose on a couple of occasions when there was a need for urgent action--really urgent action. The main problem that arose in that connection was when sometime in early or mid April--and I cannot remember when--the FAA [Federal Aviation Administration] regional office in Honolulu, without a word to anybody, suddenly declared Tan Son Nhut airport no longer safe for American commercial aircraft. This came just at a time when I was still heavily engaged in trying to hold Pan Am's feet to the fire to keep flying. It was also quite unjustified because, when it was done, the situation in the general area of the airfield had not changed from what it had been for a couple of years before. Apparently, the FAA decision was based on some questionable intelligence assessment which they received from PACAF [Pacific U. S. Air Force Command] in Honolulu. This was just the kind of thing, the moment it became public, that would set off a panic. If I had called the State Department a committee would have met the next morning and started discussing this. So I just simply bypassed it. I called the NSC [National Security Council] staff in the White House directly and demanded the recision within hours, and I got it. There were a couple of instances of that kind.

In connection with other agencies, I mentioned that Pan Am, fairly early in the game, wanted to discontinue their operations, and Hank Boudreau and I had to put a good deal of pressure on the airline to have them continue. I admit they had a real problem because they would be way overbooked on their daily flights out of Saigon. Then, when flight time came, there would be a lot of empty spaces because there were simply no shuttles, or people were booking seats on the airplane who didn't have the exit documentation.   Nevertheless, it was important to keep them flying.

I had a similar problem with Flying Tigers whom we also had to pressure to keep flying.   They did not respond and stopped when they decided they had to.   One last problem, not a significant one, that arose was with the Seventh Day Adventist Hospital.   That hospital provided basically medical support for the whole American community.   I was told at some point--I think it was again around mid April--that they wanted to pull out.   So I, along with Boudreau and Dr. Eben Dustin, who was our medical officer, went out to see the Seventh Day Adventists and persuaded them to remain.   That was very important to us because there was in the background, of course, always the possibility of casualties, and that was our medical support.   That problem was resolved satisfactorily.

After some exchanges of communications between ourselves and Washington, Ambassador Martin went to see Thieu on April 20.   The details of that conversation are recorded in the embassy cable traffic, and I don't know to what extent that traffic has been released.   However, in general I can say that what he told Thieu was that the decision as to what to do was, of course, entirely up to him.   But, if he should decide to resign, we would assist him and get him, his family, and a small number of his close assistants into a safe haven.   Thieu resigned on April 22, two days later announcing that resignation in a very bitter speech.   I do not blame him for being bitter, incidentally.   He had a right to be.   He resigned that day.   Two days later on April 24 we had arranged for a special U. S. aircraft at the airport to take him, his family and a few assistants to Taipei.

We began packing and sending out embassy files and records at the beginning of April or maybe it was even early March.   This was the kind of thing that we could do quietly.   Nobody would see that.   Things could be packed up in the [file] room and shipped out.   They were going all the way back to the United States.   We also, for example, had the bubble, the classified conference room, that had to be gotten out.   That's a rather large and unwieldy thing and, of course, that was a visible act.   Most people really don't know what it is when they see big pieces of plastic lying around in the courtyard; so that was sent out.   Whatever documents that were not sent out at the time or taken out by us individually in our briefcases towards the end were destroyed, including some during the night of April 29-30.   In any event, everything was either sent out or destroyed. Nothing fell into anybody's hands.   This was not a Tehran situation.   I get rather upset every once in a while when I read stories about the situation in Tehran having the greatest intelligence loss since the evacuation of the embassy in Saigon.   We didn't lose anything.

Also the same applies to the consulates general. They had either sent back or mostly destroyed all their files and records. That's true for all four of them.

There was a research reactor in Da Lat, the so-called Triga reactor, that had been part of the U.S. AID [Agency for International Development] program many years before. After Tet 1968, there was some nervousness in certain circles in Washington about the fuel elements of that reactor. I recall distinctly then when I was director of the Office of Atomic Energy the State Department was approached by the Atomic Energy Commission to get those fuel elements out. Ambassador Bunker quite correctly just ignored that nonsense. In any event, we did want to get the fuel out in April of 1975. Again, it was one of those things where we wanted to act in time but not before time.

For about a week before we finally decided--and I did--to move those fuel elements, there were a couple of special C-130 aircraft standing by at Clark Field in the Philippines with technicians and the equipment necessary to pull the fuel elements out of that small reactor. I finally permitted them to come in and go ahead with that. I believe it must have been around mid April. Then we did preserve the proper forms because I asked the Vietnamese government to give me a formal letter requesting that we remove the fuel elements. They did so. It was a slightly hectic operation. The NVA [North Vietnamese Army] was beginning to approach the area. This was in the highlands, of course. It took all night, but it was done and properly done.

Let's keep in mind that at this point we had been operating around the clock C-141 and C-130 flights from the airport since Monday, April 21. In the middle of that week and the latter part of that week a kind of a lull set in on the battlefield. There wasn't much by way of North Vietnamese offensive action. They were beginning to approach Saigon. It was shortly after that a rather tough battle at Xuan Loc where the ARVN [Army of the Republic of Vietnam] had really distinguished themselves and fought very well indeed. At that time there was, of course, some speculation as to the reason for that lull. There are two possibilities. One was that it reflected a political decision in Hanoi to have the whole business end in some form as an ostensible government of national reconciliation which they always said they had wanted. This would have been, of course, a complete farce. There was the idea of negotiating with Duong Van Minh who had replaced Thieu. He was, therefore, from their standpoint the ideal candidate with whom to negotiate this charade or farce.

The other possibility, of course, was that, having conducted extensive offensive operations, they simply had a logistical problem and needed to regroup and reorganize. There is still a third possibility--that it was a combination of both of those things. In any event, the first option I mentioned, if it was ever considered, was dismissed. In retrospect it is probable that the lull was due to a need to regroup, reorganize and look after their logistics.

However, none of this affected our evacuation operations which, as I said, continued. On Thursday I decided that the time had come for us to evacuate the last of the wives, who were simply the wives of senior officers, including my own, Hank Boudreau's wife, Marinka Bennett, the wife of the political counselor, and one other lady and two children which we still had. They were the children of the consular officer, Peter Orr, whom we had to retain because we needed him in our operation. I also had Mrs. Martin on that list, but her name was deleted by the ambassador. In order to do this we had the Army send in a U-21 from Thailand because we didn't want to have the departure of the senior wives noted out where most of the evacuation was taking place. We also needed to maintain the fiction that they were simply going to Bangkok for an extended weekend. That was done on Friday, April 25.

The lull, as I mentioned, did continue through Sunday, April 27. Early on Monday morning, April 28, it became quite clear that the North Vietnamese were actively resuming their offensive operations. At about six o'clock in the afternoon on Monday, April 28, a number of A-37 aircraft, obviously manned either by North Vietnamese or defecting South Vietnamese pilots, attacked the flight lines at the Tan Son Nhut airport.

At the time that occurred, I had just gone out of my office and gone out into the second courtyard of the embassy in the area where the swimming pool and the snack bar were located. This was an area where we were assembling evacuees to bus them to the airport. I was told there was a problem of a delay, and I had gone out to look into that just at the time that the air strike in Tan Son Nhut took place. Now, there have been some rather lurid accounts of that particular event. When the strike took place, it precipitated a certain amount of quite unnecessary rushing around and a bit of upset. I might note parenthetically here that, being a veteran of the Italian campaign of World War II including the Cassino Line, the Anzio beachhead and quite a few other events, I can differentiate between unfriendly high explosives coming down in your immediate vicinity, in which case you would have a very strong, direct personal interest, and something that is happening a mile or two away. In that case you can afford to take a detached professional interest in what is going on. This strike out at Tan Son Nhut, lurid descriptions in some books to the contrary, was in the latter category. It was quite a distance away. There was no immediate danger to the embassy or anybody in the embassy. This did not prevent our very solicitous, protective marines from immediately surrounding the minister with weapons drawn in order to protect him.

On April 15, sometime earlier, we had activated an evacuee holding facility out at the DAO [Defense Attaché Office] compound which is out at the airport. The system was that anybody being evacuated by fixed-wing aircraft--which, as I mentioned, were operating round the clock beginning April 21--would come out there or be bussed out there either from the embassy itself or from some other designated locations in town, notably staff housing areas. [The evacuation system] was continuing at that late date until the air strike on the flight line at Tan Son Nhut at six o'clock on Monday evening. That attack, in which at least one C-130 was destroyed, in effect ended the fixed-wing airlift. After we had rather quickly assessed the situation, and in the course of the next hour, a decision was made that it would be too risky to continue fixed-wing operations out of Tan Son Nhut because of the danger that we might lose an aircraft full of people.

The people that were out at the DAO compound remained there. The people that were in the embassy remained there for the time being. After we had made the decision to discontinue fixed-wing operations, the rest of the evening was taken up with reviewing the final plans for the increasing likelihood, but not yet a decision, that we would have to go to a helicopter evacuation--which is technically known as option four of "Frequent Winds"--the following day. That went on throughout the early evening. Shortly after midnight--the night from Monday to Tuesday morning--the ambassador decided that he and I should return to our residences and try to get some rest in view of the likelihood that a lot of major and crucial decisions had to be made the next day. I got back to my house between one o'clock and two o'clock in the morning. I tried to get some sleep.

It is important for all concerned to get some sort of rest. Otherwise, they become useless. With regard to most of the staff, we had earlier worked out a shift system. Because we had designated certain elements of the mission to worry about various categories of potential evacuees--the defense attaché to worry about the Vietnamese military, the political section to worry about politicians, and other people to worry about relatives of Americans, etc. These things had gone on a shift basis somewhat earlier so that nobody would work more than about twelve hours or so. That was the attempt that was made. For the absolute senior staff, it was on a more irregular basis. You got what rest you could whenever you could.

The helicopter evacuation plan called for some of the helicopters to land on the roof helipad and others--notably the rather heavy CA-53s that the roof pad could not support--to land in the courtyard of the embassy where this famous, beautiful banyan tree was located. It always was obvious that, when push came to shove, the tree would have to come down. One of the problems here, however, was that the tree was not only large but it was also very visible from the street. The streets were getting increasingly crowded as panic was beginning slowly to develop in the city of Saigon. The removal of the tree would be a visible act that would undoubtedly spread like wild-fire throughout the city.

As I was returning from the outer courtyard, surrounded by my solicitous marines, to go back to my office to assess the situation and try to find out just what had happened out at Tan Son Nhut, I was passing the tree. As I was passing the tree, one of our Seabees [U.S. Navy engineers] was vigorously but somewhat ineffectually chopping away at the tree with an axe in what was quite clearly a self-initiated attempt to clear the area for use as a helicopter landing zone. As I entered the embassy chancery building, I called the security officer to have the Seabee cease and desist promptly from the rather ineffectual and somewhat premature efforts, and to bring in some power tools such as chain saws, etc., have them ready, but not to take any action regarding the tree until instructed and until the time was right. I then forgot about the tree and turned to other things. As a matter of fact, I'm not sure that Graham Martin ever knew anything about the tree.

I didn't really get any sleep. I got to bed between one and two and dozed off for a while. At about 4:15 A.M. I was roused from my dozing by a series of explosions out in the direction of the Tan Son Nhut airfield and the defense attaché compound. About ten minutes later, at about 4:30 A.M., the phone rang and the report--I don't recall now whether it was directly from the defense attaché or from an officer at the embassy chancery--was that there had been a rocket attack on the DAO compound and that two of the embassy marine security guards out there had been killed.

That, of course, ended the rest period. I got up, showered, went down, and my majordomo, my butler, gave me some breakfast. I packed some extra underwear, an extra pair of socks and a couple of little things in my briefcase. I had a last conversation with my butler who had previously told me that he wanted to remain. He was an elderly man. I made some final arrangements with him to get some money to him in addition to money he had already been given--that's dollars, not piasters. After having a little breakfast, I went back to the chancery. Ambassador Martin arrived from his residence just a little bit later on. We jointly began to review the situation, getting reports from General Smith out at Tan Son Nhut as to the details of the rocket attack, which continued intermittently throughout the area.

Other facilities were also being spotted, but it was the first time at a little after four that morning that an attack appeared to be targeted specifically on an American installation. The cause of the death of the two marines was a direct hit on the sandbag emplacement where they were. Ambassador Martin decided to go out to Tan Son Nhut and review the situation personally with General Smith. While out there, he had a telephone conversation with General Scowcroft back in Washington which, however, did not result as yet in a definite conclusion on whether or not we would continue fixed-wing airlift rather than go to option four of the evacuation plan.

Ambassador Martin then returned to the embassy.   Meanwhile, it became very clear that damage to runways at the airfield and other things made it quite impossible to continue a fixed-wing airlift.   Ambassador Martin then got on the telephone again, this time from the chancery, with General Scowcroft. A decision to go to option four of "Frequent Winds", the helicopter airlift, was made between 10:30 and 10:40 on Tuesday morning.

We were using Air America, that is, our own helicopters, first in the morning to move people from the assembly areas either to the embassy or to the DAO holding facilities out at the airfield. Later on we were using the Air America helicopters to move evacuees directly out to the fleet. The plan called for the marine ground security force to arrive at the DAO compound at Tan Son Nhut--which had priority on the evacuation under our plan--one hour after the option four execute order was given.   To illustrate that plans would go wrong, the ground security force arrived three hours later and not one hour later.   The first helicopter evacuees using fleet and Marine Corps helicopters were lifted out on the same choppers that brought in the security force.

This was between one and two in the afternoon.   That delay cost us something at the end of the whole operation. I found out much later that the reason for that delay was that there had to be some cross-loading out at the fleet because some of the marines who were supposed to come in to secure both the DAO compound and the embassy compound were not on the same ships as the helicopters.   They had to move people around. By early or mid-afternoon, the embassy was surrounded by masses of people--mobs. The security situation became increasingly risky. It was only with some difficulty that we managed to get into the compound some people for whose evacuation we had really special responsibilities--for example, Tran Quoc Buu, the leader of the Vietnamese Labor Federation, and his people; Buu Vien, the minister of the interior and Tran Van Lam, the former foreign minister who had signed the Paris agreement. Nonetheless, all this was accomplished, but the security situation was really getting touchy. I, therefore, called the general who was out at the DAO compound and told him that we urgently needed about a platoon of additional Marines in addition to our embassy guards in the compound in order to maintain the security. These arrived about an hour later.

I was not in Ambassador Martin's office when he had the conversation with Washington which resulted in the decision to execute the helicopter lift, but several of the other senior staff people were. I was busy in my own office doing various other things on the telephone. After the decision was made, Hank Boudreau walked over into my office, told me the decision was made, and I went back to see Graham Martin to have it confirmed to me directly. I then walked out and told the security officer now to chop down that tree. The tree was chopped down long before anybody was ready to arrive by helicopter in the embassy courtyard. Timing was, indeed, quite adequate.

By the time we're talking about, all Americans still in the area were either at the DAO compound or in the embassy compound. A little bit earlier some of the last ones, including some journalists, had arrived at the compound and gotten through into the compound, but only with some difficulty in getting through the crowds. I should be quite accurate here. All those who wanted to leave--there was one fellow, a contractor who turned out later on somehow not to get the word. It was his own fault. He was left behind. Then, of course, there were a couple of journalists who stayed on deliberately.

The priority was evacuation from the DAO compound at Tan Son Nhut. So most of the initial lift by helicopter went out of the DAO compound. That operation was completed by 8:00 in the evening on Tuesday. On its completion, General Smith and the few remaining DAO staff left a few minutes after eight that evening. That ended that phase of the operation. Up until that time, we had relatively little lift out of the embassy compound. It is correct, of course, that that lift--which was really only beginning in the mid-afternoon out of the embassy compound--did involve the lighter helicopters, the CH-46s--from the roof. The heavy ones, the CH-53s, were from the courtyard where the famous banyan tree had been. We were putting as many as 70 people into a CH-53, which was overloading it somewhat. Since many of them were Vietnamese, they were rather small.

All these poor people were desperately trying to do was to get into the compound with the hope that somehow they might be taken out. There was an occasional shot fired from outside the compound, but we could not really determine whether that was directed at an incoming helicopter or not. In any event, it did not in any way interfere with the operation. At this point, we did have enough marines to secure both the inner and the outer embassy compound, although occasionally someone might have slipped in who shouldn't have. It did not affect anything.

In the course of the evening--and I can't remember exactly when it was, but I suspect it was around 8:30 or 9:00 in the evening--the military suggested that we suspend further helicopter operations for the time being and resume them at first light the next morning. The ambassador and I vetoed that very promptly and insisted that we would have to continue the operation throughout the night. That insistence was based both on what the intelligence [sources] were still able to gather about the North Vietnamese--and there were some that were still available to us--and on a judgment that the situation around the embassy, even with the larger Marine detachment, was becoming increasingly untenable.

At that point we may have had somewhere between 1,000 and 1,500 people in the compound, both American and Vietnamese, with a heavy preponderance of Vietnamese.   During the night, therefore, the lift continued, although at times there would be long intervals which, in our view were excessive, between arriving helicopters from the fleet.   I understand, and I think we understood then, that there were deep problems of refueling, fatigue of the crews, etc. Yet it was clear that the operation definitely had to continue and could not be stopped and resumed the next morning. They could see their way in. The situation in the courtyard was dealt with by having embassy cars parked around the perimeter of the courtyard with the headlights on. That illuminated the courtyard situation, which was a tricky thing for the pilots. It was very tricky because of walls and antennas and other things nearby that they had to get over before they could clear the courtyard with their heavy loads.

One of the things that became a matter of some concern is that sometime during the time around midnight or a little bit later it began to rain very lightly. Remember, we were now in April and at the beginning of the monsoon. The mere fact of water on the hulls of the helicopters added to their weight. So we had one very critical moment where a pilot with a load full of people tried to lift out of the courtyard and could not get enough altitude. He had to put back down, and they had to unload some people before he could get out. They did not want to get off. So that was a moment of great concern because, if we had an accident in the courtyard with a broken helicopter, that would have finished the lift out of the courtyard, and we would have had to rely entirely on the smaller choppers coming in on the roof.

As I said, we could put as many as 70 people in the CH-53s, and I think the maximum number of CH-46s might have been about 40. Close to two-to-one difference. At the same time, we were also destroying a few last documents by burning up on the rooftop.

There was no panic among any of the people. We had people waiting in the courtyard. We had people waiting in the stairwell of the chancery building to go up to the rooftop, but there was no panic. At one point, when we had reduced the number still waiting to a more manageable proportion, we abandoned the outer embassy courtyard--the area where the swimming pool, the snack bar and the administrative section was--and removed everybody into the inner courtyard, which gave us also a smaller perimeter to protect against the crowd outside.

As to priorities, well, you know, your priorities as far as we were concerned--the first obligations, of course, were to Americans. Certainly, the second was to any high-risk Vietnamese, to our employees. But we did not have a priority question as such arise. The small group that in the end was left behind, largely because the entire lift operation began about two to three hours later than it should have, was a mix of Vietnamese and Koreans.

At about four o'clock in the morning, the ambassador and I went to the remaining communications set-up, the last one.   We sent our final message.   The date-time group of that message was 291215 Zulu which, of course, is Greenwich time.   The message said, "Plan to close mission about 0430, 30 April local time.   Due to necessity destroying commo [communications] gear.   This is the last message from Embassy Saigon."

After that message was sent, the communicator disabled the communications set-up.   He got in line to leave.   We were not, however, out of communications because we still had a link all the way back to Washington through a radio of a marine with the marine security force and the major commanding that force.   After we sent the message, there was really nothing much else for us to do.   We waited while the operation was continuing to try to get as many people out of the courtyard as possible.   At some time a little later--it might have been around 4:30--a very peremptory message did come through direct from the White House where they were monitoring the situation directing the ambassador and the remaining staff to leave by the next helicopter.   We considered that for a while and let the operation continue for a while longer.   Finally, after some consultation between myself and the marine major, we decided that the time had come for the ambassador and the rest of us to leave. Initially, through an error we all went downstairs rather than upstairs because we thought we were going to leave on one of the bigger helicopters.   But, that was not to be.   The ambassador and remaining staff trooped on up to the rooftop where one CH-46 was just landing and another one was hovering not far away.   As the CH-46 landed, Ambassador Martin along with George Jacobson, Tom Bolgar and a few others started walking towards the helicopter.   Some of the rest of us began to follow, but that crew chief knew when he had his man.   He waved the rest of us back, and the helicopter took off.   It had some other people on it.   It had some remaining mission warden guards on it who helped the control of all of this and a few other people, but it was not entirely full.   Shortly thereafter, the next CH-46 put down on the rooftop, and the rest of us--which included Hank Boudreau, John Bennett, Bronson McKinley, Jim Devine, Jay Blowers and the last mission warden guards boarded that helicopter which became really very jammed and crowded. We stayed up on the rooftop for about twenty to twenty-five minutes because the marine major, who was doing a very competent job of running things out in the courtyard, was using the helicopter's radio to firm up his final plans for extracting the marine detachment which was the final step, of course.   So we sat there for about twenty minutes while he was working that out over the radio.   We lifted off according to my records at 5:20 in the morning.   As we were leaving the Saigon area, I could look out the helicopter and I could see the approaching North Vietnamese columns with their headlights out and beginning to enter the outskirts of the city. Our exit was covered by armed aircraft from the fleet. That had been the case throughout.

There was no interference. There was no attempt to interfere. I think that was probably intentional. It took about 45 minutes to get out to the fleet. Our helicopter landed on the *Denver*, which was an LPD, a landing platform dock. It had marines on it and assault boats and helicopters. The ambassador and those with him, meanwhile, had gone out to the *Blue Ridge*, so we were separated at this point. Arriving at the *Denver* the first thing that the navy made sure of was that nobody had any weapons on them. I was deprived of one little mace thing that I had with me. I think Boudreau was deprived of a revolver he had which I'm not sure he ever recovered. Except for that, they were very solicitous and gave us a lot of food to eat. They gave us an initially rather crowded place to sleep, but that was sorted out later on.

The fleet stayed out. After the evacuation was completed--the marines, incidentally, were extracted from the compound by about seven o'clock in the morning or a little bit before, perhaps, moving up through the building gradually and abandoning the courtyard which was immediately taken over by the crowds. They took away typewriters and anything else they could find.

There were no incidents [in the marine departure], and there were no casualties of any kind throughout except the two marines that were killed early on in the day by that direct hit.

The fleet did not move out. The fleet remained on station, anchored out in the South China Sea about 25 miles offshore or something like that for a number of days. They picked up additional people--Vietnamese coming out on boats and barges. All told, about another 60,000 people came out on boats and barges while the fleet stayed out there. They were mostly put on some MSTS transports that were with the fleet. I have forgotten just how long we stayed out there, but I think it was about three or four days before we sailed into Subic Bay.

13

Nicaragua, 1979:
Somoza Out, Sandinistas In

Nicaragua has occupied a peculiarly important place in our attentions during this century. United States Marines landed there in times past in response to real or imagined challenges to our national interests. We have encouraged amenable political factions and supported two generations of Somozas as virtual dictators of Nicaragua. In 1978 the assassination of a newspaper editor set off an explosion of violence, which Somoza was unable to crush. He became politically isolated, and the country was thrown into turmoil.

LAWRENCE A. PEZZULO was ambassador to Uruguay when the situation in Nicaragua approached crisis proportions. He was recalled to Washington to be part of a working group trying to come up with a solution. In July 1979 he was appointed United States ambassador to Nicaragua. Following is Ambassador Pezzulo's account.

Pezzulo: In early 1978 one of Nicaragua's major editors, Pedro Jaquin Chamorro [whose widow later was elected President of Nicaragua], was shot down in the streets. Even though I don't think Somoza was responsible for this, the country went up in flames. Suddenly Somoza's position, which had slowly been deteriorating over a long period of time, became untenable. He over-reacted, brusquely using the National Guard to attack towns, firebombing and the like.

After a particularly brutal attack by the National Guard in the town of Esteli, the OAS [Organization of American States] called a special session and passed a resolution which led to the naming of a three-member commission consisting of representatives from the United States,

Guatemala, and the Dominican Republic to go to Nicaragua to see if they could help in some way to bring about an end to the hostilities.

When they got there they found that the Nicaraguans were completely polarized: Somoza with a few cronies and the national guard were on one side; and everyone else, right, left, and center in opposition. That realization came to them very quickly, because the three delegations had spread out over the country and had spoken with all sectors--newspaper editors, politicians, church leaders, campesinos, everyone. They received a repetition of the same message: "We've had enough. We've had enough." That led to a period in which the OAS mediators were dealing with Somoza on the one hand and with the multi-partied opposition on the other to see if there was some way to resolve the conflict. The opposition ultimately organized itself into a national front, a coordinated front, and demanded that Somoza leave, after which they would form a transitional government which would lead to general elections.

Negotiations went on for about three and a half months. They were ultimately thwarted by Somoza and collapsed. When they collapsed, Pete Vaky and Bill Bowdler from the State Department, who had put a tremendous amount of effort into it, were exhausted. They had been fighting back and forth with the NSC [National Security Council] and the White House, because they thought more pressure should be put on Somoza by the United States. They felt that if Somoza would leave the presidency there was a chance for a peaceful transition to some kind of democratic government.

It failed and we [the U.S.] withdrew from the scene a bit. When the mediation effort failed, the Sandinistas, who were divided into three divisions or factions, came together into one faction, with the aid and assistance of Fidel Castro. In fact, they went to Cuba and signed a unity pact. The Sandinistas then began planning the armed overthrow of Somoza, with the assistance of Cuba, Venezuela, Costa Rica, and Panama. I think it's fair to say that we in the United States, the State Department and the intelligence services, were just not watching carefully enough. While everybody knew something was amiss, the antennas were not all that attuned. The Sandinistas were now building up for a major military campaign against Somoza. I don't think that was generally known. In fact, I was called back [from Uruguay] in early May 1979 to attend a meeting in Costa Rica to discuss Central American policy. It was a three-day meeting to look at Central America, because Central America was clearly in crisis. The report on Nicaragua basically focused on how we would convince Somoza to step down at the end of his term in 1981. There was not a whisper about impending civil war. Nobody was talking about imminent attack.

One of the interesting things is that in this meeting we had in San José in May, I asked what we were doing with this leftist group. The

Sandinistas by then had a name; before then they weren't called the Sandinistas, it was just sort of a melange of different leftist groups. I was told that we had no contacts. We had never talked to them, which just shocked the pants off of me. I said, "I can't believe this. You tell me we're not talking to these people."

By the first week in June the war was on; we had a civil war. I mean, they were starting to topple cities. Furthermore, our ambassador to Nicaragua, a political appointee, had picked up and left Nicaragua in the spring without authority or so much as by your leave. So we had no ambassador, and the embassy staff was inexperienced. There was no reporting or analysis coming out of Managua. A civil war was going on but no ambassador, and an embassy which wasn't functioning.

I got a call one day [while in Uruguay] and was told, "We'd like you to go to Nicaragua." I agreed and left shortly thereafter, going first to Washington for meetings. Over the next three weeks we were meeting almost daily, either at the NSC, or elsewhere. What we put together was basically a policy that said, given the circumstances, the only thing the U.S can do now is try to hasten the departure of Somoza and to end the war. We thought that if we could end the conflict, and we were probably the only nation who could do that, we could get some political momentum to bring about a transition that was somewhat democratic, or at least participatory. I don't think anybody had great high hopes, however, because in the middle of a civil war it's hard to figure out what's going to come after.

When I arrived in Nicaragua I couldn't land in the city--I couldn't land at the airport because it was cut off from the city. The Sandinistas were in between. So I flew in on a small airplane that dropped me off at a landing strip on the coast. They picked me up in a car and drove me up to the capital. Then the siege ended because the Sandinistas had really put themselves in a very exposed position, so they retreated one evening to the city of Masaya. Yet there was constant firing and shooting. The major battles were out, away from the city, although there was a constant closing in on the city. You felt as if you were in this little enclave, which was not going to hold too long; and that if you were going to strike a deal and get this thing done you had better get on with it.

It becomes a fascination with people who are analyzing things to death [in Washington] while events are changing quickly on the ground. Here I was dealing with the war, and I kept getting commentary from Washington from people who were sitting up there dreaming up new schemes. One of the crackpot ideas--it's crackpot in hindsight--was that we could suddenly construct a transitional government of "wise men." It borrowed from a concept considered eight months earlier during the mediation effort. Simply put, we would approach people who had already been identified as leaders in the community, all of whom were in hiding, and some of them had left the country--and propose to them that they form this group of "wise men." Well, the problem was they didn't trust the U.S. government anymore. They had exposed themselves eight months before, when suddenly--when the moment of truth came, to get Somoza out, we couldn't deliver. They weren't about to expose themselves again in the middle of a civil war.

But in Washington's mind, especially the NSC, it was doable. It was Brzezinski and some of the people around him. I think people were groping for straws. They were hoping to come up with some sort of miracle in the middle of a very nasty situation. What I was concerned with, as the situation started to deteriorate and the war came closer and closer into Managua, was that if we failed to remove Somoza, after all this chipping away, we'd end up with nothing. The only thing we had to deliver, and I kept saying this in various forums, was Somoza. And if we failed to get him out and stop the bloodshed, then we had nothing.

The other idea, which I thought more possible was to preserve some elements of the National Guard so that you would have a transition with some members of a security force who were disciplined and capable of retaining some balance. Now again, in hindsight, that was illusory. What made it impossible was Somoza himself. I really miscalculated how frightened he was. I think what happened at the end proves that he thought that the national guard would kill him. Unfortunately, I couldn't get to the guard directly, and my military attaché couldn't get to them either, because they were fighting a war.

I talked to a lot of people. I met most of these wise men. They were squirreled away around the city, and we'd go out and find them. I spoke to the archbishop [Obando y Bravo] as much as I could. In fact, the two of us were caught in the middle of a fire-fight. I was talking to him and they started a fire-fight around us, and we had to break off our discussion. He was then an archbishop. He became a cardinal, I guess, about four years ago. I had known him before, and he was one of the first people I called on. A very nice gentleman. He's gotten harder as time has gone on, because life has become difficult for him. But he's a sage old gentleman, who watches, and listens, and was very, very critical of Somoza for a long time. So I conferred with him just to get a sense of what he saw happening. And I told him what we were doing; I wanted him to know. I said, "This is what I'm doing, and I want you to understand if there's any question in your mind. This is the route we're on."

He said, "Well, that's a fine route. Try to get this war ended. This country is bleeding to death. And anything I can do I'll be glad to do." He was working hard eight months before, during the mediation effort. He was trying to do everything possible to get the mediation to succeed. He saw it for what it was--the last really peaceful chance to end that conflict.

And I met with other politicians. I met with the few diplomats that remained; there weren't many left, because it was a war zone. But we'd meet for lunch, or we'd meet one another in the office. It was not the kind of place you could go out and wander around in. They had curfew from five o'clock in the evening, until, I think it was eight o'clock the next morning. So you were buttoned up in the evening. It was very restricted.

I'd met Somoza years before, during the earthquake in 1972. The first one [meeting with Somoza during the Civil War] was "one on one"; I figured that I owed it to him, just from a courtesy point of view, to make it "one on one." So I went in alone. And that's when he had Congressman Murphy [from Staten Island, New York] with him, and his foreign minister. In fact, Somoza remarked, "You're alone?" I replied, "I thought that would be a courtesy to extend to you, if you wanted to speak to me alone." After that I was accompanied by a team. Usually I brought somebody with me from Washington, and then later I had a DCM [Deputy Chief of Mission] who was with me--a new DCM. So it was usually myself, a DCM, and another advisor; there'd be three on our side, and he'd have anywhere from three to six. It varied.

They were very business-like meetings. We knew he was taping them, by the way. But he would go through these rhetorical diversions every once in a while. I guess it was time for him to make his speech--and he'd go through a long speech about how much he liked the United States. He'd say, "I'm a Latin from Manhattan." He spoke beautiful English and knew the United States better than I did. He'd been every place. And I think he honestly liked the United States of America. There's no question in my mind. He was a very charming rascal.

So he'd regale with stories of how he'd helped the United States here, there, and the other place. He'd done our business for us. How could we be doing this to him? And the Communists were going to come in, and so on. He went on, and on, and on. He would belabor people in the Carter administration, whom he really had a burn against--and Carter himself. So you had to listen to all of this because this was all for the tape.

Somoza, you have to keep in mind, was really wired into our system in a way that's hard to understand. He had very good intelligence on what we were doing at the highest levels. For that reason a lot of people were very intimidated by Somoza, because he could pull levers. In fact, one day, it was about our third or fourth conversation, he called Washington and tried to open a dialogue there. He was told, "You've got our man. You talk to Pezzulo." Washington called me and said, "We just wanted you to know that." And the next time I walked in Somoza said, "Hey, you've got a lot of power, haven't you?" He said, "They told me from Washington I've got to deal with you." He always had had somebody in Washington he could appeal to, and then he could play with our ambassador.

But then he'd get down to the business at hand and talk about various things. My concerns were the timing of his departure; and this national guard issue--setting it up and getting the right commander, and part of the time, waiting for Washington to agree that we had to start the countdown. I was trying to push the countdown--the 72-hour countdown.

Managua at night was like a battlefield--firing, and so on. Then you just had the sense of this thing closing in on you. We were getting constant reports on how much ammunition the guard had left. Somoza was making excursions--or trips out--for resupplies.

We had cut off supply to the guard. We had stopped some supplies that were coming from Israel. We stopped them on the high seas--diverted the ships. We were telling his former suppliers in Central America, Guatemala and others, to cut it off. They did. So his materiel was slowly running down. We knew that. We also knew the opposition forces were building up. So you could just sense a closing in. There was no way of knowing when it would break; so you tended to want to get the darn scenario in place.

What struck me then was how--and I think it's true, the field tends to have a different view of the world from Washington. It's just a natural reality. You're sitting in one place, and they're sitting in another. Also, I think there was a lot of lyricism on the part of Washington as to what you could do under the circumstances. Maybe it's natural, when you're sitting up at Washington, you figure you have more options than you really have. I didn't see the options, and I kept saying, "I don't see these options--not now." These things are not going to be realizable, except for the National Guard, which we went down the line with. And then it folded in on us.

I was discussing the future of the guard only with Somoza and his son. The planning was being done in a vacuum, to the extent that the officers in the guard were not involved. I finally worked out a scenario with Somoza in which he would step down under his own constitutional processes so there was no interruption in that and turn over power to a member of the congress, who would then invite in the junta in San José, who would begin deliberating on the transfer of power. The new head of the national guard, who would have to be named, would do the same with the Sandinista forces. And there would be a cease-fire and stand-down, and the initiation of discussions about merging forces.

The problem, we know in hindsight, was that Somoza never relayed this honestly to his own guard, because he was afraid that if he did--if they ever thought he was leaving Nicaragua and was unable to deliver what he ultimately promised them [that the United States was going to come in-- once he got out--to support them]--they would kill him. And that's what frustrated this entire play. What happened was that Somoza left. We didn't come in to the support of the guard, because we'd never promised that, but the guard, deceived by Somoza, didn't know that. They suddenly found themselves without Somoza, and without U.S. assistance, and they broke down. They collapsed. Within twenty-four hours they were gone; they had all run up to Honduras, or to other places.

It turned out that a lot of the people that we had been dealing with before were closet Sandinistas, but we didn't know that. We didn't have our ear to the ground. That embassy, I think, was a failure. I don't know why, but we never considered Nicaragua a very important country.

I think one of the unfortunate things in all of this is that there were times when people talk about possibilities, and options. You start talking and throwing out ideas. There were some people who said a few things about the possibility of a U.S. input of troops under certain circumstances. And I remember [Secretary of State] Vance, at the time, got furious. He said, "I don't want to hear that. That's something the United States is not going to do. That situation does not warrant it." I think somebody, somewhere said, "Look, as a contingency, can somebody just do . . ." You know how these things are--"Can you do sort of a contingency plan, if in case . . ." That, I think, would have become known, and I think a guy like Anastasio Somoza would have found out about it. I think he thought that at the eleventh hour [we would step in and help him]--he kept saying it in different ways: "Are you people really prepared to do this?" I think he thought when it came to the crunch we couldn't face the possibility of losing him and his regime, and we would bring in troops.

You see, he was a West Point graduate. He was very close to a lot of military officers and he cultivated them. It is altogether possible that somebody was available to tell him that kind of thing. "Look, Tacho, I just want you to know that these plans are in place." And that would have been enough to convince him that if push came to shove, the United States was going to take some military action, that he had friends up there who would take care of him.

He'd lived through scrapes before. Don't forget, this man had grown up as the son of a dictator. There were ups and downs. There were administrations that were more critical than others. He was right in saying he'd always been a friend. During the Bay of Pigs, where did we launch aircraft from? From Nicaragua. Where did we train? Nicaragua. He'd been a friend in need; he'd carried our water. You couldn't deny that. He felt that he was America's friend, and to some extent he was perfectly right. So why not, in this hour of need, have some people push these crazy guys in the administration who didn't understand his value, to come ultimately to his rescue?

So he left. There was no option. He had no supplies.

What happened was cities and towns just rose up and went after the guard. Little kids, mothers and daughters, etc. Pretty soon the guard was caught in their barracks. Where the guard met the Sandinistas as a military force, they beat them. They did it in the southern zone, where there was really a set-piece battle.

So he was facing the most impossible of circumstances. The populace had really risen up against him, and were aiding and abetting these young people. So there were a lot of illusions here. I mean, the illusion indulged in by the Sandinistas is that they won a military victory, which was not true. The Nicaraguan people rose up against their leader and threw him out, and they happened to be--they, the Sandinistas--the armed vanguard of that. But they never overthrew Somoza. They alone would never have done it. It was the Nicaraguan people who overthrew Somoza.

I went back twice to Washington. The first time was because one of these ideas about forming this wise men's group had reached the point where people thought that it should be considered again. And I went back to tell them it's no go--this thing is not going to fly, and to forget it. So that was one crucial point.

Then there was another meeting, shortly thereafter. I found it, again, to be sort of a nothing discussion. It was for the purpose of discussing the enlarging of the junta, from the five that they had begun with, to a larger number, to include more moderates. And again, I felt that this was a marginal issue of no great consequence, because the key was going to be that the people with the guns were going to have the power, and whether you now had five people in the junta, or seven people, or all moderates, or all leftists--you know, I didn't see that this was a major issue. But again, there was a sense of a great urgency about this.

There was a long discussion, and Carter then addressed it to Torrijos, who had come in to meet on this particular issue. Torrijos, the president, the dictator from Panama, who had been in and out of this issue all along conferring with us, doing some of the negotiating and some of the helpful work, at the same time that he was supporting the Sandinistas with military assistance.

What happened is that while some of us were not all that hot on it we did recommend the idea of enlarging the junta to Carter, who recommended it to Torrijos. Torrijos raised it with the Sandinistas, and they turned it down. He told them that it was an American plan. So the whole thing was a bust. In the meantime we had put together, basically, the scenario for Somoza's leaving. And the scenario was, fundamentally, that he would turn over power, constitutionally, to a senator. He selected a fellow named Urcuyo, who was an unknown sort of hanger-on, of no great consequence.   But Urcuyo, then, was to go through the process that we had laid out. He was to invite the junta from San José to come to Managua. The junta was going to come in, accompanied by the archbishop of Managua, as well as members of the international community. They were going to include Ambassador Bowdler, the foreign ministers of Venezuela, the Dominican Republic, and Costa Rica, and others.

The idea was to have a goodly number of people present from the international community, to make it a moment in history. At that point there would be a press conference at the airport, where they would discuss the process of transition to take place over the next several days and where Urcuyo would hand over power to this transitional government--the junta in San José. Then they would follow through on the promises they had made to the OAS, that they would assume power and then call for early elections, which they of course failed to do. In the meantime, the military commanders would meet, and talk about stand-down, merging the forces, and so on.

This was explained to Somoza in a very detailed way. By this time the new guard commander had been selected by us, with Somoza's concurrence, and the concurrence of the Sandinistas, through the junta in San José. The new guard commander was a lieutenant colonel, unknown to anybody--a fellow named Mejia. All the guard officers who were tainted by Somoza, which included most of the lieutenant colonels and colonels, were retired in one official act, and Mejia was made commander of the National Guard. So that was taken care of.

While we were talking about this with Somoza, Bowdler was talking to the junta in San Jose. So everything we did, everything I negotiated with Somoza, the junta was party to, even to the naming of the new National Guard commander.

So Urcuyo was to take charge of the country. He was then to invite the junta from San José, and a whole series of things were to happen. Somoza left at three o'clock in the morning, the morning of July 17. Before that he had had the ceremony in which he had passed the baton to Urcuyo. Urcuyo, then, was supposed to do a series of things. By about six o'clock in the morning we saw the thing unravelling. I got to him (Urcuyo). We had been through two meetings where we went through every one of these issues. He claimed to be ignorant of all these things, and said, "I don't understand this. I'm the president of Nicaragua."

It was then that I told Washington that Somoza had backed away from the agreement. This triggered the call from [Under Secretary of State] Christopher to Somoza in Miami. Somoza quickly chartered two yachts and got out of the United States. But he had clearly given Urcuyo the other message, that he was to stay on, not let the Communists come in, and goodness knows what.

My theory is that Somoza was afraid that if he ever went to the guard and said he was leaving, and they were going to turn over power to the Sandinistas, they would have killed him. And he lied to Urcuyo. Now, Urcuyo (too) was just a plain liar, because he sat in on two meetings when I explained the scenario step by step to him, and then I had my DCM,

Tom O'Donnell, go over to his hotel, and go through it with him again, minutely. And he was just a plain, bald-faced liar. Mejia was duped. I went to tell him that very day. Then I went up to see the president (Urcuyo) with him, and we had a pretty stormy session. This was the second meeting. He denied all of this, and said he was insulted, that I was telling him what to do, and all this kind of nonsense. By this time I think Mejia was starting to smell a rat, plus the national guard was starting to collapse. I told Urcuyo. "My friend, you're going to be a president without a country. What are you talking about? This thing will not hold. It will only hold under the scenario we set up. That's all agreed--with the Sandinistas, with everybody. You can't do this."

So it began to collapse. A day later he ran out of the country. Then because it was collapsing, I made the recommendation to Washington that I be pulled out right away, with some part of the embassy, accompanied by a public statement criticizing Somoza for having broken the pact. If we didn't do that it would look as if this was our plan all along. They agreed, and I left on the morning of the 18th.

Tom O'Donnell, then, was left to hold this little group together. He met with Mejia--by this time Urcuyo had fled the country--Mejia said, "Can I meet with Umberto Ortega [the head of the Sandinista armed forces] to see if we can work this out?" But it was too late, and Mejia had nothing to deal with; he had no armed forces left. His air force had run away, his infantry had run out to Honduras, and the poor devil was stuck. So he eventually got on a plane and flew to Guatemala. It was over. The National Guard had disappeared. Then the Sandinistas just drove into the country and up to the capital on the 17th and took over.

What was portrayed in the press was exactly what people were saying. "Who are these? Aren't they Communists? How do we deal with them?" In fact, when I came back to Washington shortly after the fall of Somoza, they put me downstairs with the spokesman. The first question was, "Are these people Communists?" And the position we were taking at the time was, "Look, we don't want to prejudge something like this. Let their actions speak for what they are. These people have gone through a terribly painful period. The Nicaraguan people have suffered. And we're going to take them at their word, that they're going to put a democratic administration into being. Yet during this period of need we're going to be as helpful as we can. We're not going to be driven to make judgments about it."

So I kept the tough issues to a very bilateral kind of thing. In public we were supportive, and we were trying our best to give whatever assistance was needed. They responded, I thought, quite well, given what they thought we were, and suddenly finding themselves in a governing role. They were--and Nicaraguans in general--are very gracious people; they happen to be that kind of people. So you can meet with them, and the conversations will always be at least civilized.   Even though they got heated, they were civilized.   And they really respected the fact that we had done some of the things we did; they respected that.   But they resented, very much, our long-term support of Somoza, and so on.   So you'd have to go through that.

And the questions that arose early were who are these guys?   I mean, are they going to work themselves into a lather?   Are they ever going to turn over power to anybody?   And what's the role going to be of the Cubans?, and so on.

It wasn't too long before it became clear that the Cubans had an in that nobody was going to compete with.   The Cubans had fought with them; the Cubans were their military advisors.   The Cubans are very good at ingratiating themselves because they know the culture.   And Castro was bigger than life to the Sandinistas.   To them there were very few heroes that they could think of that would supercede Castro.   So that quality was there.   I think all of them rather aspired to be pint-sized Castros.

I found two things that we had to worry about.   One was their export of revolution, because they were fascinated by the romantic idea that they were the new revolutionaries.   Castro had told them, "You're the new generation."   This guy is a world-class snake oil salesman.   He really is a mesmerizer.   He's a real, real article; but he's a snake oil salesman.   No matter how good he is, he's a snake oil salesman.   He convinced these guys that they had brought about a new concept of revolution.   His [Cuba] was almost an antiquated model; this [Nicaragua] was the new model, and the new model had two new elements in it.   One was religion; it had the church.   And the second; it had people from the private sector.   In other words, it was a total societal overthrow.   And it had all the elements of a new revolution.   But this was baloney.   They were just taken in by this.   And they were taken by the idea that they could play a role way beyond Nicaragua.

In fact, I remember one of them telling me--I think it was Umberto Ortega.   He said, "You know, you are very fortunate to be here at this time, because you can see from us how things are going to play out all through Latin America."   He said, "We're going to be the model all through Latin America."   Here you have a young guy, 32 years old, who has just become all blown up with euphoria, who attained power because of the fortunes of the draw. The Sandinistas didn't win a victory, they just slid in on a series of circumstances that were fortuitous for them.   Nonetheless, it gave them this heady feeling that the whole gosh-dang continent was going in their direction, Chile, and all the rest of Latin America.   They felt, "We are the center of the universe."

Now what was happening, which made this thing very credible to them--every cuckoo nut around the world was there.   We had extremists from Peru.   We had the Montoneros from Argentina. Miristas from Chile.   The

Tupamaros from Uruguay.   We had the PLO [Palestine Liberation Organization].   We had North Koreans; it was the first time I saw the North Koreans. We had revolutionaries from Africa. I mean, you walked around, especially at the Intercontinental Hotel, and it looked like some sort of a Hollywood stage.

Then you had all the people who were looking for happenings. You know, Hollywood starlets, and musicians, and goodness knows who else. They were all there. And these guys were booted up to stardom. They were heady as hell. They really believed they were supermen. It was very dangerous; it seemed to me it was very dangerous for these people to think that they could do these things, when they couldn't even run the country. Nicaragua was in terrible shape.

I used to talk to them about relations with their neighbors, and relations with us. Basically the line I took was that they should attend to their own needs at home, but their doing so became problematic. I mean, it was there right in the beginning. And they would argue at great length that, you know, you don't understand that there's sort of a harmonic feeling here, throughout this region. All these other societies are not going to make it; they're going to topple. And I'd say, "You're going to pay a price. We are not going to sit idly by. Forget it. If you want this regime to survive, you'd better tend to your own business. As long as you tend to your own business, at least people can be tolerant of some of the screeching. But if you start fooling around . . !"

14

Terrorism, Coups, and Other Violence

From the ambassador's perspective, it is a dangerous world out there. In some areas coups d'état and violence seem to be an almost accepted part of political life. Though the United States government may be completely neutral as to the issues involved and the embassy and American establishments not themselves targets, they can be caught in the crossfire, and the protection of American lives and property becomes of prime concern to the ambassador.

At times, U.S. embassies and American establishments have themselves been targets of groups bent on venting their anger over U.S. policies. American property has been attacked and burned and American lives have been threatened. Murder and kidnapping of Americans, including ambassadors, have been all too frequent. It is the duty of the ambassador to do all that is possible to insure that American lives and property are protected, insisting on the cooperation and assistance of the local government to this end.

There is no book of instructions to advise an ambassador what to do or how to act in times of crisis. Decisions must be made quickly on the spot; there is no time to ask for advice from Washington, which under the best of circumstances is not geared to making quick decisions. Often there is little that an ambassador or embassy can or should do except to keep heads down, to make sure that Americans are safe and to keep informed as to what is going on.

Always in the back of the ambassador's mind in times of crisis is the question: "Should American personnel be evacuated?" To help him make this decision, there is the expertise and experience of the embassy attachés and other staff. Foreign diplomatic colleagues and host country nationals or officials can be of help. But in the final analysis it is their instinct and past experience that ambassadors must rely upon to tell them what they should do.

The accounts of crisis situations which are described in this chapter illustrate the suddenness with which they arise and how little time an ambassador has to respond to them. They point up how valuable the embassy staff can be in such situations and how together they can perform the important duties required of them at such times.

LIBERIA (1980)

One of the nastiest coups in Africa occurred in Liberia during the time ROBERT POWELL SMITH was ambassador to that country, 1979-1981. He was out of the country but raced back to Monrovia when the long-standing government of President Tolbert was overthrown by Sergeant Sammy Doe, who conducted a virtual bloodbath of his opposition.

Smith: President Tolbert was very nice. At the same time, we would have to fuss at the foreign minister or the president several times about human rights violations, imprisoning people and then keeping them without charge, that sort of thing. But the main problem was that the Americo-Liberian clique, and they were a small minority in the country, in fact, ruled the country. They controlled the court system, the police, the armed forces, the parliament, everything about life in Liberia.

And, again, inevitably perhaps after my experience in Ghana, I had come back to the States on a medical evacuation and was an outpatient at the Mayo Clinic in Rochester, Minnesota, when I got the inevitable call at one o'clock in the morning from the desk officer in Washington saying, "Mr. Ambassador, the secretary would like you back in Liberia like yesterday. There's been a coup." We did not anticipate that coup. I would like to be able to say we saw it coming. We did not, although we knew there was great unhappiness.

In this case, in April of 1980, a group of enlisted men in the armed forces were down on the beach near the presidential palace drinking beer and they had their weapons with them. One thing led to another and, to make a long story short, they got a group together and went into the presidential palace and murdered President Tolbert. They tracked down virtually the entire cabinet, senior parliamentary leaders, and other prominent Americo-Liberians, and it was a blood bath.

I got back on the next day, on the first flight in. The young man who had taken over the country was a 29-year-old master sergeant named Sammy Doe. He was semi-literate, could barely read and write his own name. He could, in fact, barely speak proper English. I literally, at times, would resort to pidgin English to communicate with Sergeant Doe after he became head of state. It was a real body blow, not because we had anything against the indigenous peoples of Liberia, and we knew the faults of the old regime, but at the same time, the blood bath that followed was inexcusable.

There were a few frantic days, and they were frantic because this unleashed this latent hatred which was there on the part of the enlisted men in the armed forces. The first order Doe gave was that you no longer have to obey the orders of your officers either in the police force or in the army. You can imagine the kind of chaos that resulted from that. So they were stopping people on the street, dragging people from their beds and murdering them. In the case of the cabinet, they were tying them to stakes on the beach and executing them by firing squad.

This was despite the fact that in the morning I had again gone to see Sergeant Doe and given him a personal appeal from President Carter to spare their lives. He heard me but made no commitment. That afternoon my public affairs officer burst into my office and said, "Mr. Ambassador, my God, they have done it. They've shot all of them. They've killed all of them, eight or nine lined up on the beach tied to stakes." So it was a bloody mess.

Worse yet, we had the obvious concern about these ignorant, poorly educated, almost illiterate enlisted men being gotten to by the other side and being turned around and having Liberia wind up as a Communist state. The Soviets were there and very interested in all this, although they were completely nonplussed by the coup. However, they immediately saw an opportunity here and tried to move in on it. I must say, I think one of the major things that saved us there was not, certainly, the charm or good looks of the American ambassador. It was, rather, the presence of a U.S. military mission that had been there for decades, headed, in my tenure, by a tough, charming Texas full colonel in the U.S. Army named Bob Gosney. As the head of the U.S. Military Mission and, in that capacity, he had helped train Master Sergeant Doe. Master Sergeant Doe adored Colonel Gosney, and called him "Chief." He referred to him always in the third person as "the Chief."

I very quickly became cognizant of this and I started taking Colonel Gosney with me when I went to see Sammy Doe. This helped enormously because he respected and had total confidence in Colonel Gosney. He knew little and cared less about communism and the Soviet Union. There was nothing ideological. This was a genuine tribal upheaval to get rid of the hated upper classes and to bring more privileges to the underprivileged. So Sammy Doe was not then and is not now a politically ideological person. But I can't emphasize strongly enough how helpful it was to have had this small group of American army officers, consisting of a group of lieutenant colonels and majors. They had, instead of lording it over the enlisted men of the armed forces as their Liberian counterparts did, being Americans they would learn these fellows names, including Sergeant Doe's, and they were warm and cordial to their underlings. As a result, Sergeant Doe quickly passed the word that whatever "the chief" says, goes.

So I had the members of my military mission out in their vehicles literally patrolling the streets. And when they would see a drunken or doped up Liberian soldier holding a group of civilians at gunpoint or something, trying to rob them, or rape them or whatever, one word from one of my American officers would stop that dead in its tracks. They would stop, salute, and say, "Yes, sir," and go on about their business. It saved lives, literally saved lives, this personal relationship that they had established. And that really sustained us for a very lengthy period before their government was formed and Sammy Doe came up with a foreign minister who was bright and well educated with whom we could deal.

The problem was that Sammy Doe and his immediate cohorts were to me, in a very personal sense, murderers. They had murdered William Tolbert, who was a very dear friend of mine, and the other members of the cabinet with whom I had been very close. And yet, here they were, the new government. It was clearly not in our national interest to see the country go down the tubes, so it fell to me to do what we could to sustain this young man in steering him along a certain course. This we managed to do with great difficulty.

However, that led to a situation in which he came to lean on me and the embassy almost too much. He would summon me at all hours of the night to say, "Mr. Ambassador, we have a problem." He would state the problem and wait for me to come up with a solution. So at times it came very uncomfortably close to running a country that you really don't want any part of, and always putting out the fires and fears that he had. He had a fear that Houphouët-Boigny, president of the Ivory Coast, whose daughter was married to Tolbert's son, was going to invade Liberia with the help of French troops.

So it was a question of hanging in there and doing what we could to moderate the behavior of Sergeant Doe and his government. I think we were relatively successful, as was my successor, Bill Swing, who had a long tenure there, about five years, pumping in a great deal of American aid, especially to the military, since the unhappiness of the military with their lot in life was one of the main causes of the coup.

It was an exciting time. The secretary ordered me to evacuate American dependents. We had to get them out of the country right after the coup when the troops were running wild. So it was, perhaps, the most exciting time in my Foreign Service career, but not the most satisfying.

We felt we were really operating in a goldfish bowl or under a microscope, I should say. Human rights pressure inevitably came into this picture after the coup, but strangely enough, there was not a great deal of congressional pressure. Everyone was sickened, of course, by what happened out there. However, you can't reverse that and I think everyone saw that what we had to concentrate on was where do we go from there. I had to keep reminding people of some of the things that the previous government had done and why the depths of anger being felt by these people was quite genuine.

MYANMAR [BURMA] (1976)

The instigators of an unsuccessful coup d'état by a pro-American group in Burma (now Myanmar) in July 1976 had hoped to promote meaningful, joint venture investment from the United States. When the coup failed the leader of this so-called "Captains Coup" sought asylum in the ambassador's residence. DAVID LAWRENCE OSBORN, then ambassador, had to make a decision, and quickly.

Osborn: There was strong and growing sentiment among the ordinary people of Burma for somehow getting rid of their particular socialist system--the Burma Socialist Program Party or "BSPP." Now during the time that I was there, a group of junior military officers began to plot in earnest to knock over the government and to install a degree of free enterprise-oriented democracy. The embassy was not aware of this plot, and of course had no part in it.

One of the plotters' hopes was that they could promote meaningful, joint-venture investments from the United States. These junior military officers (later called the "Captains Coup Plotters") plotted a coup to overthrow the government, which, by coincidence, was to occur very near the time of our July 4 celebrations, in 1976--the bicentennial year celebrations. The young plotters did in fact attempt to launch their coup, but they blew it.

At the time it happened, that evening in July of 1976, I was attending a dinner party at the Pakistani ambassador's home, when I was called home and learned, on getting back to my residence, that the leader of the "Captains Coup" group was seeking asylum in the residence. This presented us with a problem, because the embassy and its code room had been shut down; we did not maintain a 24 hours [watch]. It would have been impossible for me to go to the embassy and have a telephone conversation, or a telegraphic exchange with the Department, without alerting the Burmese that something was up. So I had a consultation with my acting political counselor, and the acting CIA station chief; I decided that we would have to handle this on our own, without immediate reference to the Department.

What I decided to do was to offer the captain his free choice: on the one hand, he could take shelter in the embassy, with the understanding that he would have to be turned over to the Burmese when and if they came and made a proper request for his release. On the other hand, if he so desired, we would take him to any part of Rangoon that he designated, and drop him at the roadside, with no questions asked, and he would be on his own and free to try to escape. He thought it over for a while, and then chose to take his chances on trying to escape. So, true to our promise, we took him and deposited him near the [Sule] Pagoda, and he took it from there. As it turned out, he was able to hide out for only a matter of a few weeks; a couple of weeks later he was, in fact, picked up by the Burmese police, and imprisoned. Ultimately he was put on trial for his part in the coup attempt, and was probably executed, I fear.

EGYPT (1964)

LUCIUS DURHAM BATTLE had barely arrived at his new post as ambassador to Egypt in 1964 when his embassy was attacked and its library burnt by a crowd protesting U.S. actions in the Congo.

Battle: The burning of the American library in the embassy compound was a dramatic event and has been much discussed. I was still making my introductory calls. This was around Thanksgiving or about two months after I arrived. All embassies had received alerts from the Department advising that there could be trouble in connection with the Congo issues. There were large numbers of black students in Cairo and elsewhere. The Egyptians had made an effort to have a large number of African students in order to try to increase their influence in the continent. So embassy Cairo was an obvious target.

I received this alert over Thanksgiving weekend. I read the instructions which said if a building was ever invaded and could not be defended, even if files were in danger, the marines should not fire. They were to use fire-arms in only very circumscribed circumstances. On Thanksgiving Day, I read the president's proclamation at the English church in Cairo. We drove home after service, passing the embassy compound. All was quiet since it was a holiday. We had dinner about 2 P.M. I settled down with a brandy and my children were playing chess with some of their friends. I had let my car go, which was a blessing.

The phone rang; it was the marine guard saying that the compound was under attack. There were people all over the place throwing bricks, tearing up the flower pots and in general rampaging. The marine asked whether I could come. I asked him whether I could get through and he thought that I could. So I walked, since my car and driver had long left. It was not a long walk, so I went. I put on a raincoat since it was a chilly evening. I told Srey, the majordomo, to pull down all the blinds, to lock up and not let anyone into the house, to lock all the gates and to prepare for possible trouble.

I walked to the embassy, and it was a disastrous situation. In order to get there, I had to pass both the fire and police departments buildings. In neither case, did I see any activity. I passed these buildings and went to the embassy. As I arrived, the fire crackers were being thrown right into the building, right into my office. The marine barracks were on fire as was the library. I walked very slowly and the mob let me go through. The marines were all lined up behind the door; I could see them. They yelled at me to run, but I thought that if I did that, I would be killed. So I walked through the crowd; I pushed one guy who stood in the way, aside. The crowd waited long enough for the gate to swing open so I could get through. Then it went back to rioting again. Now it seems the funniest thing in the world. I wasn't quite sure what to do; I asked each marine to take a fire extinguisher, of which we had a number. I took one, although I had never used one in my life, and headed for the library fire.

By the time we got there, it was a gigantic blaze. There wasn't anything we could do; we couldn't even get close enough. Unfortunately, that fire was so spectacular, as the photographs taken at the time will show, that every article written in the next six months in the U.S. included mention and pictures of it. The burning of U.S. libraries was common problem in those days. The articles would use the Cairo's burning as an example; *Life* included the pictures in one of its editions; a lot of publications did. Every time there was a fire at any post, the Cairo library pictures were used as an illustration, because they were the best pictures available. The stories might be general in nature or about an event somewhere else, but the pictures were always that of our fire.

I stayed up all night at the embassy; the police and the fire departments finally showed up, unnecessarily late. I think the Egyptians were embarrassed; they didn't know what to do about the incident. The ministry of foreign affairs representative came to the embassy, but I got absolutely no satisfaction. They gave me no response. The chief of police came to ask whether I was all right. I told him that I was okay and that was about the extent of that conversation. I showed him the damage. By that time, the mob had broken up. If the Egyptians had done more immediately, the press might have reported it differently. If they had apologized or committed themselves to compensation for the building damage, that would have made a big difference. But they didn't do that. Ultimately, after many weeks, they did the right things. As we pieced the story together, it was apparently a mob of African students who were protesting the Congo developments--the U.S. airlift out of the Congo.

The next day, I went to protest the absence of appropriate protection and the slow response by the police and fire departments. The foreign office became very indignant that I protested; they didn't respond; they didn't apologize. They expressed regrets that the incident had occurred, which wasn't satisfactory. So we had a mess. In a few days, I received instructions to see Nasser. It was probably the first substantive appointment I had with him. I had presented my credentials, but that was purely ceremonial. We met alone in his residence on the outskirts of Cairo and he said to me: "You are very young to be the American ambassador." I looked younger than I really was. I replied: "You are too young to be president. We are exactly the same age and you have done a lot better than I have." He laughed; he thought that was very funny. After that, he would often laugh and we used to laugh together. He expressed his deep regret; he said he would give a thousand books in his own name for the library and he would give us a new building to be selected.

I don't think the Egyptians ever intended for the riot to occur, but they had given a permit for the demonstration.

MOROCCO (1971)

Diplomats are not fond of diplomatic receptions; the food is usually not very good, it is hard on the feet and one is meeting the same people over and over again. STUART WESSON ROCKWELL, ambassador to Morocco from 1970 to 1973, saw the birthday celebration for the King of Morocco turn into an assassination attempt which left some 130 persons dead. The king, however, escaped injury and the coup failed.

Rockwell: This was the king's annual celebration of his birthday [July 14, 1971], which took place at his summer palace south of Rabat, between Rabat and Casablanca, at Skhirat. It usually involved all the notables of the realm and all the chiefs of foreign diplomatic missions. It was a stag party, and everybody was very informally dressed in sports clothes. There were opportunities for golf, tennis, swimming and clay pigeon shooting, but the party ws mainly for a huge banquet at mid-day in this summer palace. It was a very sportive affair, supposed to be, until just as we were about to go in to sit down to lunch, we heard these sort of popping sounds, and somebody said, "Oh, the king has arranged fireworks for us this year."

And when people started to fall with blood pouring out of them, we realized that the palace was being attacked, and the king's entourage, especially the military members, rushed out to defend it and were cut down. The rest of us were trapped inside or out on the golf course or wherever we happened to be. There must have been a thousand guests there, at least. Eventually, the guard was overcome and the attackers forced us all out of the palace and required us to lie down in front while they searched for the king, who had hidden in the men's room of the palace, which they didn't know about, with some of his key people. They never found him until the very end, but at that time, the command of the rebels had figured out that the king had fled to Rabat somehow, so they had gone to Rabat to try to catch him.

When the subordinates finally uncovered him and realized that contrary to what they had been told, the king, instead of being endangered by devious foreign types and disloyal Moroccans, was being endangered by themselves, they reversed their attitude and declared their loyalty to him.

The king dispatched General Oufkir to Rabat to get control of the city, which was being attacked by the rebel group. In fact, the ministry of information had been seized and the radio was under rebel control. So the ringleaders were court-martialled instantly and shot.

It turned out to be an offshoot of this problem I mentioned earlier, that the head of the military household of the king was a very personable officer who was personally affronted by the degree of corruption and felt the king was not doing enough about it, and felt that the king should make way for the crown prince. He got the cooperation of Colonel Ababou, who was the head of the cadet academy at Fez, and owing to his position as the head of the military household, it was possible to infiltrate during the night 1,000 or 1,200 of these young men, cadets, into the surroundings of the palace. They were the ones that attacked the palace, who had been told apparently that the king was in danger, and that it was their patriotic duty to liberate him. What happened, apparently, was that Colonel Ababou decided that this was a good opportunity to get rid of the king and establish a sort of Libyan-style republic. The fact of the matter is that Colonel Ababou asked the head of the military household where the king was, and the man knew where he was, because I saw him lead the king into his hiding place, and he didn't let on. So Colonel Ababou had him executed right then, right on the spot, as being a traitor to the cause. So there were two people with different motives.

We were lying on our faces outside the palace until the king was uncovered by the cadets who were left in charge, and as soon as they laid down their arms, everything returned to normal. It was very strange. I mean, there we were with all our limousines parked down in the parking lot. Although the Belgian ambassador had been shot dead and the Syrian was wounded, we all went back to Rabat, and the countryside seemed perfectly normal. People were selling fish by the roadside, there were swimmers at the beaches. It was hard to believe that this bloody event, which must have cost the lives of about 130 people, had occurred only two hours or so ago.

EGYPT (1981)

Being an ambassador means being in proximity to the leaders of the host nation at ceremonial events, including those where large bodies of heavily armed men parade in front of the dignitaries. Senior diplomats in troubled countries are aware that their work can bring them perilously close to potential targets of assassins. This diplomatic nightmare became reality for ALFRED LEROY ATHERTON, Jr. in Egypt [ambassador from 1979 to 1983] on October 6, 1981, when President Anwar Sadat was murdered. Atherton and his staff quickly informed resident Americans and Washington of developments and maintained an alert until the scene had returned to normal.

Atherton: There was a kind of a sense of foreboding in the atmosphere. There had been an authenticated aborted attempt to assassinate Sadat once before that. So one worried a bit. But because this was a military parade, it was controlled by the military and security was in the hands of the military. Our area was a secure area that people couldn't get into without credentials being checked. There was the sense that nothing could happen here.

I was there, sitting in the reviewing stand where the diplomatic corps sat with the British and Canadian ambassadors not too far from the Israeli ambassador plus the visiting delegations that happened to be in Cairo, including one, I think either Chinese or North Korean delegation that was further back in the reviewing stands. On the other side, Sadat and his cabinet, senior officers and other distinguished guests all sat down in the front. Behind them on tiered reviewing stands, to the right were the diplomatic corps and the visiting delegations, and on the left were the attaché corps and visiting military dignitaries.

We had two senior American generals in town at the time, who were guests of the military. One was the deputy commander in chief of CINCEUR Europe. His name was Klink Smith. The other was General Pactin, who was the commander of the rapid deployment task force that later became the Central Command. It was the command with responsibility for preparing against contingencies that might arise in the Persian Gulf. They were the ones under whom the joint military exercises took place every year. So General Pactin and General Smith were both there as invited guests of the Egyptian military; they were sitting down in the front row along with the vice president and all of the religious dignitaries; so our two generals were down in the area just a few rows behind Sadat. Their staff of military aides was sitting with our defense attachés, our military and others on the military side.

And the parade went on and on and on, with occasional disruptions. A vehicle would break down occasionally and had to be hand maneuvered out of the way. There was one live demonstration of paratroopers who made a precision drop and came down right in the circles that were drawn on the ground in front of the reviewing stand. They came up and saluted the president.

There were flybys, and I did have one chilling moment, because in one of the very low flyovers, the planes came straight at the reviewing stand, then at the last minute pulled up. And I suddenly found myself thinking, "You know, what a way to. . . . ! if somebody really wanted to wipe out the president, his whole government, and anybody else, their planes, if they had that mission and decided to do it, we would be perfect targets." Well, anyway, we all watched them fly away.

Near the end of the parade, along came the heavy artillery with their crews sitting in the back of the trucks pulling their heavy guns. One of them stopped in front of the reviewing stand. The crew scrambled out. Well, our assumption, and it was certainly Sadat's assumption that this was going to be another one of these scenes for the president, as the paratroopers had been. They were going to come up to the stand and salute the president.

The president stood up to take the salute. We all were watching. And at that moment, suddenly hand grenades were thrown and machine guns began to be fired. Clearly this was the assassination attempt at Sadat.

I didn't witness anything else, because, along with all of my colleagues, I was down, hugging the ground as fast and as far as I could. But there was a lot of shooting, and you could hear the shots. I could hear occasional bullets whizzing by. It was just luck who got hit and who didn't. A number of people in the diplomatic reviewing stands did get hit.

They were after Sadat, certainly, but they were firing at random to keep down any potential counterfire from the security forces that might have protected us. As it turned out nobody did, because his own security had let their guard down, thinking that this was something that the military had charge of and therefore they didn't have to worry. My security detail was several rows behind me in the reviewing stands. The Israeli had his security in back of mine, I guess. I think we were the only ambassadors that had personal security guards. I had this Egyptian guard at the time, provided by the Egyptian government.

Anyway, it was total chaos. When the firing stopped we all stood up and looked down at the front. There was a jumble of chairs upside down. They had already carried Sadat out and gotten him into a helicopter that was standing by, and we heard the helicopter leave.

Michael Weir, who was the British ambassador, and I were side by side. With all that training as a political officer that I had gotten I immediately began seeing who was there, comparing notes. Is that Mubarak? Is that the minister of defense? Who isn't there? Who's been hit? Where's Sadat? Sadat was nowhere to be seen. But we did try to get some impression of what the damage had been. We only learned sometime later that there had been 8 people killed in addition to Sadat and some 30 people had been wounded--some diplomats, the Australian commercial officer. The Belgian ambassador was hurt, and one of these Chinese or Korean delegation members I remember seeing as I was leaving, had been hit in his wrist, bone shattered--his hand sort of dangled. It was a pretty bloody scene.

Well, the assassins ran out of bullets, and they had no escape plan. I guess they expected to be killed in the process. They were all captured, and eventually they were tried, and several of them were executed. It was ascertained that this was an Islamic fundamentalist cell that had infiltrated the military from the outside, got themselves military uniforms and used forged papers and substituted themselves for the crew of this artillery prime mover. One of the elements of the trial charge was that this cell was not in the main stream of the Moslem Brotherhood but was a spinoff, a group dedicated to violent overthrow in order to establish an Islamic Koranic rule in the country.

But clearly Sadat had become to them the personification of evil, because he had made peace with Israel, because of his lifestyle and because he was seen as anti-Islamic. He had done all the things that the Islamic fundamentalists disapproved of. So it was no surprise that there were cells of extremists in the Islamic fundamentalist group who were out to destabilize the regime, including assassination and acts of violence.

It wasn't the first time; there had been other attempts earlier in the Sadat period. There had been an attack on the military industrial training school in Cairo at one time. The remarkable thing wasn't that the attempt took place, I suppose, as much as that they were not a grassroots group; they didn't begin a groundswell of revolution of opposition to the regime. Even the disaffected didn't want to go to this kind of violence, but these were not a grassroots group. They didn't begin a groundswell of revolution and of opposition to the regime. Even the disaffected didn't want to go to this kind of violence for the most part. And so they didn't even represent the mainstream of Islamic fundamentalism. They were the extreme wing of Islamic fundamentalism. They didn't represent the mainstream, in those days of the Moslem Brotherhood, which had decided to cooperate within the law.

But it was not a new phenomenon. The Moslem Brotherhood and Moslem opposition to westernization or secularization of the regime dated back to the 1930s. They had tried to destabilize the Nasser regime, and that was why Nasser had a number of their leaders executed in the early 1950s and kept many of them in jail. After having given Sadat a very good chance to be a good Islamic leader they began to go after him.

In any case, there was utter confusion. It wasn't quite clear whether Sadat had been killed or whether he had been wounded. We saw the vice president with a little bandage over his forehead, so obviously he was all right. The minister of defense had gotten a superficial wound, but he was all right too. Probably the reasons why not more of the leaders had gotten killed were twofold. First, the very first opening move was the throwing of the hand grenade. I was told later by the minister of defense it had bounced off his head; that was why he had this little scar. But the grenade didn't go off. And then there was one man whose job it was to kill Sadat. He came up with his gun and pulled it on Sadat. We've seen some of the pictures of this. He was up, actually up, aiming the gun down, because Sadat by that time had fallen to the ground. Others were simply providing covering fire for the man whose job it was to kill Sadat. They were not targeting other individuals, but they weren't trying to avoid killing other people--and they did kill other people. But the target was clearly Sadat.

Anyway, the question was: How do we get out of here?   By that time I was being urged to stop counting and get away.   Somebody had organized the diplomatic cars, which had been parked out behind the reviewing stand, and gotten them into some kind of order.   I went and found my car and driver, and we headed back to the embassy.

I had a radio in the car which not many of the other ambassadorial cars had, so I was able to get on the radio as soon as I got in the car and called the embassy and talked to the DCM, Henry Precht, who was at the Embassy, and said: "First of all, please tell Betty," my wife, who I knew was going to be watching this on television at the embassy. She had turned down an invitation to go and sit in the ladies' reviewing stand with Mrs. Sadat, up behind where the president and all of us were, and was watching this at the embassy; so I said, "Please tell Betty I'm all right. I'm on my way back." I told Henry it looks here as though it was a single assassination attempt.   But we couldn't tell whether there was a follow-up plan or whether there was going to be an attempt to take over the usual targets: military headquarters, television stations, and so forth.   I told him he'd better get a team and get people scattered around to do as much reconnaissance as you can.   Well, Henry had already started doing these things.

I learned from Betty what went on at the embassy while they were watching the parade on television.   Suddenly the screen went crazy, and it was clear that the cameras were pointing in the air and in all directions. Henry just said right away, "Something's happened." He got on the phone and opened the line to the operations center in Washington and said, "I don't know what's happening, but clearly something is happening that is very serious--keep the line open, and we will report to you as soon as we get some facts."   So we were able to get Washington pretty early and report that there had been an assassination. I was all right. I didn't know yet whether the president was alive.   There were others who saw some bodies down there. The senior bishop of the Coptic church was killed. Then we had to worry, are all the Americans accounted for?   By the time I got back to the embassy a few general officers had arrived.   They had been down in the reviewing area but had escaped any of the bullets. They were worried about their aides, who had been sitting in the reviewing stand.   Well, we had to find out what had happened to the military aides; we had to establish a task force; we had to get word out to the American community and to set up an information center to answer the inevitable questions.   Is this something to be worried about? Is it the beginning of a revolution? Is there going to be disorder and chaos?

Our initial reporting was that it looked like an isolated event, no indication that there would be a follow-up or trouble anywhere else. The Egyptian radio and TV were showing soap operas at that point, and playing light music and no news at all was coming over.   We assumed that meant that everyone in the government was getting themselves together to try to take stock of what had happened and to let everybody know who was in charge. I had a phone call from Mrs. Reagan who wanted me to talk to Mrs. Sadat. I said I would convey a message to her but I wouldn't be able to see her that day. Mrs Reagan wanted Mrs. Sadat to know that she was very concerned.

Then, the most bizarre phone call was one from the minister of defense, Field Marshal Abu Ghazala, who had been the military attaché in Washington and was considered very much a friend of the Americans and one of the strong advocates of U.S. military cooperation. He phoned me and said, "I just want to let you know that everything is under control in the country, the government is bereaved and the president has been seriously wounded but it is not life threatening, and I have no choice but to accept that until we have evidence to the contrary."

Just at that point I had a telephone call from former President Carter. He wanted to know what had happened to his friend Sadat. And I said, "All I can tell you is that there has been a serious attempt on his life. He certainly had to have been seriously wounded by all of the fire that had gone on, but I have just been told by the minister of defense that he wasn't killed." This is in Carter's book, that he had been reassured by my report.

But there was a period of almost seven hours, between the time of the assassination attempt and when the Egyptian government announced the death of the president, while we were still in doubt. We kept getting urgent requests from the American press corps to confirm that the president had been killed. And I said, "I can't. We are waiting for the Egyptian government to announce it. I can't announce it." I got a certain amount of criticism in fact, including the press corps from the department, that we were behind the power curve on this.

The CBS correspondent, a woman correspondent, whose name I've forgotten, was the first to go on the air and announce that the president had been killed. Of course, we were asked to confirm it. My instructions were that it was not up to the American ambassador or the American government to announce the death of the president of Egypt. It was up to the Egyptian government.

I later learned that she (the correspondent) was outside the military hospital in Maadi, where the helicopter had taken Sadat and had taken Mrs. Sadat behind him too. The correspondent had gotten hold of the doctor coming out of the hospital, one of the surgeons or an assistant. She had said "What about the president?" And he had said "He's dead." And so she went on the air and announced it. But it was not official.

We told Washington not to confirm it, but that they should be prepared. Then the radio and the TV began to play and chant verses from the Koran. I tried to call the family; I tried to call the foreign minister, and I tried to call various other people in the government. I kept being told that they were all at a meeting. Of course, they were. They were having a meeting at senior level of government to make sure that authority was maintained. The Arabic language radio came on and announced that Sadat had been killed, that the government was intact, order would be maintained. Everyone should remain calm. So we had our confirmation--about seven hours after he had been killed.

ITALY (1981)

Italy would seem to be the ideal place to be an ambassador. The country is beautiful, the people gracious, the food delicious and Americans seem to be well liked. In the 1970s and 1980s, however, Italy was the seat of a small but deadly terrorist organization, the Red Brigades, and a favorite place for terrorists from the other side of the Mediterranean. MAXWELL M. RABB, then ambassador to Italy, tells how the plot by terrorists to kidnap him was foiled.

Rabb: When I came in [1981], Italy was number one on the list of terrorist countries, insofar as prevalence of that practice is concerned. I stepped into this situation. So many Italians, journalists, and businessmen were either shot in the back of the legs or killed or kidnapped and their children were kidnapped.   It was a terrible mess as as far as I was concerned, from the very moment I went there, I always had seven to watch me.   If I ventured out, I had a police car in front, two riding shotgun in my car.   Then, in the back car, an unmarked police car with Italian policemen in plain clothes. I did whatever they asked me to do. I never once broke the rules. I never sneaked off to jog or to take a walk without them. It was very difficult. There were six different groups that they had identified and either grabbed or sent out of the country, who tried to kill me.

The first one was October 12, 1981. Qaddafi [of Libya] had failed in his attempt to knock out of the skies two American planes. His two planes had intended to blast a carrier. They lost them. So the next best thing was to get a symbol. I was the symbol.

All that I know was that I made a speech on Columbus Day in, in this case, Milan. I left the place, went to my hotel. I had been in the area travelling for about two or three days. I had nothing but dirty laundry.

At about 6:30 in the morning, the telephone call at the hotel came in from my DCM who said, "Don't say anything to me, just listen and do as I tell you. Take the 11:00 plane--I think there was an 11:00 plane at that time from Milan to the United States--and don't say anything more. Just go there."

He hung up the receiver. Boy, if that wasn't a mystery. Anyway, I got on this plane. I didn't know what the devil I was doing. I had nothing but dirty clothes with me. I then found out that I was to be assassinated the next day when I returned to Rome. The police did pick up the six men. I have a picture of one of them, the hit man. The Italian police were good enough to give me this in secret. He was a young man, about 36 years of age, an attractive young man, but he had the job of killing me. The others were captured in this hotel--I forget which one it was--on the floor. They were all kneeling on the floor when they were hit, with a map of the embassy, with my picture there on the floor and with my biography there.

Anyway, I went to the States, and that was one [attempt]. There were several others like this. At that time they, the Italians, were fairly soft on them. They sent them out of the country. But then, of course, came the Dozier case [the kidnapping of an American general in Italy by the Italian Red Brigade].

BOLIVIA (1969-1973)

Bolivia is a poor, land-locked country with a long history of domestic violence and coups. With the rise of the communist movement in Latin America, some Bolivians were receptive to the siren call of anti-Americanism. This hostile environment required that extraordinary precautions be taken to ensure the safety of Americans and particularly of ERNEST VICTOR SIRACUSA and his family during his tour as ambassador in that country, 1969-1973.

Siracusa: In Bolivia at that time most of the upper classes were fine people, reasonably disposed toward the United States. At the lower end was the Indian peasantry, benefiting somewhat from the drastic land reforms of the early fifties, but otherwise put upon by everybody; and the miners, manipulated, exploited, and influenced by the leftist labor unions. Add to this mix the extremely leftist, marxist-dominated university system and the leftist "intellectuals" and youthful hot-head politicians, all devoted to inflaming student passions and exploiting the poverty of the people, and you had an incendiary mixture. Their *modus operandi* was intimidation. The almost random firing of automatic weapons out the university tower just a few blocks from my residence was a reminder of their threat.

The United States and Americans became the targets. The university is on the main road going down from La Paz proper to the lower, residential suburbs, giving the students a strategic spot for mischief as they could block and command the road. One night, unaware that there was activity at the school, two of our carryalls were stopped, tipped-over and burned by the students. Fortunately, the drivers and passengers were able to escape unharmed. On another occasion our cultural center, near the university, was sacked and then confiscated. Also, our marine guard residence was twice attacked and looted, once with gunfire injury to the "gunny-sergeant" in charge.

On another occasion the students, under cover of launching an AID-sponsored literacy program, departed for the Amazon region with "literacy" banners flying. However, the trucks really contained heavily armed students who had been induced to attempt to start a revolutionary guerrilla movement in that area. After considerable fighting, and suffering casualties, this ill-advised student rebellion was put down by the military. One unintended victim of this debacle was President Ovando's son. After having been flown (unauthorized) over the "war zone" by one of the fighter pilots, he died in a crash into Lake Titicaca, where the pilot was thrilling him with a demonstration of low-level aerobatics.

In June 1971 I sent my family home. By that time (during the Torres regime) we had had many attacks on American installations, including the seizing and destroying of our cultural institutes around the country. There was also a more or less constant propaganda barrage against me. For a while, until my protests forced its cancellation, the nightly news broadcast over the government-owned TV station ended its opening panorama shot of the spectacular city of La Paz by focusing sharply on a wall with the graffiti slogan *"Muera Siracusa"* (Death to Siracusa).

Next came terrorist threats against my children. One day the guards captured someone in the park across from the residence, who had been observed tracking and recording their movements. Investigation indicated that this might be a possible life-threat against my youngest daughter. Therefore, as soon as my oldest daughter was graduated from high school my family left, she to enter university and my wife to work toward a degree in anthropology.

The move was a timely one as we discovered shortly thereafter that the minister of government in the Torres regime was a secret member of the ELN terrorist group. This was critical information as all of our guards were Bolivian police officers, seconded to the embassy. We trained and paid them and, while they worked for us, their ultimate Bolivian boss was the same minister of government.

Upon being informed of this, Washington decided to send for my protection an especially trained force of four marines to served as a PSU (personal security unit). Since marine guards normally function only as guards of embassy premises, we had to obtain special permission for these marines to work outside. Thereafter, and until the overthrow of the Torres regime several months later, everywhere I went I was accompanied by at least one marine, in addition to my chauffeur and Bolivian guards. We always traveled with a follow-car, and sometimes with a lead-car as well, and invariably over changing and circuitous routes. Happily, after the Torres regime fell, our situation in Bolivia changed drastically. The PSU was sent home and a new sense of optimism and hope grew as the quickly marshaled U.S. assistance-backed changes in the beginning of the Banzer administration. The exile of the more militant political hotheads and communist agitators, and the government's gaining some control over the university extremism, made a quantum difference as their ability to intimidate the populace ended.

A few months later my youngest daughter returned to Bolivia, and later my wife as well. For our last two years Bolivia was a very pleasant place to be, as the country was embarked upon several years of solid progress and economic betterment. While we continued to have Bolivian guards, I moved freely about the country, having real and rewarding contact with the people at all levels.

JORDAN (1970)

The Middle East continued to seethe following the 1967 war. By 1970, Palestinian guerrilla organizations had developed into formidable military units and were threatening the stability of several local regimes. Jordan became an uneasy host to these elements, who considered the United States an enemy of the Arabs and a friend of their bitter enemy, Israel. In April 1970 the anti-American sentiment boiled over, threatening the lives of U.S. personnel from mob violence. Given this atmosphere, HARRISON MATTHEWS SYMMES, the ambassador to Jordan, feared for the safety of Assistant Secretary of State Joseph Sisco and advised against his planned visit to Jordan. King Hussein was displeased.

Symmes: By early 1970 we were really in something of a quagmire, and about that time it was thought it would be a good time for Joe Sisco to make a visit to the area, that he would go to Cairo and Tel Aviv and ultimately Jordan. He was to come to Jordan from Tel Aviv. Well, he got to Tel Aviv, and at that point apparently the king decided--now whether this was a ploy, whether he had something to do with it, whether some of his staff had something to do with it, or however it came about--he let the Fedayeen demonstrate. In letting them demonstrate against Sisco's visit, he withdrew protection from around the embassy, from the cultural center and certain other locations in Amman in order, as they said at the time, to avoid inciting the Fedayeen. So one morning in April 1970 I went as usual to the embassy. (My route was always varied). Sisco was over in Tel Aviv, and there had been a mounting press campaign and radio campaign about "We don't want Sisco, blah, blah, blah." And I was in close touch with Joe, of course, over in Tel Aviv. When I arrived at the embassy that morning, there were no troops about. No armored cars, no Bedouin guards. And a surging mass of people in combat fatigues and one thing or another were fanned out around the embassy. I managed to get into the embassy, and the next thing I knew--there were a few soldiers around--an army captain came in and was brought up to my second-floor office to see me. He said, "The Fedayeen have requested that you lower the American flag."

And I replied, "I'm not going to lower the American flag. This is a diplomatic mission. Why are the armored cars and the protection not here?"

"We didn't want to have them here in order to avoid inciting the mob."

"Well, I think you'd better do something about the mob."

By this time they were throwing stones and bottles at the buildings, and we had all the shutters down. We were prepared of course for mob violence, and we had rigged up a device so that halyards of the flag were sort of halfway up the pole and they could be pulled over to an upstairs window so you couldn't just pull the flag down. Well, one of the mob shimmied up the flag pole and got the halyard and pulled the flag down. And then they started tearing it up. And, as I said at the time, it was like dividing up pieces of the true cross. You could buy a piece of the American flag down in the *suq*. It had been liberated that day. The mob were breaking windows and by this time they had set some embassy cars on fire. The embassy nurse narrowly escaped from her little building out in the garden. The mob uprooted all of the roses in the garden, pulled up plants, etc. Meanwhile, of course, I was trying to get through to the foreign minister, the prime minister, the king. Nobody could be found. They were all at a parade at the army general headquarters. So I did all the proper things to get messages to them as quickly as possible. I looked across to one of the other hills where the cultural center was located. It was up in smoke! I got a telephone call that the mob had gotten into the cultural center and they were burning the books. They had such a fire that the iron shelving melted. So the cultural center was just completely demolished. Finally, I got through to somebody in authority, and I said, "Look, you've got to get the military or the police or somebody out. Lord knows how much longer the embassy is going to be able to hold out." Ultimately, they did get the mob dispersed. They brought in some troops and so on.

That afternoon I was able finally to get through to someone to get an appointment with the king and went out to his residential palace. He was there with Zaid Al-Rifa'i, Chief of the Royal Diwan, who was later prime minister--one of his nefarious advisors--but very refined. I, of course, told the king that I was very concerned about what had happened, that I hoped he had a full report about it and that there would be restitution of what had ben destroyed in terms of physical property. He never said he was sorry. His sidekick never said he was sorry. I said, "I think in view of what's happened, we are going to have to consider some way maybe to postpone the Sisco visit."

He said, "Oh, no. That would certainly not be possible. You mustn't postpone that visit whatever happens. I am in charge here and I can assure you that Mr. Sisco will be safe." "Well, the plan calls for him to cross the Jordan River and then to be motored up to Amman, which would provide very tricky places for an ambush."

"Oh, no. I'll have my helicopter pick him up and fly him to Amman."

"Well, the Fedayeen have got all kinds of assault rifles and hand missiles, and I don't think that would be particularly safe."

"As long as I'm in control of this country, Mr. Sisco will be safe. He must come."

I then reminded him of December 1958 when I'd gone out with Bill Rountree on a trip around the Middle East. We'd ended up in Baghdad and been attacked by a mob and so on. Before we'd gone on to Baghdad, we had visited both Hussein and Nasser, who had warned us not to go, that if we went we were going into a trap and so on. Bill and I went, anyway. Although we had recommended we not continue the trip to Baghdad, Loy Henderson who was in charge at the time--Dulles was sick and Herter wasn't there--said we had to go and we went and almost lost our lives.

So I reminded the king of this and said, "You know, we didn't take your advice then, and Bill Rountree wished we had when we got there. Maybe this is one of those times, Your Majesty, that we should think about a way to avoid having Sisco come. We could come up with a very good public relations rationale. We could get him sick. There are all kinds of things we can do and just postpone the visit."   He said, "I shall regard Sisco's not coming as a deliberate personal insult and I shall consider you responsible."

So I went back to the embassy with that and communicated all this to Joe and to Washington and made a recommendation that Joe not come in the circumstances. I didn't think the king was effectively in charge of the situation, and even if he tried to be in charge, I didn't think he would succeed. Given what the mob had just done, we did not know what would happen if he came. I thought Joe's life would be in danger, and not only Joe's life, but the whole American community would be in danger. It was just too easy to cut our losses, in other words. So I sent word back to the Department--Joe concurred in it, Wally Barbour [American Ambassador in Israel] concurred in it--and the Department agreed that I should say Mr. Sisco had unavoidably been forced to postpone his visit and would not be coming. An illness or something like that--I've forgotten now the rationale, but a perfectly good one. I was told to communicate that to the king the next day. So I had that message written out and called up the palace and spoke to Zaid Al-Rifa'i, Chief of the Royal Diwan. He said, "His Majesty is not available and he has asked me to take any message that you may have. What can I do for you?"   I said, "Well, this is for His Majesty's ears only and I'd really like to see him. I think it is terribly important for our two countries."

"His Majesty is just not going to be available to do it." Well we hemmed and hawed and he said, "Bring it to me." I said, "Well, I'd like for you to go back to the king and see what can be done." He called up later and said the king wasn't going to be available. About 9:00 that evening, I was watching a home movie with my family and I got a call from the prime minister to come and see him. He said the king had requested my transfer to Washington. He said that he had advised against it. I said, "Well, I hope you can go back to him. I think its a very bad idea. I don't think it's going to be good for our relations on either side. Apart from any personal effect on me, I just don't think it's going to look good for Jordan. I'm due for a transfer anyway. I've just been waiting for orders, why not let the thing go through?" He said, "Well, we'll keep it quiet so you just get word to Washington."

Of course, the next day it was all over the papers. That's a typical sort of Hussein way of acting.

15

The American Ambassador
and the Future

The experiences recounted in this book by American ambassadors and their deputies are from the latter half of the twentieth century, a period that saw the rise of the United States of America as the one major world power. The same period saw the collapse of the old order, the colonial empires of Great Britain, Belgium, France, the Netherlands, Portugal, and finally even of the Soviet Union. Having the Soviets and Communist movement as the clear enemies of the free world gave some sense of focus and order to American foreign policy towards other nations, and in 1992 it can be said that American foreign policy was triumphant, at least for the short term. These ambassadors were, in effect, successful field commanders in a worldwide diplomatic battle against the Communist forces. What will the accounts of American ambassadors be like taken from men and women who serve during the twenty-first century?

While it is always dangerous to predict the future, certain trends seem to speak of as great if not greater role for our ambassadors during the next century. The United States with all its warts and blemishes has emerged as the only power that can project policy leadership throughout the world. While the record can be uneven it has pushed for matters of world concern such as democracy, human rights, protecting the environment, economic cooperation, and fighting the narcotics trade. Issues may change but the United States predictably will be in the forefront and American ambassadors will continue to be on the cutting edge of American foreign policy in their countries of assignment.

The issues raised in this book will continue and will not be resolved. While there will be calls for a depoliticalization of ambassadorial appointments, both career and non-career ambassadors will be with us during the next century. There are strengths as well as weaknesses in having some ambassadors appointed from outside the Foreign Service. There is no guarantee that an all-professional ambassadorial corps would be better. The political ambassador is as American as apple pie.

There will continue to be questioning by policy makers, or policy kibitzers, as to the value of embassies abroad on the grounds that with instant communications and faster travel experts in the State Department or White House can take care of any situation that arises. This is doubtful. The world is not getting less complicated. Nationalism and ethnic strife are more pervasive than during the period of the empires; the colonial lid is off, and it is possibly going to be an even messier world out there. The ambassador on the spot with his or her staff is needed to know the ground and the players, something that cannot be done from Washington.

As was illustrated in this book, when events are fast moving and Americans are in danger, or American interests are in jeopardy, the ambassadors write their own instructions; there is not time for interdepartmental debate in Washington. Policy makers in the White House and State Department need the input from the field, even in tranquil times or places. Ambassadors are not only creatures of crisis, they also oversee our normal interests abroad. These include such matters as promoting American trade, supervising the immigration process, assisting tourists in trouble, and informing the host governments and people of our stands on various issues. Equally, tension will exist between the home office and the field, a situation that is unlikely ever to be resolved.

Despite the change in power relationships in the world the American ambassador is not going to find it any safer. Terrorist attacks on our ambassadors and embassies will always have to be reckoned with. The United States has too high a profile for them not to be a target for extremist groups who want to attract attention. Unless there is a remarkable return to civility throughout the world, American ambassadors will continue to be targets and require protection.

Our ambassadors will be also faced with natural disasters, civil conflict, and wars which threaten their embassies and other Americans caught in the country. It will be up to the ambassador to see to their protection, while at the same time keeping Washington informed of the situation and maintaining ties with the host government.

Despite these problems and dangers which our ambassadors may have to face, there will always be more than enough highly motivated, qualified men and women eager to be called by the president and asked to serve abroad as ambassador of the United States of America.

Appendix A

President's Letter to Ambassadors

The White House
July 10, 1990

Dear Mr./Madam Ambassador:

I send you my very best wishes and appreciation for your efforts as chief of the United States mission in (full official name of country/at)/(at international organization). We are entering a new, exciting time of change in international relations. The postwar era is drawing to a close. As leader of the democracies, our nation faces an historic opportunity to help shape a freer, more secure, and more prosperous world, in which our ideals and our way of life can truly flourish. As president, I intend to advance these objective and United States interests around the globe, and I look to you, as my personal representative in (country)/at (international organization), as my partner in this task.

As my representative, you, along with the secretary of state, share with me my constitutional responsibility for the conduct of our relations with (country)/(International organization). I charge you to exercise full responsibility for the direction, coordination, and supervision of all executive branch U.S. offices and personnel in (country)/at (international organization), except for personnel under the command of a United States area military commander, personnel under the authority of the chief of another U.S. mission (for example, one accredited to an international organization), or personnel detailed to duty on the staff of an international organization.

The secretary of state is my principal foreign policy advisor. You will receive policy guidance and instructions from him or from me. Except in the most unusual circumstances, as I shall determine, messages on policy proposals and policy implementation will be sent to you through official Department of State channels. You will normally report through the secretary. I want to emphasize that the secretary of state has the responsibility not only for the activities of the Department of State and the Foreign Service, but also, to the fullest extent provided by law, for the overall coordination and supervision of United States Government activities abroad.

You are to provide strong program direction and leadership to all executive branch agency activities to carry out United States foreign policy. It is also your responsibility to foster conditions in which our regional or worldwide activities can achieve success. I have notified all heads of departments and agencies accordingly and instructed them to inform their personnel in the United States and abroad.

You should cooperate fully with personnel of the U.S. legislative and judicial branches in (country)/at (international organization) so that United States foreign policy goals are advanced, security is maintained, and executive, legislative, and judicial responsibilities are carried out.

You should instruct all executive branch personnel under your authority of their responsibility to keep you fully informed at all times of their current and planned activities, so that you can effectively carry our your responsibility for United States government programs and operations. You have the right to see all communications to or from mission elements except, those specifically exempted by law or executive decision.

As commander in chief, I retain authority over United States armed forces. On my behalf you have responsibility for the direction, coordination, supervision, and safety, including security from terrorism, of all Department of Defense personnel on official duty in (country)/at (international organization), except those personnel under the command of a U.S. area military commander. You and such commanders must keep each other currently informed and cooperate on all matters of mutual interest. Any differences that cannot be resolved in the field should be reported by you to the secretary of state; unified commanders should report to the secretary of defense.

I expect you to report with directness and candor. If there are policies or programs with which you or personnel under your authority disagree, the secretary of state and I will always welcome the opportunity to consider alternative courses of action. Nevertheless, there can be only one United States policy, which I expect you and all members of your mission to follow and articulate.

I am committed to a lean personnel profile overseas for reasons of foreign policy, security, and economy. Thus, it is my policy that overseas staffing be tied directly to the accomplishment of specific national goals, and reduced whenever and wherever possible. I therefore want you to assess regularly the staffing levels and overall costs of every element of your mission to make certain they are consistent with our overall efforts to reduce the official U.S. presence abroad. You may initiate changes when you believe the staffing of any agency is either inadequate or excessive to the performance of essential functions. Every agency under your authority, including the Department of State, must obtain your approval for any change in the size, composition, or mandate of its staff. You must make the hard choices, and I expect you to relate mission resources directly to priority policy and program activities, genuine need, and safety. However, you should be aware that overall staff reductions notwithstanding, some diplomatic missions may, as the need arises, be asked to accept augmentation to meet new and pressing national security demands.

If an agency head disagrees with you regarding staffing, he may inform the secretary of state, to whom I have delegated responsibility for resolving such issues. In the event the secretary of state is unable to resolve a dispute, the secretary of state and the agency head will present their respective views to me, through my assistant for national security affairs, for decision. In such instances, both the secretary of state and I will uphold the party arguing for the best use of increasingly scarce resources.

The protection of all United States government personnel on official duty abroad and their accompanying dependents is a crucial responsibility in this dangerous time. You must always keep security in the forefront of your concerns. The security of your mission is your direct, personal responsibility. I also expect you to support strongly counterintelligence and counterterrorism activities that enhance security both locally and in the broader international context.

I know you share my total commitment to fair and equitable treatment for all, regardless of race, color, creed, sex, or national origin. It is your duty to demonstrate our shared commitment to equal employment opportunity. I expect you to run your mission in an atmosphere free of discrimination. From my own personal experience as an ambassador, I know that there are many ways you can foster a positive climate in this important regard by your own emphasis and example.

I also expect the highest standards of professional and personal conduct from all United States government personnel. Public service is a trust requiring government personnel to place public duties above private interests. Accordingly, they must abide by the highest ethical standards. To ensure that the American people retain complete confidence in the integrity of their government, government personnel must abide not only by the letter of regulations but also by the spirit of public service. You have the authority and my full support to ensure that ethical conduct is a hallmark of our presence overseas, both on and off the job.

I am sure you will represent the United States with imagination, energy, and skill. You have my full personal confidence and best wishes.

Sincerely,

George Bush

Appendix B

Interviews Used in Text

Note: the date given is the date of the first interview; several of the interviews consisted of more than one session.

Ambassador Alfred L. ATHERTON, April 1990
Ambasador William ATTWOOD, Dec. 14, 1988
Ambassador Lucius D. BATTLE, July 1990
Ambassador Ralph E. BECKER, Feb. 9, 1988
Ambassador John O. BELL, June 17, 1988
Ambassador William Tapley BENNETT, Jr.
　　June 16, 1988
Ambassador Maurice BERNBAUM, Jan. 13, 1988
Ambassador Richard BLOOMFIELD, May 6, 1988
Ambassador Davis Eugene BOSTER, Oct. 20, 1989
Ambassador William D. BREWER, Aug. 2, 1988
Ambassador Theodore R. BRITTON, Jr.
　　Mar. 29, 1989
Ambassador L. Dean BROWN, May 17, 1989
Ambassador John R. BURKE, May 26, 1989
Ambassador Findley BURNS, Jr., Nov. 2, 1988
Ambassador Walter C. CARRINGTON, Mar. 9, 1988
Ambassador Frederic L. CHAPIN, Mar. 22, 1988,
Christian A. CHAPMAN, Mar. 3, 1990
Ambassador Carleton S. COON, Jr.,
　　Oct. 25, 1989

Ambassador William R. CRAWFORD, Jr.
   Oct. 24, 1988
Ambassador Walter L. CUTLER, Sept 15, 1989
Ambassador William N. DALE, Sept. 19,
Ambassador Shelby C. DAVIS, Oct. 9, 1988
Ambassador William True DAVIS, Jr.
   Mar. 20, 1989
Ambassador Olcott H. DEMING, April 20, 1988
Ambassador Eileen R. DONOVAN. April 7, 1989
Ambassador Everett DRUMRIGHT, Dec. 5, 1988
Ambassador Angier Biddle DUKE, Apr. 4, 1989
Ambassador Donald B. EASUM, Jan. 17, 1990
Ambassador Hermann F. EILTS
   Aug. 12, 13, 1988
Ambassador David B. FUNDERBURK, Aug. 17, 1989
Ambassador Samuel R. GAMMON, Feb. 2, 1989
Ambassador Lincoln GORDON, Sept. 30, 1987
Lindsey GRANT,   June 30, 1990
Ambassador Brandon GROVE, Dec. 19, 1990
Ambassador Raymond A. HARE, July 1988
Ambassador Arthur W. HUMMEL, Jr.
   July 13, 1989
Ambassador John Wesley JONES, May 11, 1988
Ambassador William B. JONES, Feb. 14, 1989
Ambassador Jack B. KUBISCH, Jan. 6, 1989
Ambassador Carol C. LAISE, Apr. 17, 1989
Wolfgang LEHMANN, May 7, 1989
Ambassador Cecil B. LYON, Oct 26, 1988
Ambassador Douglas MacARTHUR II
   Dec. 15, 1986
Ambassador Edward E. MASTERS, March 14, 1989
Ambassador Richard C. MATHERON, March, 1989
Ambassador Robinson McILVAINE, Apr. 1, 1988
Ambassador Jay P. MOFFAT, Nov. 15, 1989
Ambassador Langhorne A. MOTLEY, Mar. 7, 1991
Ambassador Edward W. MULCAHY, Mar. 23, 1989
David G. NES, April 1991
Ambassador Herman W. NICKEL, Aug. 31, 1989
Ambassador David L. OSBORN, Jan. 16, 1989
Ambassador Edward L. PECK, July 1989
Ambassador Lawrence A. PEZZULO, Feb. 24, 1989
Ambassador Maxwell M. RABB, Aug. 2, 1989
Ambassador Stuart W. ROCKWELL, Oct. 5, 1988
Ambassador Claude G. ROSS, Feb. 16, 1989

Ambassador Ernest V. SIRACUSA, May 1989
Ambassador Robert P. SMITH, Feb. 28, 1989
Ambassador Robert S. SMITH, April 14, 1988
Ambassador William P. STEDMAN, Jr.
    Feb. 23, 1989
Thomas STERN, Oct. 2, 1987
Ambassador Robert A. STEVENSON
    Sept. 19, 1989
Ambassador Harrison M. SYMMES, Feb. 25, 1989
Ambassador Malcolm TOON, June 9, 1989
Ambassador Horace G. TORBERT, Aug. 31, 1988
Ambassador John W. TUTHILL, December 1987
Ambassador Marshall W. WILEY, Apr. 18, 1989
Ambassador Jean Mary WILKOWSKI, Aug. 23, 1989
Ambassador James W. WINE, Apr. 4, 1989
Ambassador Robert F. WOODWARD, May 5, 1987

The work of the following volunteer interviewers were used in this book, Willis Armstrong, John Bovey, William Brewer, Lee Cotterman, Gordon Evans, Stuart Kennedy, Arthur Lowrie, Dayton Mak, Robert Martens, Henry Mattox, John McKesson, Richard Nethercutt, Bertha Potts, Dorothy Robins, Leonard Saccio, Malcolm Thompson, Arthur Tienken, Horace Torbert, and Henry Zivitz.

These transcripts are on deposit in the Special Collections Room of Lauinger Library , Georgetown University, Washington, DC

Appendix C

Master Organization of a
United States Diplomatic Mission

Master Organization of a United States
Diplomatic Mission*

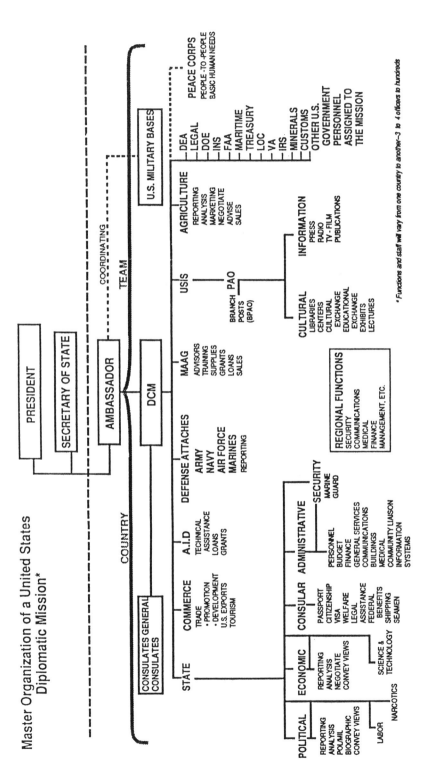

* Functions and staff will vary from one country to another—3 to 4 officers to hundreds

DGPER; D.E. L'Heureux
Rev. 9/89

Index

About the Authors

DAYTON MAK and CHARLES STUART KENNEDY, former foreign service officers, are in the Foreign Affairs Oral History Program at Georgetown University. Mr. Kennedy is also the author of *The American Consul: A History of the United States Consular Service* and, with William D. Morgan, *The U.S. Consul at Work*, both published by Greenwood Press in 1990.